THE POWER OF GOD

Access, Purpose, and Mystery

Martin Kaonga

While books are designed for general use, please consider the following safety precautions: Ensure that the content of this book is appropriate for the intended age group. Keep this product out of reach of young children unless specifically designed for their age group. Supervision is recommended for children under 3 years of age due to potential risks such as small detachable elements, sharp corners, or the possibility of paper cuts. Avoid exposure to fire, heat sources, or water to maintain product integrity and prevent hazards.

EU Conformity Declaration
This product complies with the following safety regulations and standards to ensure consumer safety and product quality: Regulation (EU) 2023/988 of the European Parliament and of the Council on General Product Safety (GPSR): The Consumer Product Safety Improvement Act (CPSIA), Section 101. The Californian Safe drinking water and toxic enforcement act. (Proposition 65) EN71-Part 1: Mechanical and Physical Properties EN71-Part 2: Flammability EN71-Part 3 Migration of certain elements.

Published and Manufactured by Softwood Books
EU Responsible person: Maddy Glenn
Office 2, Wharfside House, Prentice Road, Stowmarket, Suffolk, IP14 1RD
www.softwoodbooks.com
hello@softwoodbooks.com

EU Rep:
Authorised Rep Compliance Ltd., Ground Floor, 71 Lower Baggot Street, Dublin, D02 P593, Ireland
www.arccompliance.com
info@arccompliance.com

Text © Martin Kaonga, 2025

All rights reserved.

Without limiting the rights under copyright reserved above, no part of this publication may be reproduced, stored, or introduced into a retrieval system, or transmitted, in any form or by any means (electronic, mechanical, photocopying, recording or otherwise) without the prior written permission of both the copyright owners and the publisher of this book. This book was created without the use of artificial intelligence tools. The author does not grant permission for this manuscript to be used for training AI models or other machine learning purposes.

Paperback ISBN: 978-1-0686502-2-2

Hardback ISBN: 978-1-0686502-3-9

Dedication

To every believer who has ever asked,
"Why is this so hard?"

May you come to know that the power of God is not distant, but present, within you, for you, and working through you. This book is for the weary, the wondering, and the waiting, that you may rise in the strength of His might and fulfil the calling placed on your life.

Contents

Preface	7
Chapter 1: Why Do I Struggle to Do God's Work?	9
Chapter 2: Defining the Power of God	14
Chapter 3: The Uniqueness of God's Power	26
Chapter 4: How Powerful Was the First Human God created?	54
Chapter 5: Divine Power and Human Failure: A Paradox in the Garden?	71
Chapter 6: The Power of God and His creation	88
Chapter 7: Manifestations of God's Power	126
Chapter 8: God's Power and Our Earthly Mission	163
Chapter 9: Accessing the Power of God	232
Chapter 10: How God's Power Works	312
Chapter 11: When Can we Access the Power of God?	322
Conclusion	334

PREFACE

We all ask the same questions at some point in life: Why am I here? Why is doing the work of God so hard? Why do I feel powerless, despite my faith? In quiet moments, when the noise of daily obligations fades and the ache of purpose rises, our hearts long for something more than survival. We long to live lives of meaning, impact, and spiritual vitality. And yet, many of us walk through life weary, confused, or defeated, wondering where the power is that we read about in Scripture, sing about in church, and hear proclaimed from pulpits.

For many believers, "God's power" is a familiar phrase, quoted in prayers, echoed in hymns, and revered in theological language. But for all its familiarity, it often remains elusive in lived experience. Why do we, with sincere hearts and spiritual zeal, still struggle to do God's work? When is His power truly available to us? Are we missing something? And why does His power sometimes feel absent in our greatest moments of need?

This book was born from that tension, the space between the promises of divine power and the felt reality of human weakness. It is not a collection of easy answers or spiritual clichés. Instead, it is a journey of rediscovery. At the heart of this journey lies a divine paradox: that God's power is not simply about doing more, but about becoming more fully aligned with His purposes. It is not a resource to be used, but a mystery to be received, one that transforms us from the inside out.

Throughout these pages, we will explore what the power of God truly is, not just as a theological concept, but as a dynamic, relational reality that shapes creation, history, and the life of every believer. We will trace its manifestations in Scripture, examine its role in creation and redemption, and reflect on how it empowers our earthly mission. We will also wrestle with difficult but necessary questions: What is our role in accessing God's power? What blocks or limits it in our lives? How does sin, suffering, or spiritual dryness affect our experience of divine strength?

We will look not only at access and purpose, but also at mystery. God's power is not a button we press or a formula we master. It is a holy presence, marked by love, often revealed in weakness, and always aligned with His greater purposes. Sometimes it is displayed in miraculous ways; other times it is known only in the quiet endurance of faith, the unexpected strength to forgive, or the courage to keep going.

Each chapter is crafted to guide you, from wrestling with personal struggles to uncovering deep spiritual truths. Together, we will reflect on why God's power is unique, how it relates to humanity, and how it equips us to live purposefully. We will challenge assumptions, reframe expectations, and ultimately discover that divine power is not reserved for the spiritually elite, it is available to all who trust, surrender, and believe that their lives carry divine significance.

This is not just a theological study. It is an invitation, to know God more deeply, to walk in greater faith, and to live with the strength that only He can give. Whether you are feeling dry, discouraged, or simply hungry for more of God, this book is for you.

May each chapter stir your spirit, renew your mind, and embolden your heart.

Let us begin the journey into access, purpose, and mystery, and discover what it truly means to live by the power of God.

CHAPTER 1
Why Do I Struggle to Do God's Work?

Have you ever gone on a virtual tour of the universe, which displays God's complex, artistic, orderly, and intelligent creation? This is the product of His will. What converts His thoughts, words, and actions into physical, spiritual, or emotional realities is His divine power. God used this power to create the world and to make man, and He continues to use the same power to sustain His creation. Unlike earthly energy systems that waste energy, God perfectly uses all the power He supplies to accomplish His purposes.

With His power, the LORD effortlessly achieves 100% efficiency and effectiveness in executing everything He conceives, speaks, and does. He brings about results with precision, accuracy, and integrity. The combination of God's creative intent, the full deployment of His divine resources, and His omnipotent power ensures that whatever He does perfectly matches the expected outcome. There is no disconnect between what He thinks, says, or does and the resulting physical, spiritual, or emotional realities. The life and ministry of our Lord Jesus Christ clearly demonstrated that everything prophesied about Him was fulfilled with perfect accuracy.

After His baptism, Jesus received the Holy Spirit, who empowered His three-year earthly ministry. The Bible is full of examples of the Spirit descending on individuals whom God had assigned special tasks. Those who obeyed God and followed His instructions always accomplished their mission. Jesus instructed His disciples to wait in Jerusalem until they received power from on high to spread the gospel to all nations. Without the anointing of the Holy Spirit, no godly task can be effectively accomplished. The origin of this power is so perfect that whatever God creates has the potential to function at full capacity.

Fearfully and wonderfully made in the image and likeness of God, believers are expected to carry out their tasks with excellence and integrity. We have the potential, the resources, and the ability to do every good work that God prepared in advance for us. Like our Father, there should be alignment between our intentions, our actions, and the results they produce. Paul reminds us in his letter to the Ephesians: *For we are His workmanship, created in Christ Jesus for good works, which God prepared beforehand that we should walk in them* (Eph. 2:10, NKJV). Everything we are meant to do is already part of God's plan, and He has provided what we need to accomplish it. The power to carry out our mission is already within us.

As Christians, we are blessed because the same power that raised Jesus from the dead and seated Him at God's right hand in the heavenly realms is at work in us (Eph. 1:19–20, NIV). God has assured us that His divine power has given us everything we need for life and godliness through the knowledge of Him who called us by His own glory and goodness (2 Pet. 1:3, NKJV). Paul also declares, *I can do all things through Christ who strengthens me* (Philip. 4:13, NKJV). If we abide in Christ and He abides in us, then what we think, say, and do will produce the intended results.

God's power in a believer is like a folded crane on the back of a truck. When extended into the open sky, towering above buildings, it becomes visible to people and even aircraft from a distance. In that position, it can lift and move heavy objects, an awe-inspiring sight to many. However, for the crane to safely hoist such weights, its base must be anchored on firm ground, or it risks toppling. Similarly, the power of God within you becomes evident when you apply it to your circumstances while remaining firmly rooted in Christ.

God has given every Christian a full measure of power to fulfil their calling on earth. He dwells in us, and His power is readily available to be activated in every aspect of our lives. The apostle Peter assures us that, *His divine power has given us everything we need for life and godliness, through our knowledge of Him who called us by His own glory and goodness* (2 Peter 1:3, KJV). Everything we need to live for God and carry out His will is already within us. But to what extent do we, as Christians, truly access and deploy this power in our lives?

Have you ever resolved to do God's work, only to fall short or not do it at all?

How often have you planned to rise early to pray or study the Bible, but failed to follow through? How many times have you intended to share the gospel, only to retreat when the opportunity came? Each day likely holds a record of good works God prepared for us to do—in our families, workplaces, communities, churches, and personal spiritual life—that went undone.

We resolve to study Scripture, pray and fast, give tithes and offerings, help orphans and widows, visit the sick, serve in church, or assist the vulnerable, but we often struggle to follow through. Even when we act, our performance often falls short of God's standard. We confess our shortcomings and recommit ourselves, yet the cycle repeats. Why is there such a gap between our intentions, our actions, and the results?

Some scientists explain this phenomenon in physical systems using the Second Law of Thermodynamics, which states that in every energy transformation, some energy is lost as heat, a concept known as entropy. Similarly, human effort is often marked by inefficiency. But while that may apply in physics, spiritual inefficiency stems from factors like spiritual immaturity, sin, lack of discipline, failure to recognize our divine potential, or neglect of the resources God has provided.

Ultimately, our effectiveness in ministry depends on how well we understand, access, and apply God's power. Our spiritual performance ranges from no performance - when we are disconnected from God - to near-perfect obedience when we walk closely with Him. Sadly, many of us underutilize, or never tap into, the power of God available to us.

The apostle Paul expressed this inner battle when he wrote: *For the good that I will to do, I do not do; but the evil I will not to do, that I practice* (Rom. 7:19–24, NKJV). We long to walk with God, but we often struggle to obey His commands. Have you ever felt spiritually deficient when comparing your life to the zeal and fruitfulness of the apostles, prophets, or great men and women of faith like Enoch or Noah? This awareness can feel overwhelming, and in response, we sometimes attempt to compensate with lesser substitutes rather than seeking deeper intimacy and empowerment from God.

Christians sometimes feel so powerless that they depend entirely on others to help them navigate their challenges. This sense of helplessness often leads believers to move from one church to another, hoping to find godly people who can solve their problems. Many invest heavily in conferences, seminars, and other gatherings in search of solutions. While these activities have value and a rightful place in the life of a believer - and indeed, some problems are resolved through them - they are not the full expression of what God has provided. The greater issue is that many of us underutilize the power of God within us, if we use it at all.

Having access to God's power but not using it is as ineffective as not having it. Even when we do use it, we may only tap into a small fraction. As a result, believers sometimes experience unnecessary hardships, even though they have the spiritual power to avoid, endure, or overcome them.

I was deeply touched by a movie I watched in April 2018 that illustrated this truth. It told the story of two devout Christians - a brother and sister in Christ - who fell in love and began dating. They eventually believed they were meant for each other and shared their plans with their parents. Their pastor organized premarital counselling for them. After months of preparation, their wedding was a beautiful event. To crown it all, they honeymooned at a luxurious resort.

Upon returning home, they visited their pastor, who prayed for them and gave them a Bible as a gift. They placed the Bible on a shelf in their living room with other books, and forgot about it. Life went smoothly until trouble hit. One day, the husband was unexpectedly laid off due to company restructuring, without any severance pay. He was devastated. His wife was equally shocked. How could a recently promoted man be declared redundant?

After just two months, they could no longer afford the lifestyle they were used to. When they defaulted on rent, the landlord evicted them. Strangely, the only thing they left behind was the Bible. The landlord found new tenants, and the woman was immediately drawn to the book on the shelf. Curious, she picked it up. As she flipped through the pages, something fell out, a £15,000 cheque.

Unbeknownst to the couple, their pastor had not just gifted them a Bible; he had tucked inside it a cheque that could have sustained them during their crisis. But they never opened it. That is exactly how many Christians treat the power of God within them. It is available, but unused. They live with it every day, yet fail to unlock its benefits simply because they don't realize they have it. And even when they do, they often use it sparingly.

When we face marital struggles, financial hardship, rebellious children, job loss, broken relationships, or spiritual battles, what do we do? We often turn to our parents, friends, counsellors, and pastors. While some of these supports can point us to God's power, relying solely on people short-circuits God's command: *But seek first the kingdom of God and His righteousness, and all these things shall be added to you* (Matthew 6:33, NKJV).

God is in us. He knows exactly what we are going through, and He has the solution. But we often seek human advice before we seek His. We wrestle with problems while the power of God within us remains untapped. Failing to recognize or fully use this power not only limits us, it grieves God and cuts us off from His supernatural help. This hinders us from living a purpose-filled and victorious Christian life.

When Christians are frantically searching for solutions to their problems, they are often at their weakest and most vulnerable. Even those who appear strong in the Lord can sometimes exploit such situations, taking advantage of others' desperation. While Scripture encourages believers to seek godly counsel, the process of problem-solving must always begin with God. He should be the first point of contact, and it is He who should direct us to the right counsellors, if we need them at all. Seeking God first activates His power in our situation.

If God's power to do good works is already within us, how do we harness it? The following chapters will: define the power of God and explore its unique characteristics; explain how God's power functions and how it relates to His creation and our earthly mission; and describe how and when to access God's power.

This book is designed to deepen your understanding of God's power and show you how to harness it to live a purpose-driven and spiritually empowered life.

CHAPTER 2
Defining the Power of God

How often do we hear people talking about the power of God? But do we all share a common understanding of what it truly means? The concept of *the power of God* features prominently in the Bible, in daily conversations, in Bible studies, and across various platforms. While theologians, Christians, scientists, philosophers, and institutions have attempted to define this concept, no universally accepted definition exists. Yet, we cannot use, manage, or engage with something we don't understand, least of all, a divine attribute like the eternal power of our Creator. Since our goal is to understand and harness *the power of God*, defining the phrase and exploring how it applies to the life of a Christian is a spiritual necessity.

Scientific Definitions of Power

While defining *"the power of God"* is our primary aim, it is helpful to first understand the term *"power"* in general terms. The word *power* has various meanings depending on the field in which it is used:

- In physics, power refers to the rate of doing work; it can be defined as the product of force and velocity, or the rate at which energy is transferred or transformed in a system.
- In engineering and technology, power means energy - mechanical, electrical, or otherwise - that is used to operate a device.
- In optics, power refers to the ability of a lens or mirror to converge or diverge light.
- In social sciences, power is often defined as the capacity to influence behaviour or outcomes, an ability or talent to perform specific tasks, or a legal authority to alter the rights and responsibilities of oneself or others (as defined by the *Business Dictionary*).

Other disciplines, such as computing, mathematics, arts, sports, and music, also have their own definitions of power. What do these definitions have in common?

Despite their diversity, these definitions generally share two key features: a force or influence is exerted; and a movement or change—whether physical, chemical, psychological, or behavioural. In essence, *power can be viewed as the ability to bring about change or cause something to happen, or cease to happen*. This dual condition—force and movement or influence and transformation—is what defines power across disciplines.

In summary, while the specific meanings of *"power"* vary widely across different fields, they all converge on a common essence: the capacity to exert influence or force that initiates change or transformation. This foundational understanding provides a valuable lens through which we can begin to explore and define the power of God, not merely as an abstract concept, but as a dynamic and transformative force that acts purposefully within creation and human experience. Recognizing power as both influence and movement prepares us to grasp the unique nature of divine power and its profound impact on our lives.

The Limits of Human Understanding

Although science has made great strides in understanding power through natural laws and empirical principles, it struggles to comprehend how divine power operates beyond the bounds of natural law. Attempts to define God's power using frameworks rooted in human reasoning and observable phenomena are limited. These approaches often assume that everything in the universe conforms to human perception and understanding of nature. However, as our study of the universe deepens, we often discover how much we still don't know. The power of God originates from the Creator, who transcends the created universe. He operates beyond the physical and metaphysical boundaries that humans strive to comprehend.

In December 2013, a BBC radio broadcaster interviewed people from different walks of life in Cambridge, UK. Among them was an astrophysicist, who was asked to explain his field of study to the listeners. The scientist gave a clear and informative explanation of astrophysics. However, the next question, on the current state of knowledge in his discipline, revealed a truth that many scientists are reluctant to admit and that few non-scientists pause to consider.

The interviewer asked him to share the most recent and exciting developments in astrophysics. The scientist, honest and enthusiastic, explained that researchers had recently discovered a new method for studying dark matter, but admitted that scientists currently understand only about 5% of this mysterious component of the universe.

As I listened attentively, I was struck by how often we overestimate our understanding of the universe. We tend to make impressive claims about our ability to explain cosmic phenomena using human-engineered tools and theories. The truth is, we only understand a tiny fraction of the vast universe, and our principles and technologies reveal very little of its full reality. This limited understanding partly explains why we struggle to comprehend the power of God.

Three Major Limitations of Human Understanding

While people can generally define power using observable features of nature, there are three key limitations to understanding the power of God through a human lens:

1. **We rely solely on what God has revealed to us.** God's secret knowledge remains hidden unless He chooses to reveal it. As the Bible says: *The secret things belong to the LORD our God, but the things revealed belong to us and to our children forever, that we may follow all the words of this law* (Deut. 29:29, NIV). There are aspects of God's nature, plans, and purposes, "the secret things", that remain known only to God Himself. These divine mysteries are beyond human understanding and belong solely to the Lord. However, the "things revealed" are the truths, instructions, and guidance God has chosen to make known to us through His law, scripture, and revelation. These revealed things are given so that we and future generations can understand how to live rightly, obey God's commands, and maintain a faithful relationship with Him. In essence, it reminds us to trust God's wisdom, accepting that some things remain mysterious, while faithfully following what He has clearly shown us. Therefore, our

understanding, even of the things in our immediate environment, is partial and limited.

2. **Creation has been distorted by the curse of decay.** The original goodness and order of the created world have been negatively affected or corrupted due to a curse, often understood in a biblical context as the consequence of human sin. This "curse of decay" refers to the natural process of deterioration, death, and corruption that now affects all living things and the environment. Instead of remaining perfect and flourishing as originally created, creation experiences decline, suffering, and brokenness. In short, it highlights how sin brought a profound disruption to the harmony and vitality of the natural world. After the fall, the curse affected the serpent, humanity, the ground, and by extension, all of creation. This distorts our perception of God's original design and weakens our ability to fully grasp the structure and purpose of creation.

3. **Our fallen nature affects our perception.** Because of humanity's fallen condition, often understood as the spiritual and moral brokenness resulting from sin, our way of seeing and understanding the world is distorted or impaired. Instead of perceiving truth clearly and rightly, our judgment, values, and interpretations are influenced by selfishness, pride, ignorance, or error. Our spiritual brokenness colours how we think, feel, and respond, leading us away from seeing reality as God intends. Though redemption through Christ is restoring us to the image and likeness of God, our human limitations persist. We continue to study the universe gradually, and our understanding evolves slowly, often through trial, revision, and error. Scientific theories once regarded as foundational have been discarded or dramatically revised over time. Scientific advances lead to deeper and more accurate explanations over time, within the revealed realm.

The Supernatural Defies Natural Laws

While we're still grappling with the complexities of our natural environment, there is also a supernatural realm, which operates on an entirely different plane. It requires different tools, assumptions, and principles to understand. The power that governs this realm is divine, not confined by natural laws. But because we've been conditioned to understand reality only through the lens of science, many people find it difficult, or even impossible, to explain or accept God's power.

We are accustomed to small glimpses of power in our everyday experiences and often extrapolate from them to explain larger systems. But natural power is only a subset of the greater power, which originates from God. Many scientists are comfortable working within the realm of natural power, but feel uneasy or sceptical about supernatural power, largely because it cannot be empirically tested or measured. This has led some to conclude that God does not exist, while others remain undecided or indifferent.

Scientific vs. Biblical Definitions of Power

Even though scientists, both in the physical and social sciences, struggle to define *power*, most agree that it involves the ability to bring about change or cause something to happen. But how does the Bible define *power*?

Biblical Meaning of Power

In the Hebrew Old Testament, the word *power* takes on various meanings depending on its context. While the Bible does not offer a single, explicit definition of the term, it presents numerous expressions that convey its meaning. For instance, in Genesis 16:9, the angel of the Lord tells Hagar, *"Return to your mistress, and submit yourself under her hand."* This command implies that Sarai had authority over Hagar, she had power to direct her, and Hagar was expected to obey.

Another clear illustration is found in Esther 9:29, where Scripture says that *"Queen Esther, the daughter of Abihail, and Mordecai the Jew wrote with full authority to confirm this second letter concerning Purim."* The phrase *"with full authority"* (from the Hebrew *toqeph*) means strength, force, or delegated power. Because this letter was backed by royal authority, it carried the same weight as if issued by the king himself. The administrators in the 127 provinces were therefore required to honour it, allowing the Jews to celebrate Purim.

This shows that authority (a form of power) may mean having the license, approval, or right to act on behalf of someone else. For example, a football referee is licensed to oversee a match. He has the authority to start, pause, or end the game and can discipline players. Even if the referee has limited competence, players and coaches still submit to his decisions, not necessarily because of his skill, but because of the license he carries.

However, human authority has limits. A person may be authorized to carry out a task without having the actual capacity to perform it well. In contrast, there exists a kind of authority that guarantees both license and absolute ability, a form of authority that is both backed and enabled by God. This rare and perfect authority is what we should aspire to, and it is accessible through Jesus Christ.

New Testament Usage of 'Power'

In the New Testament, the Greek word ἐξουσία (*exousia*), often translated as *power* or *authority*, appears in several contexts. In John 1:12, it says: *But as many as received Him, to them He gave the right [power] to become children of God, to those who believe in His name.* This promise is profound: faith in Jesus Christ grants believers the power, by divine enablement, to become God's children. This transformation is not symbolic but real, and it can only happen through the specific power of God that regenerates the human spirit.

Jesus further explains in John 5:26–27 (NKJV): *For as the Father has life in Himself, so He has granted the Son to have life in Himself, and has given Him authority to execute judgment also, because He is the Son of Man.* Here, we see that the power of God is life-giving and judicial. Jesus received from the Father both the authority to grant eternal life and the authority to judge all people. There are three aspects of Christ's divine power:

1. He has the power to give life to all who accept Him, restoring what was lost through sin.

2. He has authority as the Son of Man, having lived in the flesh, to judge humanity justly.
3. He is the standard of redeemed humanity and the representative of God's perfect will.

Jesus, as both fully divine and fully human, possessed a unique kind of power: the ability to give eternal life, empower believers to become children of God, and judge the world righteously. His authority is not just delegated but intrinsic, flowing from His nature as God.

Toward A Biblical Definition of God's Power

Although the Bible does not provide a dictionary-style definition of *power*, the concept emerges clearly through its narratives and teachings. Biblically, God's power is: *transformative* - it changes lives and circumstances; *life-giving* - it enables spiritual rebirth and sustains creation; *authoritative*: it enforces divine judgment and executes God's will; and *redemptive*: it restores what sin has broken.

The 'Power of God' Defined

Several scholars have attempted to define the phrase *"the power of God"* and have outlined key features of their definitions. According to Norman Geisler, the power of God refers to that which can effect change in another, or what can cause something to be, or not be, in a particular way. This power brought the heavens and the earth into existence. It is the active principle behind the intelligent and orderly creation of the universe.

Stephen Charnock described God's power as "that ability and strength whereby He can bring to pass whatsoever pleases Him, whatsoever His infinite wisdom may direct, and whatsoever the infinite purity of His will may resolve." When God said, *"Let us make mankind in our image, in our likeness…"* (Genesis 1:26), His power translated that divine will into physical reality.

Similarly, another theologian (Lard, 1993) stated that God's power is the personal activity in His will, achieving moral and religious objectives. It is the active principle that proceeds from God and gives life to the physical world.

According to Lard, this power is a constituent element of God's essence that expresses both His nature and the precepts of His will.

Despite the varying expressions, common features emerge from these definitions:
1. God's sovereign will originates from His divine nature and is executed through His power.
2. His active principle - active, creative force - brings to life whatever He conceives, speaks, or desires.
3. Creation itself was brought into existence by the power of His Word (Genesis 1).

God's power is not passive; it is the vital force that effects change, causing something to exist, sustain its existence, or cease to exist. It undergirds His nature and all His attributes.

Charnock insightfully asked: *How vain would be the eternal counsels if power did not step in to execute them? Without power, His mercy would be but feeble pity, His promises an empty sound, His threats a mere scarecrow.* Indeed, God's power transforms His thoughts, words, and actions into tangible outcomes.

This is seen clearly in Scripture when Jesus cried out, *"Lazarus, come forth!"*, the man who had been dead came out of the tomb (John 11:43–44). The power in Jesus' command resurrected the dead. Similarly, when God created Adam, He formed man from the dust and breathed into his nostrils the breath of life, making him a living being (Gen. 2:7). The breath of God, the power of life, transformed lifeless dust into a living person. This same power resides in believers today and has the capacity to transform situations, overcome obstacles, and fulfil God's will and purpose.

The biblical creation narrative, along with miracles throughout Scripture, illustrates that the power of God, often referred to as His omnipotence, is His all-encompassing active essence. It includes ability, creative force, sustaining strength, complete control over all that exists, and the capacity to do anything logically possible, as understood within religious and philosophical traditions.

In short, *the power of God* refers to His divine ability and authority to create, sustain, transform, judge, govern, and redeem all things in accordance with His perfect will and nature. This power is not limited by human weakness, scientific laws, or natural understanding. It is perfect, sovereign, and available to all who believe in Christ.

What Are the Key Tenets of the Definition of the Power of God?

Inherent in the definitions of God's power are attributes that reveal its unique and divine nature. This power, accessed through Christ, is limitless.

Take just five minutes to sit still and reflect on your day. Think about everything you said, did, thought, and even intended to do. Now, ask yourself: what proportion of those things materialized as you expected? If every thought, word, or action produced your desired outcome, you would be a superstar! But the reality is, only God's power can consistently bring to pass everything He wills, desires, or plans.

As His children, our thoughts, desires, words, and actions can also yield expected outcomes, but only if we abide in Christ, and He abides in us. Through Him, we have access to God's infinite and eternal power.

God's Power vs. Earthly Limitations

In our earthly economy, God has provided adequate power and resources to fulfil His will through us. Yet, as I studied economics, I learned a key principle: means of production are limited, while human wants are unlimited. Hence, we must prioritize and maximize resource use. Economists use tools such as benefit-cost analysis, return on investment, and econometric models to allocate resources efficiently.

Despite using some of the world's most sophisticated models and technology, projects often fail to deliver expected results. Even national economies, led by highly trained professionals, have experienced recessions. These failures reflect human limitations, including our failure to fully identify and mobilize the power of God.

The Supernatural Economy of God

The principle of scarcity does not apply in the Kingdom of God where His power is operational. When Jesus fed five thousand men, not counting women and children, with only five loaves and two fish (Matt. 14:16–19), He demonstrated the boundless nature of God's power. Not only was the crowd satisfied, but twelve baskets of leftovers remained (Matt. 14:20). How do we explain this level of divine provision?

1. *God's wisdom is flawless.* He designs with such perfection that no resource is ever lacking.
2. *God's power is part of His nature.* Whatever comes from Him is infused with exactly the power required to fulfil His will.
3. *God's resource base is inexhaustible.* His "natural capital" is infinite, supplying all that is needed for the universe.

The omnipotent God is all-sufficient, fully capable of providing for every need.

The Essence of God's Power

God's power fully expresses His nature and purposes. Can you imagine if every word you spoke immediately produced your desired outcome? That's how God's power functions, it is infinite, eternal, incomprehensible, and transformative. It cannot be resisted, restrained, or frustrated by any part of creation.

Since His power undergirds His very nature, it is intertwined with all His other attributes. To grasp this, imagine a human body deprived of energy. When vital organs like the brain, heart, and kidneys are starved, the body begins to shut down. Similarly, God's "being" is energized by His own inexhaustible power, which is essential to His divine nature.

God is The Source of All Power

All power has a source (generator), a transmitter, and a user. On earth, nations generate power through various means, hydroelectricity, solar, wind, nuclear, and so on. But regardless of the method, all power has a source.

In the universe, that source is God. He created all things, and all power originates from Him. His power is reliable, consistent, and sufficient to sustain everything according to His will. The Psalmist declared: *God has spoken once, twice have I heard this: that power belongs to God* (Psa. 62:11). Peter affirms that: *To Him be the power forever and ever. Amen* (1 Pet. 5:11). God's power is evident in:

- Creation of the universe from nothing
- Sustaining the natural world
- Governing all nations
- Redeeming humanity through Christ
- Transforming hearts by the Spirit
- Preserving the saints
- Defeating Satan and all evil

These truths expose the devil for what he is, a created being whose power is limited and derived. All creatures, including Satan and his fallen angels, draw their power from God. That's why plugging into God's power renders the enemy powerless.

Divine Unity in Power

Since God's power is part of His nature, it is shared fully by all three persons of the Trinity, God the Father, God the Son, and God the Holy Spirit. Each is fully God, equally powerful, and perfectly united. Whatever they agree upon is fully empowered to create, transform, or dissolve, as they choose. Whether in creation, salvation, judgment, or sustaining life, God's power is always sufficient, in every moment, for every purpose.

God sovereignly distributes power to His creation. For Christians, the Holy Spirit—who dwells within us—is our powerhouse, with inexhaustible reserves available to drive every aspect of our lives. God has pre-packaged different expressions of His power within the Holy Spirit, making them available for any work He has conceived or revealed to us. This power fuels and sustains processes both in heaven and on earth. However, for creation, the consumer, to benefit, we must activate or "switch on" that power through faith, obedience, and alignment with God's will.

Every creature of God can only express the portion of power that has been allocated to it, a part of the original divine power. If God is our source, we can rest assured that walking with Him guarantees access to everything we need for a godly life. As Scripture affirms: His divine power has given us everything we need for a godly life through our knowledge of him who called us by his own glory and goodness (2 Pet. 1:3, NIV).

God desires to reproduce, within us, the same model by which He powers His own nature and actions. Because the Godhead dwells in us, His divine power is resident within us. Just as the Father gave power to Jesus for His life and ministry, we have been given power to sustain every area of our lives - spiritual, physical, mental, vocational, familial, and financial - so that we may live a godly life.

However, this privileged access to God's power is conditional. It depends on our knowledge of Him, the One who has called us by His glory and goodness. Every Christian who truly walks with the Lord carries His power, which enables them to draw on the divine resources necessary for holy and purposeful living.

This knowledge includes recognizing God as the eternally powerful One, who not only has the will to empower us, but also the ability, if we trust and obey Him.

It is therefore evident that the power of God is the divine ability and strength that transforms thoughts, words, and actions into desired outcomes consistent with His will. As a child of God, you have access to this power through the Holy Spirit. But how potent is power?

CHAPTER 3
The Uniqueness of God's Power

But one truth must grow ever clearer-the truth that there is an Inscrutable Existence everywhere manifested, to which he [the man of science] can neither find nor conceive either beginning or end. Amid the mysteries which become the more mysterious the more they are thought about, there will remain the one absolute certainty, that he is ever in presence of an Infinite and Eternal Energy, from which all things proceed (Herbert Spencer, 1934)

Have you ever reflected on the fall of humanity in the Garden of Eden? Did Adam and Eve have enough power to defeat the enemy in the Garden? And do the descendants of Adam have enough power to resist the schemes of the devil today? The events in the Garden of Eden have sparked different interpretations about the power of God and the fall of humanity. Here are three common views:

1. Limited human power against a greater enemy

This view suggests that God, though all-powerful, created humans who lacked the power to overcome temptation. According to this interpretation, humans were outmatched by the serpent's cunning. While this perspective affirms God's supreme power, it implies that human wisdom and strength were too limited to resist the enemy's deception.

2. Power was available but misused

Another view holds that God gave humans sufficient power, but they misused their freedom of choice. Adam and Eve had access to God's strength but chose not to rely on it, driven instead by the desire to 'be like God.' This theory highlights human responsibility in the fall and implies that their failure was not due to lack of power, but a refusal to use it.

3. Disconnection due to ignorance or pride

A third perspective is that Adam and Eve failed to access God's power due to ignorance of their identity and privileges—or due to pride or disobedience. These factors may have severed or weakened their relationship with God.

Possessing divine power but failing to use it is like jumping out of a plane at 35,000 feet and refusing to open your parachute, whether from ignorance, pride, or deliberate rebellion. The result is catastrophic.

These interpretations offer different insights into how believers and unbelievers perceive God's power and human responsibility. The way we understand this principle profoundly shapes how we access and apply God's power in our walk with Him.

Have you ever truly considered the complexity of the universe and how it was intricately designed? Does the creation account in Genesis 1 not testify to the greatness of God's power? Often, when we try to comprehend this power, we unintentionally conflate it with cultural or mystical ideas, such as alchemy, occultism, divination, or telepathy. This confusion can limit our perception of God's power, reducing it to merely natural forces or supernatural tricks. But God's power exists beyond the confines of the created order, it is invincible, eternal, and unchanging.

Our limited understanding of, or inability to recognize and utilize, God's eternal and infinite power can hinder us from effectively fulfilling our vocations. Therefore, exploring the distinctive features of God's power will help us grasp its magnitude and apply it according to His will. This deeper understanding will ignite a desire and motivation to appropriate the right measure of divine power for our calling.

Distinctive Features of the Power of God.

Different religious and philosophical scholars have attempted to characterize the power of God, producing various descriptions of this divine attribute. This section highlights key features of God's power that can help us understand how to harness it in living a purpose-driven Christian life.

1. The Power of God is Eternal

There are several references to the eternal power of God in the Bible. However, understanding this power requires exploring God's eternal nature. All of God's attributes, His mercy, power, grace, and love, are eternal. Scripture refers to Him as the eternal God and our refuge, whose everlasting arms support us (Deut. 33:27); possessing eternal power and divine nature (Rom. 1:20); the eternally blessed God (Rom. 9:5); having an eternal purpose (Eph. 3:11); the King eternal (1 Tim. 1:17); the everlasting God (Gen. 21:33); and the One whose mercy and truth endure forever (Psa. 100:5). God's eternal nature permeates everything He is, says, and does.

Eternity is a difficult concept for us to grasp because we live and function within time, a narrow slice of God's vast, timeless realm. Our human minds are conditioned to perceive life as a sequence of events. Biblical tools like The Holman Book of Biblical Charts, Maps, and Reconstructions help us track these events with timelines, from creation to the new heavens and earth, but eternity transcends linear time.

Eternity is an awe-inspiring attribute of God, describing His timeless and everlasting existence. Though difficult to comprehend, it means that God has existed infinitely into the past and will continue infinitely into the future. He has no beginning and no end. Genesis 1:1 states: *In the beginning God...*, indicating that God existed before time, space, matter, and energy—before the universe itself. He existed in the undatable past, exists now, and will exist throughout the undatable future.

Eternity is an invisible but essential quality of God, woven throughout creation, Scripture, and theology. Without the reality of His eternal nature, biblical truth would collapse. Eternity is interwoven with God's power. Paul wrote, *For since the creation of the world God's invisible qualities, his eternal power and divine nature, have been clearly seen, being understood from what has been made, so that people are without excuse* (Rom. 1:20, KJV). The creation testifies to His eternal power, present before creation, sustaining the present world, and extending into the new creation.

Imagine walking through a tropical rainforest, observing layers of canopy, vibrant shrubs, and herbaceous plants. Monkeys and birds move among the branches. In the savannah, lions rest under acacia trees, elephants browse in the distance, and a giraffe stretches toward the sky. The sounds of birds and insects fill the air as the sun sets, and nocturnal creatures begin their song. From land to sea, sky to soil, the vast array of life forms reveals the wonder of God's creation. These spectacles are only possible through the presence of His eternal power that sustains all things.

God is eternal, and He has placed eternity in the human heart. Ecclesiastes 3:11 says: *He has made everything beautiful in its time. Also, He has put eternity in their hearts, except that no one can find out the work that God does from beginning to end* (NKJV). The One who placed eternity in our hearts has also granted us access to His eternal power, to keep us in His presence eternally. When we are empowered for eternity, nothing in this life or beyond can derail God's predestined plan for us. The same eternal power that created Satan also sustains him within God's limits. Since the Godhead dwells within us, we have access to that eternal power, which dictates what the enemy can or cannot do. *I can do all things through Christ who strengthens me* (Phil. 4:13), by His eternal power. This truth should embolden us to pursue and depend on God's power daily in our walk with Him.

The Power of God is Infinite

Although the term *infinity* frequently appears in everyday discussions, it remains almost impossible to fully comprehend. In mathematics and physics, infinity refers to a value greater than any real number, something unbounded, limitless, and beyond the confines of numerical systems. It is a concept used to describe what cannot be quantified or contained.

Infinity is considered an *incommunicable* attribute of God because it has no direct analogy in human experience. To say that God is infinite means that His being, greatness, and attributes are without limit. While mathematicians, physicists, and philosophers have attempted to define or model infinity, there has never been a universally accepted understanding of it. Yet Scripture applies the concept of infinity to God. The psalmist writes: *Great is our Lord and mighty in power; His understanding has no limit* (Psa. 147:5, NIV). As finite beings with limited lifespans and understanding, how can we truly grasp the boundless nature of God?

God is infinite in three key ways:

1. **Spatial Infinity (Immanence and Immensity):** God is present everywhere at the same time. This attribute, also called *immensity*, means that God is not constrained by physical space or geographic location. Solomon acknowledged this when he said, *"But will God really dwell on earth? The heavens, even the highest heaven, cannot contain you"* (1 Kings 8:27). Similarly, Paul declared, *"The God who made the world and everything in it is the Lord of heaven and earth and does not live in temples built by human hands"* (Acts 17:24). God transcends all dimensions of the physical universe and stretches into the unbounded, undated realm beyond creation.

2. **Temporal Infinity (Eternality):** God exists fully in the past, present, and future simultaneously. He is *Jehovah El Olam*, the Everlasting God (Gen. 21:33). *"Before the mountains were born or you brought forth the whole world, from everlasting to everlasting you are God"* (Psalm 90:2, NIV). Unlike His creation, God has no beginning and no end. There never was a time when He did not exist, and there never will be a time when He ceases to exist.

3. **Intrinsic Infinity (Perfection):** God is infinite in Himself, perfect and without limitation. Everything God has, He is and everything He is, He is eternally and without measure. Because God is infinite, all His attributes - love, mercy, truth, holiness, justice, and power - are also infinite. This means God acts in absolute freedom and authority: *"Whatever the Lord pleases, He does, in heaven and on earth"* (Psalm 135:6). Nothing and no one can frustrate His will.

This infinite nature of God is not abstract or inaccessible to believers. Through faith in Christ, every child of God is grafted into the vine and has access to God's infinite mercy, power, grace, and righteousness. No fallen human being can defeat the Devil on their own. But faithful Christians, by virtue of their relationship with the triune God, can overcome the enemy through the infinite power of God at work in and through them.

The Power of God is Driven by the Purpose and Precept of His Will

The allocation of God's power to the creation and sustenance of the universe and everything it contains is driven by the purpose and precept of His will. The term *God's will* can refer to different concepts. In this context, it refers to what God wants, intends, and desires. The pleasurable and honourable desires of God guide everything He thinks, says, and does. When God wills or resolves to do something, He surely accomplishes it. *He does according to His will in the army of heaven and among the inhabitants of the earth. No one can restrain His hand* (Dan. 4:35 NKJV).

There are two principal components of His will: the purpose or counsel of His will, which refers to God's sovereign desires or decrees, what He intends shall come to pass (Dan. 4:35; Eph. 1:11); and the precept of His will, which refers to what God commands us to do, our moral and spiritual duty (Ex. 20:3–17; James 4:17; Matt. 6:10; Eccl. 12:13; Gen. 1:26). Whatever God says or does is fully consistent with both the purpose and the precept of His will.

The eternal purpose of the will of God encompasses the principles, tenets, and plans through which He accomplishes His desires. Because God is purposeful, He does not act randomly or arbitrarily. The purpose of His will is always fulfilled and governs what He thinks, says, and does. Like a perfect architect, God has made all things for a specific purpose. The Psalmist writes, *The LORD has made everything for its purpose, even the wicked for the day of trouble* (Prov. 16:4). Paul also affirms, *…we know that all things work together for good to them that love God, to them who are the called according to his purpose* (Rom. 8:28, KJV).

We have received power to work out our salvation with fear and trembling, *for it is God who works in us to will and to act in order to fulfil His good purpose* (Phil. 2:13). When we fear God and obey His commandments, He reveals His will to us and gives us the grace to align our will with His, enabling us to fulfil His good purpose.

Our limited, human logic often leads us to divide creatures into categories of useful and useless, but King Solomon teaches us that everything, even the wicked, was made for a purpose. God has a divine purpose for all of creation: for humanity (Gen. 1:26; Eccl. 12:13), for the prophets, judges, and kings, for the incarnation, ministry, death, and resurrection of Jesus Christ, for His disciples, and for modern-day Christians.

The purpose of God's will cannot be known generally, it must be revealed. We must draw near to God to understand His purpose. It is so precious and noble that He reveals it only to those who lean on Him.

God has a tailor-made vocation for each person. He told Jeremiah, *I knew you before I formed you in your mother's womb. Before you were born, I set you apart and appointed you as My prophet to the nations* (Jer. 1:5). Jeremiah's assignment was carved out for him even before birth. It would be uncharacteristic of a loving Father to ask His child to do something beyond their ability. When God ordained Jeremiah to prophesy to the nations, He also equipped him with the ability and grace to accomplish that task.

Likewise, whatever God has called you to do, He has equipped you to do it, because your vocation is rooted in the purpose of His will. Imagine John the Baptist opening a carpentry shop, running a kindergarten, starting a consultancy firm, or pursuing any career unrelated to his prophetic mission, he would have been the most frustrated man on earth. There is unspeakable joy and peace when you discover and fulfil your calling according to the purpose of God's will.

The second component of God's will is the precept of His will. This refers to the principles, commands, or duties God requires of us. While God absolutely accomplishes the purpose of His will, the precept of His will depends on human response and obedience.

God's general precepts apply to all believers: loving God and our neighbours, praying and fasting, fellowshipping with other believers, partaking in Holy Communion, stewarding God's creation, obeying His commandments, preaching the gospel, and healing the sick, among others. In contrast, specific precepts apply to individuals and include unique spiritual gifts (teaching, prophesying, evangelism, pastoring, apostleship, etc.), natural talents (leadership, entrepreneurship, administration), and ministries of service (visiting the sick, caring for the vulnerable, and so on).

However, the purpose and precepts of God's will cannot be realized apart from His eternal and infinite power. A key part of God equipping His children involves giving them access to this power. It is intricately woven into His purpose, what He wills, speaks, or acts always comes to pass.

The fulfilment of God's desires is grounded in the flawless perfection of His nature, the certainty of His purpose, and the eternal power with which He operates. In God's divine economy, His power always matches the demands of His will with perfect efficiency.

God is precise in His allocation of power to create and sustain the heavens, the earth, and everything within them. All things, animate and inanimate, require divine power to exist and function. Scripture affirms: *He (Jesus) is before all things, and in Him all things hold together* (Col. 1:17).

Have you ever considered what keeps the components of creation functioning and intact? What makes the human heartbeat without rest for decades? What gives life its internal balance? Jesus Christ, who existed before all things, is the sustaining force behind creation and every process that maintains it.

Scientists confirm this through the principle of homeostasis, the steady internal condition maintained by all living systems. Every cell in your body constantly requires energy just to carry out life's most basic functions. That energy, ultimately, is sustained by the power of God, even down to the cellular "powerhouses." Philosopher Herbert Spencer once wrote (1934): *"But one truth must grow ever clearer—the truth that there is an Inscrutable Existence everywhere manifested, to which he [the man of science] can neither find nor conceive either beginning or end. Amid the mysteries which become the more mysterious the more they are thought about, there will remain the one absolute certainty, that he is ever in presence of an Infinite and Eternal Energy, from which all things proceed."*

The power that sustains the created order originates from God. His eternal and infinite power brought the universe and all its inhabitants into being and upholds them by the word of His power. Paul asserts, *He (Christ) is before all things, and in Him all things hold together* (Col. 1:17). According to John Gill's exposition of the Bible, *He upholds all things by the word of His power; the heavens have their stability and continuance from Him; the pillars of the earth are borne up by Him; otherwise, both the earth and its inhabitants would be dissolved. All mankind live and move, and have their being in Him. The entire frame of nature would burst asunder and break into pieces if it were not held together by Him. Every created being has its support from Him and its consistency in Him; and all the affairs of providence, concerning all creatures, are governed, directed, and managed by Him, in conjunction with the Father and the Blessed Spirit.*

Every human being, created in the image of God, has potential access to the eternal power of God. The only condition is walking in His light and in the paths of righteousness He has ordained for us. King Solomon said: *Fear God and keep His commandments, for this is the whole duty of man* (Eccl. 12:13 NIV). When we obey this command, we open the flow of God's eternal power to fulfil the purpose and precepts of His will. However, the sovereign LORD distributes and activates His power within the limits of the curse of decay upon the created order, which remains under His control.

God, who made us, loves us, and designed us to do good works, has prepared those works in advance for us to do (Eph. 2:10). The Bible assures us that God conceived our lives from conception into eternity, allocating His eternal power to our eternal life in alignment with the purpose and precepts of His will. The Psalmist declares: *Your eyes saw my substance, being yet unformed. And in Your book they all were written, the days fashioned for me, when as yet there were none of them* (Psa. 139:16 NKJV).

Are you not thrilled by the reality that God conceived your eternity? God saw you as a foetus and watched as your body grew and developed in your mother's womb. He captured every detail of cell multiplication and differentiation, from the fertilization of the egg to your birth and into the future that only He can see.

A vehicle manufacturer typically provides a manual with each vehicle. This manual itemizes and describes all the parts of the vehicle, provides symbols that will appear on the dashboard if a key part malfunctions, specifies the fuel and lubricants, the horsepower, tire pressure, weight of the car, and other specifications to help the owner manage the vehicle for optimum performance.

Similarly, God determines the power needs of everything He thinks, says, and does with perfect precision. He allocates power to activities and processes based on absolute needs because of His ability to measure and distribute power perfectly. Since God prepared an inventory of all the parts of your body in His book, including the days ordained for you before you were born, He also determined the total eternal power required to create and sustain you for eternity.

God knows every part of your body, its position, and its function relative to all other parts. He who created the universe and everything in it knows exactly how much eternal power is needed to sustain each element. Thus, God's eternal power is driven by the purpose and precept of His will.

The Power of God is Appropriated by the Holy Spirit

There are multiple dimensions of power in our societies. Power can manifest as physical force associated with fear, as governance, fame, law, and wealth in the public sphere, as the power of nature (including intelligence, orderliness, creativity, and imagination), and as the power of symbols, thought, and ritual. While power originates from God, it can be used for both good and evil. The concept of power varies across human disciplines such as philosophy, sociology, physics, mathematics, and nature, among others. Even within religious circles, there is a historical association between divinity and the power of physical and military might, especially in theocratic societies, with early Israel serving as a prominent example. However, power is ultimately a theological issue. The prophetic, priestly, wisdom traditions, and other ecclesiastical practices articulate a theology of power that is far more potent than military force. All power in the universe can be traced back to God, usually expressed as the power of the Holy Spirit.

The power of the Holy Spirit is fundamental to the fulfilment of the purpose and precept of the will of God. However, there is a significant challenge in describing and defining the Holy Spirit and His attendant power at work in us.

Contrasting views about the Lordship of the Holy Spirit in relation to the Father and the Son have led some theologians and Christians to conclude that His deity is uncapturable. The words and concepts fall short of fully capturing the person, role, and work of the Holy Spirit. The Holy Spirit does not fit neatly into our human-sized logic or conceptual frameworks. Some reject the truth that the Holy Spirit is the third person of the triune God, instead regarding Him merely as a spiritual force from God. In this text, however, the Holy Spirit is understood as God and the third person of the Godhead. His personhood is immeasurable and transformative, carrying life-giving power. The Holy Spirit is the eternal power from on high, enabling the work for which the Lord Jesus sacrificed His throne and His life, power to witness for Christ and to serve effectively in saving lives for Him.

The Bible describes the Holy Spirit as God's divine power. Many scriptures in the Old Testament refer to Him as the power of God (Zech. 4:6; Micah 3:8). The Holy Spirit is associated with the presence and great works of God, including signs and miracles. The Holy Spirit comes down from the throne of the One to whom all power has been given. The *Anchor Bible Dictionary* refers to Him as the manifestation of divine presence and power, perceptible especially in prophetic inspiration (*Vol. 3, Doubleday, New York, 1992, p. 260*). Luke identifies the Holy Spirit with the "power of the Highest" (Luke 1:35). Speaking of the Spirit of promise, which would be given to His followers after His death, Jesus told His disciples, *You shall receive power when the Holy Spirit has come upon you...* (Acts 1:8). The Holy Spirit is the very presence of God's power actively working in His children. The Spirit of God's Word and Wisdom possesses eternal and infinite power that activates what God thinks, says, and does. This is why there is liberty wherever the Holy Spirit is, because the power of God is at work.

Throughout the Bible, the power of God is associated with the Holy Spirit; the power of the Spirit is the power of God and the power of Jesus Christ. He is the Being through whom great works of power have been and are being performed. This power, from the Word and the Spirit, has manifested in the creation of the heavens and the earth (Gen. 1:1) and in transforming the formless and empty earth, covered with darkness, into an intelligent, orderly, and good creation, including the sky, earth, seas, day and night, seasons, solar systems, vegetation, animals, and human beings (Gen. 1 & 2). The power of the Holy Spirit brought the world into being.

In the Old Testament, the Holy Spirit empowered God's servants to perform specific tasks. Samuel took the horn of oil and anointed David in the presence of his brothers, and from that day on, the Spirit of the LORD came upon David in power (1 Sam. 16:13). David was endowed with kingly power to rule over the United Kingdom of Israel and Judah. In another instance, the LORD said, *I have filled him (Bezalel) with the Spirit of God, with skill, ability, and knowledge in all kinds of crafts to make artistic designs in gold, silver, and bronze, to cut and set stones, to work in wood, and to engage in all kinds of craftsmanship* (Ex. 31:3). The Spirit of God equipped Bezalel with unique knowledge, skills, and abilities to create various artistic crafts for building the temple of God. The Spirit also enabled him to transfer these skills to others who had different tasks in the construction work.

Through the Spirit of God, Moses parted the Red Sea, and the Israelites crossed on dry land (Exod. 14:21-22); Elisha struck the waters of the Jordan River, and it separated to the right and to the left, allowing him to cross (2 Kings 2:9-25); and Samson killed a lion: *the Spirit of the LORD came powerfully upon him, so that he tore the lion apart with his bare hands as he might have torn a young goat* (Judges 14:6 NIV). Other manifestations of the power of the Spirit include Israel's military victories over heathen kingdoms, Daniel's survival in the lion's den (Dan. 6:16-19), and the Hebrew young men - Shadrach, Meshach, and Abednego - defying the blazing furnace of King Nebuchadnezzar (Dan. 3:24-26). Although the Spirit of the LORD did not permanently dwell in God's servants in the Old Testament, He empowered them to accomplish God's will, which they would not have been able to carry out on their own.

In the New Testament, the Holy Spirit came upon Mary, and His power overshadowed her, enabling her to give birth to Jesus Christ, the Son of God

(Luke 1:35). After thirty years of growth and preparation for His earthly ministry, the Holy Spirit descended upon Jesus in the Jordan River and empowered Him to perform signs and wonders. His three-year ministry epitomized the expression of God's power through the Holy Spirit. Jesus was filled with the Spirit (Luke 4:1), led by the Spirit (Luke 4:14), and empowered by the Spirit to preach the gospel and perform miracles (Matt. 12:28; Isa. 61:1-3). Acknowledging the power of the Spirit, Jesus proclaimed: *The Spirit of the LORD is upon Me, because He has anointed Me to preach the gospel to the poor; He has sent Me to heal the broken-hearted, to proclaim liberty to the captives, and recovery of sight to the blind, to set at liberty those who are oppressed"* (Luke 4:18 NKJV). Luke also records that Jesus returned to Galilee in the power of the Spirit (Luke 4:14). Jesus depended on the Holy Spirit for His life and ministry.

When the Spirit of the Lord descends upon a person, signs and wonders follow. Luke testifies of the great works of Christ when he writes: *How God anointed Jesus of Nazareth with the Holy Ghost and with power, who went about doing good and healing all who were oppressed by the devil, for God was with Him* (Acts 10:38 KJV). Jesus preached the good news of the Kingdom of God, saved sinners, healed every disease, cast out demons, raised the dead, cleansed lepers, fed the hungry, and met the diverse needs of the people. The Holy Spirit also empowered Him to endure the cross, face death, rise from the dead, and ascend to heaven where He sits at the right hand of the Father. Jesus, the Son of God, needed the Holy Spirit for His life and ministry on earth. We, too, need the Holy Spirit to live a purpose-driven life.

After the ascension of Jesus Christ, His disciples were empowered by the Spirit to preach the gospel, heal the sick, and perform other works of ministry (2 Cor. 2:12; Acts 2:43; 3:1-7; 9:39-41). On the day of Pentecost, the Holy Spirit came upon the disciples, and they were filled with the Holy Spirit and began to speak in other tongues as the Spirit enabled them (Acts 2:4 NIV). The Spirit-filled Peter, who had previously denied Jesus three times, boldly preached the gospel, and three thousand converts were baptized and added to their number on that day (Acts 2:14-42). The anointing of the Holy Spirit manifested among all the believers in the early church through the dispensation of spiritual gifts, including speaking in tongues, evangelism, prophesying, teaching, wisdom, and apostleship, among others.

Through the power of the Word and Spirit, the redemption of humanity was conceived and brought to fruition. We, the redeemed of the LORD, are sealed, filled, and baptized with the Holy Spirit. When He comes upon us, He gives us wisdom, knowledge, and understanding of the truth, takes possession of our abilities, and imparts spiritual gifts that qualify us for service in the body of Christ. The Holy Spirit empowers believers for service, to witness, for spiritual warfare, and for boldness in their testimonies.

Every follower of Christ who is sealed, filled, and baptized with the Holy Spirit walks in the light of God and performs good works in alignment with the purpose and precept of God's will. Such a person is led by the Holy Spirit to seek first the Kingdom of God and His righteousness. When you allow the Holy Spirit to lead you, you gain access to the same power that raised Jesus from the dead and seated Him at the right hand of God the Father.

God's Power is Transcendent and Immanent

Although the terms *transcendence* and *immanence* do not appear in most versions of the Bible, they are commonly used in theological literature to describe the nature of God's relationship with humanity. Both Judaism and Christianity affirm that God is transcendent, exalted, above, and beyond us. As theologian John M. Frame explains, God's transcendence refers to His royal dignity and His exercise of control and authority over all creation. It conveys the idea that God is not part of the created order and cannot be fully grasped by human understanding.

Scripture supports this view. Through the prophet Isaiah, the Lord declares: *My thoughts are completely different from yours, says the LORD. And my ways are far beyond anything you could imagine. For just as the heavens are higher than the earth, so are my ways higher than your ways and my thoughts than your thoughts* (Isa. 55:8–9, NLT). Descriptive biblical terms that reflect God's transcendence include *exalted* (Psa. 57:5), *dwelling in the heavens above* (Psa. 8:1), *enthroned on high* (Psa. 113:5), and *the Most High* (Psa. 97:9). These expressions portray God as wholly other, surpassing the limits of the created order.

However, God's transcendence does not imply distance or disconnection from creation. Rather, it highlights His sovereign rule and kingly authority while affirming His personal, covenantal engagement with the world. God is not inaccessible; He has revealed Himself in Scripture and through relationship with His people.

By contrast, *immanence* means that God is present within creation, near, knowable, and intimately involved in human affairs. As King, His control and authority are expressed through His close and personal presence, particularly with His people. God's immanence is central to biblical redemption: *Emmanuel, God with us.* This is the covenantal presence of the Lord, not only existing throughout the universe but also intensifying His presence in specific places and circumstances.

John Frame emphasizes that God is *omnipresent*, present everywhere, not merely because He created and governs all things, but because creation serves His redemptive covenant purposes. Frame concludes that transcendence and immanence together describe the royal dignity and presence of the God who came to dwell among His people in Jesus Christ, Immanuel.

Covenantal presence, in theological terms, refers to God's intentional and gracious relationship with humanity, established through divine covenants. In this relationship, God promises to be present and faithful to His people, who in turn are called to live in obedience to His will.

The transcendence and immanence of God together define the scope and accessibility of His eternal and infinite power. These relational attributes mean that God's power, though it transcends creation—is also present, near, and available within it. Because God is both omnipresent and omnipotent, every place and every person is equally close to His throne of grace, and His power is always accessible.

In contrast to human systems, where power diminishes with distance from its source, God's power remains undiminished regardless of space or location. For example, the 2024 Statista Research Department reported that the United Kingdom lost around 25 terawatt-hours of electricity during transmission in 2022, about 8% of its total supply. Similarly, the influence of political power often varies with geographical proximity. But God's royal authority, through His transcendence and immanence, means we have constant access to the "full voltage" of His power anywhere and anytime.

Jonah prayed to the Lord from inside the belly of a great fish (Jon. 2:1–10), while Elijah prayed for rain atop Mount Carmel (1 Kings 18:42). Neither location diminished the effectiveness of their prayers. God's power does not fade with distance because, through the Holy Spirit, the Godhead dwells within believers. Every Christian, therefore, has access to the power of the transcendent and immanent God.

The Omnipotence of God

We often sing and read about the Almighty God, but do we truly grasp how powerful He is? Christians frequently recite verses and prayers that proclaim God's omnipotence. Even some unbelievers acknowledge or reference this power. But what is the depth of our knowledge and understanding of God's omnipotence, and how does it shape our faith and Christian living?

The omnipotence of the Lord our God transcends the limits of human understanding. Not even the most advanced science or technology can quantify His power. To help Isaiah reflect on God's greatness, the Lord posed a profound question: *Who has measured the waters in the hollow of His hand, or with the breadth of His hand marked off the heavens? Who has held the dust of the earth in a basket, or weighed the mountains on the scales and the hills in a balance?* (Isaiah 40:12, NIV)

This vivid imagery is meant to stretch our perception and awaken awe at the unimaginable scale of God's power. His eternal power is revealed in creation, in the incarnation of Jesus Christ, through Scripture, and in the work of the Holy Spirit. The God who made the universe knows the volume of the seas, the weight of the earth's dust, and the mass of the mountains and hills.

David also recognized the omnipotence of God when he wrote: *The heavens declare the glory of God; the skies proclaim the work of His hands. Day after day they pour forth speech; night after night they reveal knowledge. They have no speech, they use no words; no sound is heard from them. Yet their voice goes out into all the earth, their words to the ends of the world* (Psa. 19:1-4, NIV). Creation speaks. Creation sings. Creation testifies. All of it displays the power of God.

When we look to the skies - the vast display of light, stars, and planetary movements - we see the handiwork of the Almighty. The speech of the day is evident in the sun, the birds in flight, vegetation thriving on land and sea, and the intricate ecosystems beneath our feet. Land animals, marine creatures, and human beings with their inventions all bear witness to aspects of God's creative power.

Even the moon, stars, and nocturnal creatures display incredible wisdom embedded in creation. The voice of creation resounds throughout the earth, but no created being can fully comprehend or measure the totality of God's power.

A Zambian comedian once recited a prayer typical of charismatic Christians, humorously describing God by invoking His names and qualities. While the tone was comedic, it nonetheless acknowledged the greatness of God's power. It's not surprising that atheists and agnostics often reference such portrayals in debates about the existence of God. But if we truly understood the power of the Almighty, its ability to bring things into existence out of nothing and to radically transform situations, we would long to tap into it and learn to depend on it consistently. So, what is the omnipotence of God?

The omnipotence of God animates His perfect nature and expresses His will, plans, and purposes. Theologian Stephen Charnock described it this way: God has a powerful wisdom to attend His ends without interruption; a powerful grace to save sinners; a powerful mercy to remove our misery; a powerful love to redeem humanity from sin through His Son; a powerful justice to lay all misery upon offenders; a powerful truth to perform His promises; and an infinite power to bestow rewards and inflict penalties. Behind every mighty act of God lies His mighty power.

Three well-known biblical events test the human perception of God's omnipotence. One such moment occurred when the Israelites were trapped—the Red Sea before them, mountains on either side, and the Egyptian army pursuing from behind. Paralyzed by fear, they forgot who had delivered them. The Psalmist reflects on this moment, saying: *Who can utter the mighty acts of the LORD? ... We have sinned with our fathers, we have committed iniquity, we have done wickedly. Our fathers in Egypt did not understand Your wonders; they did not remember the multitude of Your mercies but rebelled by the sea, the Red Sea* (Psalm 106:6–7, NKJV). He identifies two reasons for their fear:

1. They did not understand God's power, despite having witnessed the ten devastating plagues in Egypt.
2. They did not remember God's abundant mercies, how He had freed them from 430 years of slavery and even enabled them to leave with Egyptian wealth.

Even with the cloud and pillar of fire, the visible presence of their Deliverer, above them, they were still overwhelmed by fear. Their preoccupation with idol worship and a deeply rooted slave mentality blinded them to God's omnipotent presence.

How often, in moments of pressure, do we act the same way, feeling as though the world has closed in around us, forgetting the God who has already done the impossible in our lives?

Despite their disobedience, God parted the Red Sea and destroyed the Egyptian army, once again demonstrating His power and delivering the Israelites for His name's sake. As the Psalmist declares: *Nevertheless, He saved them for His name's sake, that He might make His mighty power known* (Psa. 106:8).

The same power that delivered the Israelites from slavery in Egypt was available to carry them safely across the Red Sea. But God knew they could not recognize or access it. Still, in His mercy, He sent an east wind that parted the sea, allowing them to walk across on dry ground, between towering walls of water. Then, using that same sea, He brought judgment upon Pharaoh and his army.

This miraculous deliverance demonstrated that God has complete control over creation and can command it as He wills. His power was not distant, it was available to the Israelites. Yet, like them, aren't there moments when we forget that the Godhead and His power dwell in us, even in life's storms?

Another moment that tested human understanding of God's omnipotence occurred when the Lord visited Abraham and Sarah to announce the birth of Isaac. Sarah laughed in disbelief, unable to fathom that a woman far past childbearing age could conceive and give birth. But the Lord said to Abraham: *Why did Sarah laugh, saying, Shall I surely bear a child, since I am old? Is anything too hard for the LORD? At the appointed time I will return to you, according to the time of life, and Sarah shall have a son* (Genesis 18:13–14). These questions not only exposed Sarah's unbelief but also reaffirmed God's limitless power. No situation is too complex for Him to resolve.

At the time, neither Abraham nor Sarah fully grasped the potency of God's power. Sarah assessed her circumstances based on her knowledge of human biology. But she wasn't alone in her doubt, Abraham also struggled to believe. His willingness to have a child with Hagar (resulting in Ishmael) reveals his uncertainty. Even after Ishmael's birth, Abraham asked God if Ishmael was the promised son, but God insisted: Sarah would bear the child of promise, Isaac.

Like Abraham and Sarah, we often give up on God's promises because of our physical circumstances or human reasoning. We judge possibilities by natural laws, scientific understanding, and personal experience. In today's world, where science is regarded as the final authority on life, Abraham and Sarah would have been completely written off as infertile and beyond hope.

Science would categorically deny the possibility of a 100-year-old man and a 90-year-old woman conceiving naturally. At that stage in life, such a couple would be considered to need care, not to give it. But such human assumptions are flawed, because God is the source of all life.

He is eternally and infinitely powerful, capable of creating, restoring, and rejuvenating anything, even what appears lifeless or beyond hope. God created natural laws, but He is not bound by them. He can operate both within and outside of them.

What we often forget is that God is the Creator of everything in heaven and on earth, and He can change conditions at any time to fulfil His will and for His pleasure. When God introduced Himself to Abraham as "God Almighty" (*El Shaddai*) before promising that Sarah would bear a son within a year, He was affirming His sovereign power over nature.

Can we really blame Abraham and Sarah for doubting? After all, they had waited 25 years for the fulfilment of God's promise, and by then, their bodies had clearly succumbed to age-related reproductive decline. But God had no reason to panic, because He is eternally powerful and not bound by natural laws. In fact, He created those laws, and His power transcends them.

Has God promised you something that you've dismissed as impossible because of your perceived natural limitations, just as Sarah did? Believe your Creator, because at the appointed time, He will fulfil His promise.

Abraham wasn't the only person in Scripture to struggle with belief in the face of an impossible situation. Other prominent figures in the Bible also expressed doubt when God asked them to carry out what seemed like unusual or unrealistic tasks.

Moses, for example, doubted God when the Israelites complained about manna and demanded meat. Moses responded with scepticism, saying: *The people whom I am among are six hundred thousand men on foot; yet You have said, I will give them meat, that they may eat for a whole month. Shall flocks and herds be slaughtered for them, to provide enough for them? Or shall all the fish of the sea be gathered for them, to provide enough for them? And the LORD said to Moses, Has the LORD's arm been shortened? Now you shall see whether what I say will happen to you or not* (Numb. 11:21–23, NKJV).

In human terms, Moses had every reason to be concerned. As the leader of Israel, he likely tried to calculate how much meat would be needed to feed over 600,000 men, not counting women and children. He would have known that slaughtering their livestock could jeopardize their sacrificial system. And the idea of fishing enough from the sea, especially in the wilderness, seemed logistically impossible.

Moses may have considered different potential sources of meat, and he couldn't just understand why God decided to provide meat to Israelites in the wilderness. He decided to alert God to the magnitude of the problem he had created for Himself. He told God they had two options. They either had to slaughter the flocks and herds, which would eventually affect their supply of animals for sacrifices or catch all the fishes from the sea, and this would require many and experienced fishermen, if the sea had enough stocks to meet the needs of Israelites. If you imagine how stressed Moses was, trying to figure out what was logistically and biologically possible, you will agree with me that he had limited options to what was humanly possible.

Although Moses had witnessed God's power in Egypt and at the Red Sea, he still underestimated what God could do. But God reminded him of His limitless power, asking, "Has the Lord's arm been shortened?" Then, to Moses' amazement, God sent a wind that brought quail from the sea, not fish, and piled them around the camp. The quail were spread two cubits deep (around 89 to 103 cm) and extended a day's journey in every direction around the camp.

Moses must have been stunned. Quails are typically land birds, not sea creatures. Yet here they were, delivered in a miraculous quantity far beyond what he could have imagined. Scholars estimate that each person gathered at least two homers, roughly 200 litres, of quail. This was no symbolic act; it was an overwhelming demonstration of God's provision and power.

As Christians, we are often tempted to approach problems by relying on past experiences or the resources we are familiar with. However, God has the power to create, transform, sustain, and even destroy according to His will. He generates power to accomplish any task He chooses.

We can never fully comprehend the nature or magnitude of God's omnipotence, and we often underestimate His power. How often do we question our ability to fulfil God's call based on our own perceived limitations?

If God promises to do something in your life, or commissions you to perform a task, it is not your responsibility to figure out how He will do it. He is omnipotent. His word carries the same power as His will. His mighty power enables Him to accomplish all things according to His will and good pleasure.

The Challenge of Understanding the Power of God

According to Wikipedia, an individual's physical strength is determined by two main factors: the cross-sectional area of muscle fibres recruited to generate force, and the intensity of that recruitment, along with factors such as joint angles and limb length. If God's hand can hold the waters of the seas, how vast and powerful must it be?

Despite all our technological advancements, humans cannot accurately or precisely measure the total volume of water in the seas. For example, if the UK's Environment Agency were to commission a water engineering company to measure the amount of water in the North Sea, it would be an enormous undertaking, costly and likely inconclusive. There is no guarantee the results would be either accurate or precise.

Now imagine trying to weigh all the soil on the African continent or to determine the mass of Mount Everest. The hand of God is described in Scripture as able to hold the seas, scoop up the dust of the earth, and weigh the mountains and hills. While humanity struggles to even conceive the methodology to attempt such tasks, God knows their exact dimensions and mass. His power is truly beyond comparison.

King Nebuchadnezzar came to understand God's might when he was driven from his palace to live in the wilderness, grazing like cattle and dwelling among wild animals. After seven years, when his sanity was restored, he praised God and declared: *All the people of the earth are nothing compared to Him. He does as He pleases among the angels of heaven and among the people of the earth. No one can stop Him or say to Him, 'What do you mean by doing these things?* (Dan. 4:35, NLT).

This was the same king who had once boasted of building the great city of Babylon by his own power. But his humiliation revealed to him that God's power is irresistible and sovereign. God reduced a proud king to an animal-like existence, and from that experience, Nebuchadnezzar concluded that all people are as nothing before God. The Lord does whatever He pleases in heaven and on earth, and He answers to no one. How dangerous it is to toy with God's power, yet both believers and unbelievers do so again and again.

Miracles throughout history have demonstrated God's power. As the Psalmist declares: *He alone performs great miracles* (Psa. 136:4). A miracle, by definition, is an event not attributable to human power or natural laws and is therefore recognized as the work of God. While science can describe the origin, structure, and behaviour of things according to natural laws, miracles transcend these laws. Because they defy scientific explanation, miracles are often dismissed by scientists and sceptics as illusions, but they remain undeniable testimonies of God's omnipotence.

Human beings usually perform tasks that can be explained through natural or scientific laws. By contrast, there are events that can only be accomplished supernaturally. For example, Jesus called Lazarus back to life after he had been dead and buried for four days. When faced with a blind man, Jesus spat on the ground, made mud with His spittle, and applied it to the blind man's eyes, and he regained his sight. There was no medical operation or scientific explanation for what He did. All the miracles performed by the apostles were not the result of any inherent power in their words, hands, or objects. While Christians can perform miracles by leveraging God's power, God alone is the true and legitimate miracle worker.

The Bible is filled with examples of miracles. God parted the Red Sea, allowing the Israelites to cross on a dry seabed between walls of water (Exod. 14:21-22). Other notable miracles include the parting of the Jordan River, allowing the Israelites to enter Canaan (Josh. 3:15-16), the protection of Daniel in the lion's den (Dan. 6:21), and the raising of Lazarus from the dead (John 11:38-44). These miracles demonstrate the unrivalled omnipotence of God.

God's divinity and power are eternally linked and are evident to all human beings. In his letter to the Church in Rome, Paul wrote: *For since the creation of the world, God's invisible qualities, His eternal power and divine nature, have been clearly seen, being understood from what has been made, so that people are without excuse* (Rom. 1:20). Some Gentiles in Rome dishonoured God because they worshiped His creations rather than the Creator, which triggered God's wrath. Paul explains that there was no excuse for this idolatry, as the truth was plainly visible through creation. This verse highlights three aspects that the Roman Church needed to understand.

First, there are two qualities of God that the human eye cannot see, His eternal power and His divinity. Many have used these invisible attributes to argue against the existence of God. Some Christians have also struggled to understand these qualities. For example, if we fully understood the nature of God, we would not struggle with unbelief or commit sins that we would never consider if God were physically present. We deceive ourselves when we gossip, steal, fornicate, commit adultery, falsify information, cheat, or commit other sins. But how about if such sins are committed in a human-constructed environment, like a house, office, school, or hotel? Would others discover them? People may not uncover sins committed in secret or in our minds. But the omnipresent and omniscient God sees and knows everything because He lives in and around us. Whenever we observe created things, we should be reminded of God's presence and His power.

Second, Paul emphasizes that since the creation of the world, God's eternal power and divinity have been clearly seen through the things God has made. God reveals Himself to every human being in three ways: outwardly through His visible works, creation (the book of nature) and the incarnation of Christ; inwardly through our conscience (the mind perceiving what the eye cannot discern); and through the Word of God.

Although God is invisible, His great works (the universe or cosmos) reveal His nature. According to Wikipedia, the term 'universe' is commonly defined as the totality of existence, including planets, stars, galaxies, the contents of intergalactic space, and all matter and energy. This represents the totality of God's creation, with which humans interact, whether physically or remotely.

The extent to which an individual interacts with the universe depends on their environment. However, God has made provision for everyone to discern His eternal power and deity through nature. The outward manifestation of God's attributes through creation strengthens our faith, which we build through the Word and our conscience. God also enables us to perceive His divine qualities through our minds, which can see what the eye cannot discern.

Every human being has a conscience that, alongside God's self-expression through creation, enables them to discern His eternal power and divine nature. In his second letter to the Roman Church, Paul writes: *Even Gentiles, who do not have God's written law, show that they know His law when they instinctively obey it, even without having heard it. They demonstrate that God's law is written in their hearts, for their own conscience and thoughts either accuse them or tell them they are doing right* (Rom. 2:14–15, NLT). Anyone who understood that Israel was a chosen nation inadvertently concluded that Gentiles would not have the antenna for God's law and let alone to practice it. Paul must have keenly observed the Gentiles and realized that they acted according to justice, mercy, temperance and truth, the practice of which was consistent with the Law of Moses although they had no access to the written law. However, while conscience testifies to moral truth, it is through both conscience and creation that God's eternal power and divine nature are made plain to humanity.

Have you ever observed unbelievers conducting their civil affairs in a way that aligns with Christian principles, exhibiting natural justice in debates or demonstrating strong moral values in their behaviour? Perhaps you've even heard people praise an unbeliever's good works to the point of saying, "He is as good as a Christian."

When we pay attention to the conduct of some unbelievers, we may notice behaviours that reflect Christian values. Paul makes a similar observation in Romans 2:14–15, noting that Gentiles, who do not have the written Law, sometimes instinctively follow it. This moral instinct is guided by their conscience, which acts as an internal witness to God's law written on their hearts.

It is argued that God has deposited divine light, often described as God-consciousness or the light of nature, into the soul of every human being. This inner witness reveals moral truths, testifies to one's integrity, and affirms what is right. According to Scripture, God has endowed every person with the capacity to perceive His eternal power and divine nature through both creation and conscience (Rom. 1:19–20). This means that no one has an excuse for idolatry or for denying God's existence.

The apostle Paul argues that God's eternal power and divine nature have been clearly seen in the created world, so much so that any denial of Him is a suppression of the truth. Human faculties are designed to discern these attributes. Therefore, failure to acknowledge God's existence reflects not ignorance, but a voluntary turning away from truth.

People respond to this divine revelation in different ways. First, there are Christians who believe in God but have not fully understood His nature. As they seek Him sincerely, He will reveal Himself more clearly. Second, there are the indifferent—those who, despite the witness of nature and conscience, remain undecided or apathetic about God's existence. Third, there are atheists who assert that there is no God. Scripture teaches that such a stance is not based on a lack of evidence but on a conscious suppression of truth (Rom. 1:21). These individuals disregard both God's works and the testimony of conscience, resisting the righteousness of God.

David declares in Psalm 14:1, *The fool says in his heart, There is no God.* This statement reflects the spiritual and moral implications of denying God: it is not merely an intellectual position but a failure of judgment and moral sensitivity. To deny God's existence is to ignore the very foundation of human identity and dignity, which stems from being created in God's image.

Recognizing God's invisible qualities in nature leads to a life aligned with godly values, sensitivity to moral truth, reverence for creation, and the pursuit of righteousness. Conversely, those who reject God disregard the evidence around and within them, often leading to a life detached from the moral order God has established.

Is it justifiable to call someone a fool for denying the existence of God? According to Psalm 14:1, *The fool says in his heart, There is no God*. This statement is not a casual insult but a moral and spiritual assessment. In biblical terms, a *'fool'* refers to someone who wilfully rejects God's revelation, not merely someone lacking intelligence. The Psalmist likely draws this conclusion based on four foundational ways in which God has revealed Himself to humanity:

1. Through Creation (Nature) – God's eternal power and divine nature are clearly seen in the things He has made (Romans 1:20).
2. Through Conscience – God has written His law on our hearts (Romans 2:15).
3. Through Scripture – The Word of God reveals His will, character, and plan for humanity.
4. Through Jesus Christ – The fullness of God's nature has been made known in Christ (Hebrews 1:3).

While every human being has the right to either accept or reject this revelation, the Psalmist implies that denial of God stems not from lack of evidence but from a rejection of what is already known inwardly and outwardly.

That said, there are also people who believe in God but live contrary to His nature. Despite their knowledge of God, their lives are governed by the desires of the flesh, the eyes, and pride (1 John 2:16). Can such a person still be considered a child of God? According to John 1:12, those who receive and believe in Christ are given the right to become children of God. This relationship involves a covenant union with Christ, sealed by the Holy Spirit.

As children of God, we are spiritually united with Christ, grafted into Him like branches to a vine, and called to live by the Spirit. Romans 8:14 provides the litmus test: "Those who are led by the Spirit of God are the children of God." If we are truly led by the Spirit, we have access to the same power that raised Jesus from the dead (Ephesians 1:19–20), and therefore, no excuse remains for habitual sin.

Understanding the infinite power and nature of God should embolden every

Christian to live a purpose-filled life. Just as a bank account holder withdraws funds with full confidence in their balance, so too should we access God's power for fulfilling our God-given vocations. Our faith is not merely intellectual assent, but a daily walk empowered by the Holy Spirit, rooted in God's eternal character and power.

CHAPTER 4
How Powerful Was the First Human God Created?

When you watch television, listen to the radio, or scroll through the Internet and social media, what captures your attention? Most headlines are dominated by distressing news, natural disasters, economic and environmental crises, disease outbreaks, wars claiming countless lives, terrorism, human trafficking, cyber-attacks, religious conflicts, racial violence, and the moral challenges facing the Church. These stories paint a picture of a world where people not only inflict harm on one another but also seem to be losing control over key aspects of life.

Yet, amidst the chaos, good news is also reported, but it rarely gains the same traction or attention. Why is that? It seems that human nature gravitates more easily toward fear, drama, and crisis.

The state of the world today reflects the dual capacity of human beings, created in God's image, to use power for either good or evil. However, the overwhelming presence of evil has led some to question whether God, and even humanity, has any control left. If God is all-loving and all-powerful, how can He allow such widespread suffering? And if Christians are truly led by the Holy Spirit, why do we seem so powerless in the face of escalating evil?

But are believers truly as helpless as the world suggests? Or have we underestimated the power God has placed within us? Have you ever paused to reflect on the immense potential of those made in the image of God—those who carry the presence of His Spirit?

Attributes of Humans Created in the Image of God

There are certain God-given attributes in human beings that enable us to access and operate in the power of God. The extent to which we develop and express these attributes often determines how much of His power we can draw upon to fulfil the purpose and principles of His will. A clear understanding of these characteristics helps us to apply the appropriate measure of God's power in living lives worthy of our calling. Below is a summary of these attributes, which reflect the image of God in us.

Humans are God's Personal Representatives on Earth

When God created the heavens and the earth, He appointed Himself as the ruler of the heavens but delegated the governance of the earth to humanity. This responsibility required a being capable of understanding and implementing His plan for creation, one who could love, nurture, and steward the earth in a way that reflects God's own care.

For this reason, God created humans in His image and likeness, equipping us with the qualities necessary to fulfil our earthly assignment. Only those who can discern their God-given role and act accordingly are able to rule over creation effectively. God, in His wisdom, designed humanity to match the scope and scale of the task.

This model of delegated authority can be illustrated through earthly governance. For example, in southern Africa, a Paramount Chief may preside over a vast territory that spans multiple countries. Paramount Chief Mpezeni of the Ngoni people, based in Zambia's Eastern Province, also has subjects in Malawi and Mozambique. Due to the size of his kingdom, he appoints Sub-Chiefs to rule in his stead. These Sub-Chiefs are so well trained in the chief's customs and principles that they govern just as he would.

Similarly, God expects humans, His appointed stewards, to manage the earth in alignment with His will. He has provided the Word of God as the manual for governance, and this sacred task can only be fulfilled through constant communion with Him.

While being made in God's image gives us aspects of His nature, such as reason, moral responsibility, creativity, and the capacity for relationship, it does not mean we are like God in every way. We are not omnipotent or self-existent. However, we have been given everything necessary to rule creation on His behalf.

The pressing question remains: Are you and I governing the earth as the Creator expects us to? Ruling over the earth is not merely a privilege, it is the primary function of humanity.

Humans Have Unique Access to the Power of God

Humans have unique access to the supernatural power of God, an access not granted to other creatures. Non-human creation largely operates by instinct, fulfilling its God-given purpose without conscious planning. Although all creation reveals the invisible attributes and eternal power of God (Rom. 1:20), animals and plants do so naturally, without intentional worship or spiritual awareness. While scientists have observed that some animals exhibit basic forms of planning and problem-solving, their cognitive and spiritual faculties are not comparable to those of human beings.

In contrast, humans were created in the image of God, and with that image comes the capacity for spiritual communion. This divine likeness grants us access to God's power through the Holy Spirit. Since God's nature is spiritual, and humans possess both a soul and a spirit, we are uniquely equipped to engage with Him. The Holy Spirit dwelling within believers serves as the connection through which we access God's power and guidance.

God's communication with humanity is spiritual in nature. For His power to flow into a person's life, there must be a living, active connection. This communion occurs as the human spirit responds to and fellowships with the Holy Spirit. Scripture affirms this vital relationship: *For as many as are led by the Spirit of God, they are the sons of God* (Rom. 8:14, KJV). It is this spiritual bond that defines our identity as God's children and enables us to walk in His power.

Humans Were Created to Have the Image of the Mind of God

God created humans in His image and likeness, particularly reflecting His ability to reason and make judgments. Why did God choose to do this? He did not create us as mere automatons or robots. Rather, He loved us so deeply that He gave us the ability to make decisions, assess situations, and exercise freedom of choice, just as He would.

In 1 Corinthians 2:15-16 (NIV), Paul writes: *The person with the Spirit makes judgments about all things, but such a person is not subject to merely human judgments, for who has known the mind of God so as to instruct Him? But we have the mind of*

Christ. Christians, indwelt by the Holy Spirit, have the mind of Christ. This means we can make right and objective judgments that go beyond human understanding.

As believers walk in the Spirit and seek God's will, their judgments reflect His mind, making them uniquely equipped to live according to His purpose. What excites me most about this is that we, as believers, have the mind of Christ, a profound gift that empowers us to live in accordance with God's will.

Jesus said in Matthew 5:13-14: *You are the salt of the earth. But if the salt loses its saltiness, how can it be made salty again? It is no longer good for anything, except to be thrown out and trampled underfoot. You are the light of the world. A town built on a hill cannot be hidden* (NIV). Salt preserves and flavours, and so too do Christians, who, by embracing the mind of Christ, display godly character and act as preservatives of morality in society. We are called to build an ethical society, keeping the earth from moral decay.

Salt was often used by fishermen to preserve fish, and Jesus called His disciples to be salt, preserving humanity from godlessness, immorality, and chaos. As the salt of the earth, we are tasked with preserving what is good and godly in our culture. When we abide in Christ and He in us, our lives help to preserve and flavour the lives of those around us. Believers who display the beatitudes (Matt. 5:3-11) serve as a means of preventing the world's corruption and seasoning human minds with wisdom and grace. However, if we lose our saltiness, if we cease to display the mind of Christ, our ability to positively impact others diminishes.

Jesus also called His disciples the light of the world. As the light of the world, believers are called to live lives that cannot be hidden, for the Kingdom of God within them is visible to all. This light, originating from God, produces good works that bring glory to Him and lead others to the Kingdom of heaven.

As Spirit-filled Christians, we must let our light shine before others. Our lives should reflect God's love for both Him and our neighbours. Our words, actions, relationships, and even our online interactions should reflect His light. In a world full of darkness, people need to see the light of Christ shining through us to align with Kingdom principles and life.

So where are the properties of salt and light expressed? God empowers us to be salt and light wherever we are. Whether in the family, the church, the workplace, government, or in social life, our unique position as believers gives us the authority to bring God's influence into every sphere of life.

Critical thinking is a hallmark of human creation and sets us apart from non-human creation. Christians, as critical thinkers, are equipped to analyse situations through the lens of the Holy Spirit. Some may believe that only scholars, teachers, or researchers should engage in critical thinking, but that's not the case. Every believer, empowered by the Holy Spirit, is called to reason and think critically.

I'm not suggesting that every believer must become a scholar or academic to be rational. But there is no reason why a believer cannot read the news, engage in discussions, and analyse situations critically with the help of the Holy Spirit. The advantage Christians have over unbelievers is the guidance of the Holy Spirit, which leads us to explore dimensions of truth that are not accessible to the world.

Jesus Christ was a critical thinker. He grew in wisdom and stature. The Bible does not tell us that Jesus attended a special school to be able to sit in the synagogue at the age of 12, debating with scribes, Pharisees, Sadducees, and others. But He received wisdom from the Father that enabled Him to reason with any human being, regardless of their educational, philosophical, theological, or social background.

The author of Acts teaches that Paul "reasoned in the synagogue with Jews and God-fearing Greeks, as well as in the marketplace day by day with those who happened to be there. A group of Epicurean and Stoic philosophers began to debate with him. Some of them asked: *What is this babbler trying to say? Others remarked, 'He seems to be advocating foreign gods* (Acts 17:17-18, NIV). Regardless of your background, God has given you the ability to reason with both believers and unbelievers. However, developing this faculty of reasoning with people from different backgrounds requires us to invest time in studying the Word of God and relevant extrabiblical materials. For example, to reason with atheists, one needs to understand the basis of their arguments.

The wisdom to reason with others on matters of faith comes from God. Believers especially need this wisdom in the Church, where false doctrines and strange philosophies are sometimes taught. Paul also reasoned with the Epicurean and Stoic philosophers in the marketplace, where some found the gospel offensive and accused Paul of advocating foreign gods. What you consider the genuine Word of God may be mistaken for heresy, which underscores the importance of reasoning with people, either to help them understand the truth or to defend the Christian faith.

A young Nigerian comedian demonstrated her ability to reason with others in a simple yet effective way. A professor found the two comedians, a young girl and her uncle, enjoying soft drinks on the balcony of their flat. As he walked to his car, he greeted them. Just as he prepared to drive off, he remembered that the duo had recently won an award, so he turned back to congratulate them. The following discussion ensued:

Professor: "Mark Angel, I heard that you people won a YouTube Gold Award. Is that true?"

Comedians: "Yes, sir, it is true."

Professor: "Wow, you people are really trying!"

Comedians: "It is God who is doing all this for us."

Professor: "Which God?"

Comedians: "Our God."

Professor: "Where is your God?"

Comedians: "Our God is in heaven."

Professor: "Can you see your God?"

Comedians: "No!"

Professor: "Can you touch your God?"

Comedians: "No!"

Professor: "Then, there is no God."

Comedians: Eeeeh!

Professor: "Science has proven it that anything you cannot see or touch does not exist."

Comedians: "But sir"

Professor: "Shhh! Are you a graduate?"

Comedians: "No!"

Professor: "I am a Professor."

Young girl: "Professor, excuse me, 'How do you know that there is no God?'"

Professor: "It's common sense, I use my sense."

Young girl: "Where is your sense?"

Professor: "Up there."

Young girl: Can you touch your sense?

Professor: "No!"

Young girl: Can you see your sense?

Professor: "No!"

Young girl: "That means there is no sense."

Professor: Hmm!

Young girl: "According to science anything you cannot see or touch does not exist, so you have no sense."

Professor: "Eeeh!"

In this comedy, the professor used science to argue that God does not exist because we can neither touch nor see Him. However, the young girl challenged him to justify his conclusion that there is no God. The professor became vulnerable when he admitted that he used common sense to prove that there is no God.

The young girl analysed the professor's argument and understood the logic behind it. She then used the same reasoning to demonstrate that his judgment was flawed. This illustrates that critical thinking is not reserved solely for the learned. You, too, have the potential to reason with fellow believers and people in the marketplace. This is an essential tool for sharing and defending the gospel.

Many believers argue that they avoid reasoning with people on issues of Christian faith. However, if you examine the lives of the apostles, patriarchs, Jesus Christ, and His followers, you will see that debating matters of faith was an integral component of their ministry. How can you achieve your mission of being the salt of the earth and the light of the world if you cannot reason with the people God brings your way?

God has given Christians the ability to reason with others according to their measure of faith and grace. Of course, believers are to be led by the Holy Spirit in their reasoning with others. Jesus Christ warned His disciples when He said: *Behold, I send you forth as sheep in the midst of wolves: be therefore wise as serpents, and harmless as doves* (Matt. 10:16, NIV). The mission of the disciples was to share the gospel, but they needed to exercise wisdom in their ministry to avoid unnecessary confrontations. However, we must invest time in studying the Book of Scripture, the Book of Nature, and extrabiblical materials to equip ourselves to share and defend the gospel of Christ.

Creation Depends on Humanity to Fulfil its Purpose on Earth.

Many believers rarely think about their stewardship role and the fact that non-human creatures depend on humans to effectively and efficiently fulfil their functions on earth. Moses said: *When the LORD God made the heavens and the earth, no shrub of the field had yet appeared on earth, and no plant of the field had sprung up, for the LORD God had not sent rain on the earth and there was no man to work the ground* (Gen. 2:4-5 NIV). For shrubs and other plants to flourish on earth, they required two key conditions: rain to supply the necessary water for growth and humans to work the ground.

As a son of a smallholder farmer and a trained environmental scientist, I understand the importance of working the ground. During our cropping season, which coincided with the rainy season, we tilled the land to improve air circulation, water retention and drainage, and to soften the soil for easy seed germination and root penetration. These days, conservation agriculture emphasizes minimal soil disturbance, consistent soil cover, and crop rotation. Whatever agricultural practices a farmer adopts, the goal remains the same: to create a good environment that supports healthy and productive plants.

God understood the importance of working the ground to nurture shrubs and other plants, which is why He could not introduce these plants on earth until humans were ready to tend to the land. However, many believers are so distanced from the environment that they fail to see earth-keeping as their responsibility.

Some believers argue that we should leave environmental management to experts. Others believe that since heaven and earth will pass away, they can afford to be indifferent to environmental issues. But how can we be the salt of the earth and the light of the world when we shy away from our God-given responsibility? God still expects us to work the ground until He returns. We need to seek His guidance to understand what He wants us to do in this area.

Humans Were Created to Fear and Obey God

Humans are made to fear and obey God. Solomon said: *Now all has been heard; here is the conclusion of the matter: Fear God and keep His commandments, for this is the whole duty of man* (Eccl. 12:13 NIV). This verse does not suggest that humans should fear God as one would fear an abusive father. In my early childhood, my dad was very aggressive. As my schoolteacher in years 2 and 3, he made me sit alone on a stool at the front of the class and set higher targets for me than for the rest of the class. I remember times when I scored the highest marks in arithmetic and English spelling, yet still received a beating, while the rest of the class was spared.

Even worse, if my dad felt I had underperformed in class, he would punish me at home. Until he stopped treating me this way, I always associated my dad with punishment. As a result, I was so scared of him that I would look for any excuse not to be near him. I would claim I was avoiding him out of respect or love, but as a child, it was more the fear of punishment than genuine respect that defined our relationship.

However, to fear God means to revere and honour Him for what He has done and for who He is, seeking to discern and do His will.

As believers, we fear God because He is our Creator, Sustainer, Provider, and Shield. Even when He disciplines us, He does so lovingly to correct us. We are made to fear Him and obey His commandments because that is the whole duty of man. However, He does not force or coerce us into fearing Him out of a sense of duty. Rather, the fear of God and our obedience to His commands flow naturally from a strong relationship with Him, which results from the flourishing fruit of the Spirit within us. God helps us understand what we should do to maximize our fellowship with Him. We also value this relationship because it is a basic requirement for walking with Him and accessing His blessings.

When we fear and obey God, we cultivate an intimate relationship with Him and live in harmony with His will. God leverages our hunger and thirst for His righteousness to give us access to His eternal power, which enables us to fulfil His purpose for our lives. We cannot harness the power of God without fearing Him and obeying His commands.

Humans Were Blessed to be Fruitful and to Multiply

God blessed humans to be fruitful, to multiply, and to fill the earth. Moses said, *God created man in His own image, in the image of God He created him; male and female He created them. God blessed them and said to them, Be fruitful and increase in number, fill the earth and subdue it.* (Gen. 1:27-28 NIV). Fruitfulness, increasing in number, and multiplication are blessings from God. Every man and woman created in the image of God is blessed. But what does it mean to be fruitful?

Fruitfulness refers to living a life that produces good works and reflects the purpose and precepts of God's will. It is an attribute of blessedness that manifests in all primary areas of our lives, including spiritual growth, social life, physical welfare, wealth, vocation, critical thinking, and family relationships. God's desire is for humans to flourish in all these areas, and He has made provision for this to happen.

In the creational context, the fruitfulness of humanity refers to producing many offspring and increasing in number through heterosexual reproduction. Men and women made in the image and likeness of God are blessed to be fruitful.

Marriage between a man and a woman is sacred and provides a suitable environment for childbearing and upbringing.

Every offspring is a blessing and a heritage from God and should bring joy to parents. The psalmist says, *"Behold, children are a heritage from the Lord, the fruit of the womb is a reward. Like arrows in the hand of a warrior, so are the children of one's youth. Happy is the man who has his quiver full of them."* (Psa. 127:3-5 NKJV). There are traits that God has imparted to our children because they are a heritage from God. The fruit of the womb is a special embodiment of God's attributes. Sadly, the reproductive gift of humanity has been so devalued that children are recklessly aborted, abused, neglected, and belittled—compromising the godly attributes within them. Jesus cautioned His disciples: *"Whoever causes one of these little ones who believe in Me to stumble, it would be better for him that a millstone were hung around his neck and he were drowned in the depth of the sea."* (Matt. 18:6 KJV). Jesus knew what was deposited in children, and those who neglect or harm them would face severe consequences. In this context, both children in the faith and children defined by age need exceptional care to nurture what God has deposited in them.

The fruit of the womb has an inherent capacity to develop characteristics necessary for fulfilling God's purpose. Fruitfulness, in this sense, is an expression of qualities that God engraves in an offspring. God created humanity to multiply and fill the earth. The task of cultivating and keeping His garden, the earth, required a population that could effectively manage all earthly creatures and ensure they fulfilled the purpose and precepts of God's will. While God placed Adam and Eve in the Garden of Eden, a microcosm of the earth, the goal was always to fill the earth and subdue it.

Humans were made to reproduce to ensure the continuity of the species and to populate the earth. However, the multiplication of human beings is not an open-ended mandate. As resources diminish and the earth becomes filled, humans need to be wise to ensure that the demands of offspring and other creatures do not exceed the earth's capacity to recycle resources, thus ensuring that earthly creatures fulfil their purpose according to God's will.

Fruitfulness, increasing in number, and multiplication to replenish the earth and subdue it is an integrated command, a means to achieve God's will to work and keep the entire earth through humanity as His representatives. The need to increase the human population was to fill the earth and rule over it. God expected humanity to fully utilize their gifts as His image-bearers to fulfil this creational mandate. Human beings are made in the image of God, standing as His representatives on earth. We are made to represent God's authority, ruling over and subduing the rest of His creation.

Reproduction and multiplication of human beings are closely linked to their earthly mission of stewardship over God's creation. Apart from enjoying a rich sexual relationship, humans were created to populate the earth with individuals who have the qualities to cultivate and care for the earth. Ruling over the earth takes different forms based on the diversity of individuals.

God placed man in the Garden of Eden with a job to do. He had created a world, including work to be done, and He made man with a mission to accomplish that work. Logically, God could have created a perfect world with every imaginable creature in place, but He made humans to work alongside Him to actualize the universe's potential, to participate in His work. Whatever gift God has given you fits within the scope of the creational mandate to steward God's creation. Whether you are a social worker, teacher, doctor, engineer, soldier, pastor, housewife, or student, your vocation is an expression of the cultural mandate to work and keep the earth.

Harnessing the power of God involves recognizing humanity as the image of God's authority on earth and leveraging the blessedness of fruitfulness, multiplication, and the command to fill the earth and subdue it. When this inherent attribute of humanity is rightly understood, God appropriates a corresponding measure of His eternal power to fulfil the purpose and precepts of His will.

Humans Were Created to be Vocational Beings
Many Christians consider work to be burdensome and look forward to a day

when they can be free from it. Indeed, work can create stress when our knowledge and skills do not align with its demands. When we choose to work outside of what God has assigned us to do, we are likely to feel the strain of that mismatch. We were created as vocational beings to do work that God prepared in advance for us to accomplish. We need to come to terms with the fact that work is an act of worship and demonstrates that we fear and obey God.

God Himself worked when creating the universe and everything in it. Moses confirms this when he writes: *By the seventh day God had completed the work He had been doing; so, from the seventh day He rested from all His work* (Gen. 2:2 NIV). God has not stopped working. After creating the universe, He continues to uphold, maintain, guide, and sustain it by the word of His power (Heb. 1:3 AMPV). Paul reaffirms this when he says, *He (Jesus) is before all things, and in Him all things hold together* (Col. 1:17 NIV). God does not sleep or slumber as He works to keep the universe and everything in it functioning. Just as God works, humans are also created to work.

Created in the image of God, humans have the capacity to work if they follow His instructions. Moses records that *The LORD God took the man and put him in the Garden of Eden to work it and take care of it* (Gen. 2:15 NIV). If you think that work is a curse, remember that God commanded man to work the garden and care for it before humanity's rebellion. No one can fulfil their mission on earth without embracing this divine command.

It is important to discover the work that God has given you and begin to do it. This happens when a believer earnestly seeks the Kingdom of God first, along with His righteousness (Matt. 6:33). The Holy Spirit will reveal to you your specific assignment on earth. I cannot emphasize enough the importance of discovering your calling.

Paul said, *For we are God's workmanship, created in Christ Jesus to do good works, which God prepared in advance for us to do* (Eph. 2:10 NIV). He emphasizes three things: 1) God, our Maker, has created us with specific characteristics to match the work He wants us to do; 2) every believer, created in Christ Jesus, has the capacity to do good works; and 3) the believer's assignment on earth is not random, but consists of the good works that God prepared in advance. Are you doing the good works that God prepared for you in advance?

God Created Humans to be Social Beings

God created humans as social beings, with inherent needs and desires to form interpersonal relationships with others. Social bonds arising from these relationships nurture other essential needs: the need for a sense of belonging, the desire to love and be loved, and the need for sexual fulfilment. Satisfying these needs leads to a sense of completeness, and survival is ensured.

Aristotle once said: *Man is by nature a social animal; an individual who is unsocial, naturally and not accidentally, is either beneath our notice or more than human. Society is something that precedes the individual. Anyone who either cannot lead the common life or is so self-sufficient as not to need to, and therefore does not partake in society, is either a beast or a god.* We are designed to live in community and to establish networks that serve different areas of our lives. However, this can only be achieved if we commit ourselves to building these social networks.

Paul puts it this way: *Just as each of us has one body with many members, and these members do not all have the same function, so in Christ we, though many, form one body, and each member belongs to all the others* (Rom. 12:4-5 NIV). Believers thrive when they establish and maintain healthy relationships with others. They must also recognize and leverage the unique gifts of others to fulfil their purpose. This requires individuals to contribute to the overall function of the social group.

Although there are many types of social networks, an authentic community consists of people with similar beliefs and values. For a believer, family settings, Bible study groups, local churches, and other Christian associations are valuable for building a rich Christian social life. Since we live in the world, we may also be required to associate with individuals, communities, and institutions that are not sympathetic to our Christian values and beliefs. However, we must ensure that these relationships do not compromise our stand in the Lord.

A Christian who neglects the fellowship of believers is like a fish removed from its natural habitat—whether a pond, river, lake, or ocean. The author of Hebrews writes: *Let us not give up meeting together, as some are in the habit of doing, but let us encourage one another—and all the more as you see the Day approaching* (Heb. 10:25 NIV). In a gathering of believers, we learn to give to and receive from each other. The business world has understood this principle well: they believe that your networks define your net worth.

Humans Were Created as Objects of Love

How often do you hear people complaining that no one loves them? Such statements come from a vacuum in an individual that arises when he or she feels unloved. However, we should not be quick to dismiss such individuals as weak or overly sensitive. They are simply expressing their inherent desire to love and be loved. The Apostle John said: *Beloved, let us love one another, for love is of God; and everyone who loves is born of God and knows God* (1 John 4:7 NKJV). John reminds us that loving each other is something believers must naturally do because they are products of love. God is love, He loves, and He expects to be loved. As His children who know the Father, our nature is to love God and our neighbours.

Loving our neighbours is a command, not optional. It confirms who our Father is and the extent to which we know Him. Paul, writing to the Roman Church, said, *Be devoted to one another in brotherly love* (Rom. 12:10 NIV). He also writes: *Let no debt remain outstanding, except the continuing debt of love to one another, for he who loves his fellow man has fulfilled the law... Love does no harm to its neighbour. Therefore, love is the fulfilment of the law* (Rom. 13:8-10 NIV). Paul emphasizes that what drives a believer's love for another is devotion to that individual. Brotherly love should not be taken lightly—it is a matter of the heart.

Paul further explains why believers must love one another: Loving your neighbour as yourself fulfils the law, because anyone who practices genuine love does not harm his or her neighbour. God has designed us to love Him, love our neighbours, and even love non-human creation.

The qualities of humans, created in the image of God, present them as suitable rulers of the earth. However, humanity needs power and authority to discharge this function, and God has provided everything they need to fulfil this. Very few people dispute the fact that anyone made in the image of God carries His power. The question is, "How powerful is man, created in the image of God?"

Humans Are as Powerful as Their Life on Earth Demands

All creation depends on God; it begins and continues by the power of God. Similarly, when God breathed the breath of life into the nostrils of man, the Holy Spirit deposited the incredible power of Jehovah El Shaddai (God Almighty) in him, enabling him to carry out the tasks for which humans were designed. When God breathed His breath of life into Adam, he became a living soul and embodied the power and authority of God.

In Genesis 17, God reassures Abram and Sarai that they would have a child of promise in their old age, and He changes their names to Abraham and Sarah, respectively. Something supernatural happened at that moment. God breathed into Sarai and Abram, and the transformation that took place in their biologically unproductive bodies was outwardly marked by the changes in their names.

The reproductive systems of Abraham and Sarah, which were past the childbearing stage, suddenly became active. The couple defied all natural laws and conceived a miracle child. At the appointed time, Sarah gave birth, just as the LORD had promised them. The incredible power of God can turn what is humanly impossible into reality. This is the nature of the power that God gave to Adam at the moment He created him.

Apart from the unconditional power of God that sustains all creation, God provided man with mitochondrial power in his body, power from non-human creation (e.g., the sun), which supports life processes, as well as His supernatural power. By giving names to the animals God brought before him, Adam demonstrated intelligence and authority. Power is inherent in Adam's act of speaking the names of the animals, imaging the same power and authority that God exercised over all creation when He spoke the world into existence.

Before the fall in the Garden of Eden, Adam had all the power and authority to govern the earth. Within him was latent ability or power bearing the image and likeness of God. God delegated this power to humans, allowing them to exercise their freedom and use it as situations demanded.

If humans fear God and obey His commandments, they have the authority to exercise His power as needed. They have constant access to this power. Uninterrupted communion between God and His children ensured a consistent flow of power from the source to His dependents.

The extent to which God's power delivers desired results depends on two factors: the unlimited power of God and the ability of a child of God to access and utilize this power to achieve their goals. Wommack (2018) put it this way: *The power of God is like electricity. The power company generates the power and delivers it to your house. It's not your power, but it's under your control. You don't call the power company and ask them to turn the lights on. No! They won't do that. Once they deliver power to your house, it's under your command. You simply flip the switch on the wall and command the power to work. Does this mean you are the power source? Certainly not! You are not the power source, but you are the one in control of what that power does. You must assume your authority and acknowledge that the power is under your command.*

Any child of God created in His image potentially carries the incredible power of God. The Holy Spirit carries the power of God and is actively involved in the creation and sustenance of everything. Humans are unique because, at the point of their creation, they consist of three parts: body, soul, and spirit. Since God is Spirit, the spirit of man actively communes with the Holy Spirit. This is the key to the incredible power of God. Wherever the Holy Spirit is, the power of God is at work.

Anyone who fears God and obeys His commandments nurtures communion between the Holy Spirit and the human spirit, and the human body (flesh) and soul submit to the Spirit. When this ecology of relationships between God and people flourishes, we have unrestricted access to the incredible power of God. Therefore, the human beings God made in His image are incredibly powerful if they abide in God.

CHAPTER 5

Divine Power and Human Failure: A Paradox in the Garden?

The Fall of Humanity

We cannot discuss the fall of humanity and the power of God without considering the power of our adversary, against whom we contend. In heaven, Lucifer coveted the throne of grace and the power of God. Desiring the same status as God, he conspired with some angels to rebel against God, as though he had the same power as his Creator. However, he soon realized that God's absolute power dwarfed all other delegated powers. Satan and his cohort of fallen angels could not withstand the power of God, and they were disgracefully evicted from heaven and hurled to the earth.

Lucifer lost his position as an angel of God, and his ambition to establish a throne as glorious and honourable as that of his Maker proved futile. He hated God and everything associated with Him. What confused him most was watching God create man in His own image to display His attributes and power.

Humankind, created in the image of God, was given power to manage God's creation. Where did this leave Satan? He had no place in heaven, and God entrusted the earth to man. This was yet another form of humiliation for the devil, who became even more furious with God and His new creatures. He was ready to use every tactic to disrupt this new order. He examined everything in his arsenal and found that the only lethal weapon to dislodge man from the presence of God was deception.

Have you ever wondered why the Devil did not directly fight God's people, but instead subtly persuaded them to disobey their Creator? He knew that if he mishandled humans, they would use the same power that God had used to disgrace him in heaven to land another fatal blow. However, he was determined to deceive them, to prevent them from fulfilling God's will for their lives, to usurp the power of God within them, to disgrace God, and to salvage something he could claim as his own.

As the father of lies, the devil is highly skilled in deception, presenting himself as an angel of light. Of all the vices, why did the devil use deception to separate humans from their Creator? The devil tricked them into undertaking dangerous manoeuvres. First, he attempted to be like God in heaven, faced the fury of God, and was cast down to the earth like lightning — a mission impossible. Why, then, did he entice the woman to eat from the tree of the knowledge of good and evil?

Second, God made humans in His image, and they were like God. They were given a position even the devil had not attained in heaven, and they were still superior to the devil on earth. Third, the devil knew that humans had free will, which he coveted, and understood it was a powerful tool that could destroy the relationship between God and man. True to his nature, the devil aimed to steal, kill, and destroy what God had entrusted to Adam.

The new couple in the Garden of Eden was enjoying their new home and privileged relationship with the Creator as they exercised their power to cultivate and tend the garden. God regularly walked in the garden in the cool of the day to spend time with the family, to see how Adam was managing His creation, and to admire His creation, including man, made in His image.

How pleasant it was for God to look at His created order, which expressed the purpose of His will. This was the climax of His earthly project — to see His wonderful creation manifest His perfect power and glory, and to enjoy worship from His earthly creatures. Humans enjoyed the best relationship with God because He appointed them as stewards of His creation. He gave Adam a wife, blessed the couple to be fruitful and multiply, planted the Garden of Eden, provided the couple with a perfect home and food, and richly endowed the habitat with natural resources, including water, minerals, and wildlife for their enterprise.

God and humans enjoyed the beauty of the great diversity of creatures, reflecting a good, undefiled, and original ecosystem designed and constructed according to the purpose of His will. However, consistent with his usual preoccupation of roaming the earth, Satan observed the inhabitants of the Garden of Eden and was unsettled by the flourishing Garden and the relationship between God and His creation. The devil was determined to destroy God's earthly project in the Garden, but he needed to devise a strategy to trap the unsuspecting woman.

The devil knew that if he appeared in person in the Garden, the couple could easily recognize him, and his mission would be easily thwarted. Instead, he decided to use the serpent, a good creature of God, which could win the woman's trust. The devil uses the same scheme to tempt us in our families, workplaces, churches, and schools, often through our close associates or trustees, who lure us into disobeying God. By using these influential associates, he catches us off guard. We must be alert because our adversary is ready to use any device. David experienced this when he said, "They track me down and surround me, watching for the chance to throw me to the ground" (Psalm 17:11).

If only we were watchful, knowing that the agents of our adversary are always tracking us and waiting for the right opportunity to bring us down, we could avoid some of the potential sources of our troubles.

The devil groomed the serpent into the craftiest of all creatures that God had created. Whatever trick the serpent used, it managed to strategically meet the woman near the tree of the knowledge of good and evil, at the centre of the Garden.

It is unclear how the vulnerable woman was separated from her husband to face the serpent alone, although some believe he was nearby. The discussion that ensued changed the lives of the inhabitants of the Garden and their descendants for generations to come. In Genesis 3:1-8, the serpent persuaded the woman to eat some fruit from the tree of the knowledge of good and evil by asking her questions that undermined the divine truth, provided incomplete information (half-truths), questioned God's command, and dismissed the consequence of human disobedience.

The Devil asked the woman what seemed like a straightforward question, suggesting that God had forbidden them to eat the fruit from all the trees in the garden. In defending our Christian faith, we need to listen carefully to the questions that our opponents ask us, because they often sound like direct quotations from the Bible. The trick, however, could be the removal of a simple phrase or word, which may profoundly change the meaning of the statement, even though nothing seems to have changed on the surface. The Devil asked the woman whether God had forbidden them to eat the fruit from the trees of the Garden. Unfortunately, the woman misquoted God by stating that He had instructed them not to eat or touch the fruit of that tree, or they would die.

As is typical of the Devil, he distorts facts to cause the victim to stumble. However, the serpent assured her that she would not die after eating the fruit from the tree of knowledge of good and evil, suggesting that God was a liar. Dismissing divine truth and the consequences of disobeying God's commands is not uncommon in our daily lives.

Reflecting on our daily lives, we are reminded of times when we have justified disobedience. For example, while the Bible commands us to give tithes and offerings to God, the Devil whispers through our associates that God will understand if you use your tithe and offerings to settle your rent or support your parents. Of course, if we explain this to other people, we may find sympathizers who consider it a noble thing to do. However, we know the repercussions of this behaviour.

At times, the Holy Spirit will counsel you against acts of disobedience, but the Devil often downplays or dismisses the consequences of such behaviour. That is exactly what the serpent did in the Garden of Eden. It alleged that God knew that the day she ate the fruit from the tree of knowledge of good and evil, her eyes would be opened, she would become like God, knowing good and evil, and choosing blessing or evil. This statement questioned the integrity and goodness of a God who withheld the fruit that would make the woman wise and like Him. Unfortunately, her proximity to the tree didn't help. Convinced by the skilful and deceptive narrative of the serpent, the woman succumbed to the lie, and suddenly, the forbidden fruit became attractive, irresistible, mouth-watering, and a perceived source of wisdom.

The Devil succeeded in using the serpent to trick the woman and destroy the relationship between God and Adam. The serpent deceived the woman into believing that its intention was to improve her welfare, while the dialogue ultimately distanced the couple from God.

Perhaps the serpent was right when it argued that God knew that the day man ate the forbidden fruit, his eyes would be opened, and he would become like God, possessing the knowledge of good and evil, blessing and evil (Gen. 3:5). In Genesis 3:22, the Trinity confirms that after eating the fruit, humans had indeed become like one of them, possessing the knowledge of good and evil. This seems to be a curious agreement between the statements of the serpent and God. If this is the case, what was wrong with what the humans did in the Garden?

There was everything wrong with what happened after eating the fruit. We cannot answer this question without carefully analysing what occurred when the fruit of the tree of knowledge of good and evil was eaten. When God placed humans in the Garden of Eden, He gave them strict instructions for living there. God permitted them to eat freely from all the trees in the Garden, except the tree of knowledge of good and evil. He further warned them that the day they ate the fruit, they would certainly die (Gen. 2:16-17). All the trees that God planted in the Garden were good for humans, except one, which tested the integrity of the first family.

There were three categories of trees mentioned in this story: the tree of life, the tree of knowledge of good and evil, and all other trees that provided food for humans. Interestingly, eating from the tree of life kept humans alive, while eating from the tree of knowledge of good and evil could result in death. Eating from all the other trees sustained life.

We could safely say that all trees in the Garden, except the tree of knowledge of good and evil, supported human life. Therefore, the trees in the Garden could broadly be divided into two categories: those that supported life and the one that brought death to humanity. If this is true, humanity was faced with a choice between life and death. Understanding how important these two types of trees were in defining the fate of humanity, God lovingly commanded humans to avoid the tree of knowledge of good and evil, clearly stating the consequences of disobeying His command.

There may be two other explanations for God's command to Adam and Eve to avoid eating the forbidden fruit. First, allowing humankind to have the knowledge of good and evil meant they would be unnecessarily exposed to evil. This could have opened an additional temptation, and who knows, perhaps the Devil could have used this as another weapon in his arsenal. Another possibility is that this was one of the secret things of God. Moses said: *The secret things belong unto the LORD our God, but those things which are revealed belong unto us and to our children forever, that we may do all the words of this law* (Deut. 29:29 KJV). There are some things we may never understand because God has not revealed them to us.

Could God have sovereignly restrained humanity from accessing this deadly fruit to ensure they were safe? Unfortunately, that would have contradicted His own design because He created man in His image with free will—the ability to choose what he wanted to do within the environment that God provided. God created humans with the power and authority to overcome every temptation or trial.

Couldn't God have excluded the tree of knowledge of good and evil from the Garden altogether? Can we then suggest that God failed to provide a safety net to prevent the potential catastrophe in the Garden? It is important to clearly state that God is very thorough and systematic in designing and implementing His will. There was no flaw in the original design of the Garden of Eden. God planted the Garden with perfect knowledge of human needs and capabilities.

Whenever God designs a habitat for humans, He provides everything necessary for them to live a fulfilled and godly life, if they fear Him and obey His commandments. The principles of provision in the Garden are no different from those that apply to our lives today. As St. Peter said, "His divine power has given us everything we need for life and godliness, through our knowledge of Him who called us by His own glory and goodness" (2 Pet. 1:3 NIV). When God called Adam to steward His creation, He equipped him with the power to access everything he needed for life and godliness. Otherwise, how would he have been expected to fulfil this responsibility?

Unrestricted access to God's blessings could only be achieved through true knowledge of the God who called him to His glory and excellence. If humans had truly understood God and His intentions for them in the Garden, would they still have suspected that God was withholding wisdom from them?

Isn't it true that many Christians today still consult ungodly or less knowledgeable fellow believers on critical issues because they have not truly known God and His plans for them? Like us, Adam and his wife had everything they needed to fulfil their purpose in the Garden, but they chose to disobey God.

Can we truly understand how Adam and his wife were meant to fulfil their God-given assignment in the Garden without being distracted by the presence of the tree of knowledge of good and evil? The tree of knowledge of good and evil had two potential effects on those who ate its fruit: they would acquire knowledge of good and knowledge of evil. Considering that God's creation was good and fit for its purpose, humans were designed to fulfil all their functions based on their knowledge of good. If they had needed an external source of knowledge, God would have provided for this additional knowledge.

Everything humans needed for life and godliness in the Garden was available within the scope of the knowledge of good that they already had. We can safely conclude that all creatures of God were good and could be totally managed using the existing knowledge of good and the incredible power of God that humans had. There was no justification for humans to seek additional knowledge. If this is true, the only attraction of the tree was the knowledge of evil, which turned out to be an unnecessary evil.

By design, humans were inclined toward good, and everything they interacted with was created or formed to produce or respond to good. The receptors or production lines for evil were either underdeveloped or non-existent. The duality in the functions of the tree of knowledge of good and evil suggests the coexistence of two types of knowledge that were likely antagonistic. For humans to handle these two types of knowledge, they would have needed sensors and receptors that would allow them to interact with both without negatively influencing the quality of human life and functions.

Handling the knowledge of good was within the existing scope of humans, but the knowledge of evil was not part of God's original creation. Thus, the quest for knowledge likely referred to the knowledge of evil that was lacking in creation. The serpent said: *The truth is, the day you eat the fruit from that tree, you will awaken something powerful in you and become like Him* (Gen. 3:5, VTB). This statement has an accusatory tone and is subject to two possible interpretations.

First, the serpent alleges that what God told the humans regarding the command to refrain from eating the fruit of the tree of knowledge of good and evil was a lie. It claimed that humans would not die merely by eating the fruit. The serpent presented itself as the only credible source of truth.

Second, the serpent convinced the woman that humans were somehow inferior to God. It persuaded her to believe that humanity could not possess the same power, knowledge, or capabilities as God unless they ate from this special tree. The Devil may have implied that humanity was created with a defect that could only be rectified by consuming the fruit.

Third, the serpent presupposed that the humans in the Garden were deficient in their ability to distinguish between good and evil, and it implied that God was fully aware of this deficiency. Fourth, it suggested that there was something within humanity, something dormant, that could bring about the knowledge of good and evil, and eating the fruit would awaken this powerful attribute, enabling them to become like God. This accusation would present God as a malicious Creator who withheld good things from His creatures.

The serpent allegedly presented itself as a concerned ally, striving to elevate humanity to their rightful status, being like God. This scenario mirrors a very common problem in families, marriages, churches, workplaces, and various relationships. There are marriages that have broken down simply because one spouse was advised by a friend to take certain actions to make the "disadvantaged" spouse more equal to the other partner. Unfortunately, such advice has sometimes led to destructive outcomes, even resulting in divorces.

Acquiring the knowledge of both good and evil led Adam and his wife to breach their boundaries as humans and attempt to become like God. However, possessing the knowledge of evil did not guarantee the ability to manage its consequences. Instead, it deprived them of access to God's power.

The fall of humanity, as described in Genesis 3, came with severe consequences that Adam and Eve could never have imagined. First, God physically removed them from the Garden to prevent them from eating from the tree of life. Humans, animals, and plants in the Garden of Eden were the first of their kind, blessed to multiply. The Garden served as a nursery where God intended to multiply humanity and other life forms. Much like a botanical garden, which houses a collection of all kinds of plants, including rare ones, the Garden of Eden was a special facility, a breeding site, a beautiful place, a potential source of genetic material, and a place where Adam was meant to raise a family and interact with creation before their descendants spread to other parts of the world.

Being removed from the Garden denied Adam and Eve access to the blessings and benefits associated with this unique place. The ecological relationships between God, man, and creation were also disrupted. Adam, who had once enjoyed the presence of God in the Garden, now hid from Him. Creation, which had not participated in Adam's sin, suffered because of human disobedience.

After the fall, Adam and Eve realized they were naked, and innocent animals had to be slaughtered to provide them with clothing. God also cursed the land. The first marriage was shaken as Adam blamed the woman for his fall. The man who had once described the woman as *bone of my bones and flesh of my flesh* now blamed God for giving him the woman. These developments should remind us of God's desire and plan for us is to enjoy His full blessings, provided we obey Him and keep His commandments. Disobedience, however, destroys our valuable fellowship with God and deprives us of His power.

The fall of humanity derailed God's initial plan to have a holy and blameless human race. If His ultimate purpose was to be realized, God would need to find a perfect sacrifice to restore humanity to Himself, thus, the seed of a woman would bruise the head of the serpent.

Adam lost the presence of God. Since God is light and does not accept sin in His presence, He departed from Adam. With His departure, Adam lost the attributes of God that had enabled him to fellowship with his Creator and steward His creation. The image of God in Adam was now blurred, like a misty mirror. These effects of the fall imply that humanity's ability to see and describe things as God does was also compromised.

Understanding the nature of humanity and the power God designed within us provides a useful reference when assessing what we are potentially capable of. It is tempting to define our abilities based on what society tells us, but what truly defines us is what God formed and deposited in us. Every human being must discover their identity and work diligently to fully express it to fulfil their earthly mission.

What Was the Impact of the Fall on Humans' Access to God's Power?

The story of the fall of humanity in the Garden may give the impression that Adam and Eve lacked the power to resist the serpent. After all, how could they have fallen so easily at the first temptation? Could it be that God abandoned them when they needed Him most?

God is faithful and fulfils every promise He makes. When He placed humans in the Garden, He gave them authority to exercise His power to cultivate and tend the Garden, on the condition that they obeyed His commandments. God provided them with rules for living and flourishing in the Garden. If Adam and Eve had approached their conversation with the serpent with a spirit of obedience to God, they would have plugged into His power source.

However, the serpent enticed them to question God's integrity regarding the rules of living in the Garden. The premise for eating the forbidden fruit was flawed, making them vulnerable to the schemes of the enemy. By engaging with the serpent about the forbidden fruit, Eve risked falling for the lie of the enemy. In the spiritual realm, the communion between the human spirit and the Holy Spirit ended, and the flow of God's incredible power ceased.

The authority to exercise God's power that had been in humans, to be used at their discretion, was also withdrawn. Let's always remember that when we choose to act contrary to the instructions God gives us for our assignment, we lose access to His power. While God respects our free will, wrong choices come with consequences.

Consider this analogy: When a power company supplies electricity to your house, you need to plug your appliances into the wall socket and flip the switch to enjoy the power. When you switch on the appliance, there is a connection between the source and the appliance. But if the appliance is not connected, you have no access to the power supply. Similarly, when the human spirit is disconnected from the Holy Spirit, the power of God is no longer accessible.

There is another problem that arises from this disconnection: When the human spirit is cut off from the Holy Spirit, the body (flesh) becomes dominant and seeks to control the human spirit and soul. Instead of submitting to the spirit, the flesh seeks to dominate it. Knowledge of evil empowers the flesh to control all the primary areas of an individual's life. Once humanity ventured outside the realm of God's will, they became vulnerable because they were not designed to function in that environment. Adam and Eve quickly realized they were powerless and could no longer rule the Garden as they had been intended. They were naked, helpless, and hiding among the non-human creation they were meant to govern.

God removed Adam and Eve from the Garden and denied them access to the instruments of governance and His provisions for their sustenance. In addition to cutting them off from His power, He barred them from eating the fruit from the tree of life and other trees in the Garden. Humans had compromised their position and were no longer eligible to cultivate and tend the Garden. This is a sad story, isn't it? Yet, we often behave the same way as our ancestors did.

Every believer has a kingdom to govern, and God has provided the principles by which it must be ruled. Your domain might be your workplace, church, family, business, school, or any area of life where you have influence or responsibility. Wherever God has placed you, that is your kingdom to steward with wisdom, integrity, and purpose. Everyone created in the image of God has a unique gift that makes them a ruler on earth. Although God gave Adam instructions about life in the Garden, Eve was equally responsible for what happened, as she too carried a seed to care for the Garden.

So, whatever your circumstances, wherever you are, you have been created to rule over God's creation. This mandate will only expire when the Lord calls you home. How are you taking care of His vineyard? Let us remember that we will all be held accountable for how we spent our time on earth.

Do the Fallen Human Species Absolutely Have No Access to God's Power?

After the fall of humanity, a real separation occurred between God and man. Sin introduced a barrier that, on our own, we cannot remove. Consequently, God evicted the first family from the Garden of Eden. However, although humans were banished, that was not the end of God's dealings with them. On the contrary, it marked the beginning of a long, unfolding story of redemption. Even in judgment, God's mercy was present. He clothed them, protected them, and set in motion a plan to restore what was lost. The exile from Eden was not abandonment; it was the doorway to grace. Even in that moment, God promised redemption (Gen. 3:15 – the protoevangelium, or 'first gospel'). Our merciful and loving God already had a plan for their restoration, and He made provisions for His people to access His power when needed. Therefore, the fallen human species is not absolutely cut off from God's power. In fact, access to His power is precisely what grace restores. This section explains how God interacted with His people after the fall.

After the fall, the Spirit of the LORD departed and no longer dwelt in His people. He only came upon individuals assigned specific duties as they walked with God. When the LORD decided to build a sanctuary among the children of Israel, He gave Moses a vision that was detailed, intentional, and sacred. Every measurement, material, and pattern were filled with purpose. God provided architectural plans for the tabernacle, based on His will, and communicated them to Moses, who oversaw the construction, prepared a bill of quantities, and specified where the necessary materials would come from.

Briefing the Israelites, Moses said: *See, the LORD has chosen Bezalel son of Uri, the son of Hur, of the tribe of Judah, and He has filled him with the Spirit of God, to make artistic designs for work in gold, silver, and bronze, to cut and set stones, to work in wood, and to engage in all kinds of craftsmanship. And He has given both him and Oholiab son of Ahisamach, of the tribe of Dan, the ability to teach others. He has filled them with skills to do all kinds of work as craftsmen, designers, embroiderers…* (Exod. 35:30; 36:1, NIV). This highlights that God is not only a God of purpose but also of planning and precision. He chose Bezalel and Oholiab and filled them with His Spirit, granting them wisdom, understanding, knowledge, and all kinds of skills, from craftsmanship to design and teaching.

God identified every task required for the construction of the sanctuary and precisely determined the knowledge, skills, and competencies of the workers He chose to build His tabernacle. He also specified the categories of craftsmen required for the job and the size of the workforce. Those He chose, He filled with the Holy Spirit, granting them wisdom, understanding, and the ability to execute His architectural plan. Alongside Bezalel and Oholiab, other workers were stirred and gifted for various roles, from artisans and engravers to embroiderers, woodworkers, metalsmiths, builders, and masons, to accomplish the sacred work. God specified their roles, how to build the sanctuary, and how to mobilize materials for the structure.

None of the workers identified could have understood or carried out the tasks according to God's specifications without the leading and empowerment of the Holy Spirit. Moses had two key workers (Bezalel and Oholiab) who were upskilled by the Holy Spirit for various roles, including teaching other artisans. This implies that when God gives you an assignment, He will use what you have and build your capabilities to accomplish the work. What is surprising is that these workers did not attend formal schooling or university; the Holy Spirit was their teacher.

The construction of the tabernacle reveals something profound about God's nature: He is intentional, orderly, and deeply invested in both the vision and the vessel. The tabernacle was not just a physical structure, it reflected divine order, beauty, and presence. Nothing was left to human guesswork; every element had a divine blueprint, and every worker had a divine assignment.

God's approach to constructing the tabernacle highlights a critical spiritual principle: God doesn't just call; He equips. The construction wasn't merely about physical labour; it was spiritually inspired craftsmanship. The precision required could only be met by those filled with the Spirit of God, enabling them to go beyond natural talent and operate under divine direction. The LORD can also fill and empower you with His Spirit to do His sacred work.

From carving and weaving to assembling and decorating, each task was a form of worship—a visible reflection of obedience and surrender. These Spirit-filled workers weren't just building a tent; they were creating a dwelling place for God's presence. This serves as a reminder to us today: when God assigns you a task, He will provide the anointing and ability to accomplish it. His Spirit ensures that our work aligns with His will.

When the Holy Spirit leads God's people to accomplish sacred work, they don't see it as a burden. The Spirit-filled Israelites gave freewill offerings that exceeded the amount needed for building the sanctuary. Amazingly, all the construction workers had to stop their work and plead with Moses to issue a restraining order to stop the people from giving further offerings. And Moses obliged. If only we could learn how to give towards God's work as the Israelites did, we could experience phenomenal spiritual growth.

Every worker recruited for the construction of the sanctuary did so willingly. The Bible says: *Then Moses summoned Bezalel and Oholiab and every skilled person* to whom the LORD had given ability and who was willing to come and do the work (Exod. 36:2). Although there are instances where people run away from God's assignments (e.g., Jonah), God prefers to work with those who have a heart of servanthood and who willingly offer their services.

There are many other examples in the Bible where God released His Spirit on His people to carry out a specific assignment. Even then, they were able to complete their tasks according to His commandments. This reminds us that God can use a broken vessel to accomplish sacred work. Have you disqualified yourself from working in His vineyard? God can still choose to use you despite your imperfections.

In their fallen state, humans cannot host the Holy Spirit within them. The fall of man in Eden ruptured the intimate fellowship humanity once shared with God. Sin created a divide—a spiritual barrier that made it impossible for the Holy Spirit to dwell within fallen humanity. Though God still moved among His people, His presence was external, often descending upon specific individuals for specific purposes and moments in time. This is why, in the Old Testament, the Spirit came upon prophets, judges, and craftsmen like Bezalel, but did not indwell them permanently. The tabernacle and later the temple served as physical spaces where God's presence could reside among the people, but not within them.

Redemption And the Power of God

We can't fully understand the power of God in a believer without considering its manifestation in our Lord Jesus Christ. After John baptized Him in the Jordan River, Jesus received the Holy Spirit. From that point on, the Holy Spirit resided in Christ. Luke records, *"Jesus, full of the Holy Spirit, returned from the Jordan and was led by the Spirit in the desert"* (Luke 4:1, NIV). The Holy Spirit filled every area of the Savior's life. When we describe a container as being full, we mean that the substance occupies the entire space. Similarly, Jesus was filled with the Holy Spirit.

The Holy Spirit carries the power of God, which drives all His work. Jesus, filled to the brim with the Spirit, was fully empowered. When the Spirit completely fills every part of your life, He releases the full measure of God's power as He wills. This explains why Jesus was able to resist every temptation from the Devil in the wilderness. He was so powerful in His ministry that He fulfilled His mission on earth in its entirety. Similarly, we too can be filled with the Holy Spirit and fulfil our purpose on earth.

After the death and resurrection of Jesus Christ, His disciples witnessed the power of God at work more regularly than ever before. But they were promised unrestricted access to this power once Jesus returned to the Father. He said, *...you will receive power when the Holy Spirit comes upon you, and you will be my witnesses in Jerusalem, in all Judea and Samaria, and to the ends of the earth* (Acts 1:8, NIV). Jesus promised His disciples that they would preach the gospel to the ends of the earth, heal the sick, raise the dead, cleanse lepers, meet the physical needs of the poor, and do even mightier things than He did after receiving the Holy Spirit.

On the day of Pentecost, the apostles and other disciples of Jesus, who were praying in the upper room in Jerusalem, received the promise of the Lord (Acts 1:8). They were filled with the power of the Holy Spirit when He descended upon them. Every believer who accepts Jesus Christ is sealed, baptized, and filled with the Holy Spirit. Just like our Lord Jesus, if we allow the Holy Spirit to fill and lead us, we too will receive the full measure of His power.

When we yield totally to the authority of the Holy Spirit, we remain connected to the incredible power of Jehovah, El Shaddai. Jesus said, *Whoever believes in me, as the Scripture has said, streams of living water will flow from within him* (John 7:38-39). By this, He meant the Spirit, whom those who believed in Him would later receive. Access to the Holy Spirit is through Jesus Christ. When an individual believes in Christ and is saved, they are sealed and eventually filled and baptized with the Holy Spirit. Thus, the power of God is constantly available to the believer. John also reminds us that a Christian can have streams of living water flowing from within them. The indwelling of the Spirit ensures that the works and fruit of the Spirit (love, joy, peace, patience, kindness, goodness, faithfulness, gentleness, and self-control) will remain in the life of the believer.

As Christians, we often overlook or fail to fully understand that redemption through the death and resurrection of Jesus Christ restores our position as governors or rulers of God's earthly creation. Since the universe and everything in it was created and is sustained by His power, God has entrusted us, as earthly governors, with the authority to steward that power to carry out His work. God, as the Creator and Sustainer of all things (Col. 1:16-17), holds supreme authority over the universe. Yet, in His divine wisdom, He delegates a measure of that authority to Christians and other rulers, not for personal gain, but for the fulfilment of His purposes on earth.

Romans 13:1 reminds us that there is no authority except from God, and those that exist have been instituted by God. This means that those in leadership, whether in the church, governments, or communities, are accountable stewards of divine power. Their authority is not autonomous; it flows from God's sovereignty. When this power is aligned with His will, it becomes a channel for justice, mercy, order, and blessing. But when misused or disconnected from God's purpose, it leads to distortion, oppression, and confusion. True spiritual governance is not about control, it is about servanthood in power, moving in alignment with the Creator who upholds all things by the word of His power (Heb. 1:3).

As a Christian, you are a ruler, regardless of how you view yourself. If you have been adopted as a child of God, you are a partaker in His divine nature, which includes His power. Therefore, you are as powerful as your Father, provided the Holy Spirit resides in you.

CHAPTER 6
The power of God and His creation

The term "creation" has been extensively studied, debated, and often misrepresented. However, nothing could be more certain, correct, or theologically significant than its true meaning. Much time, energy, and paper have been devoted within the Christian community to discussing how the Genesis creation accounts should be properly understood.

Both Christians and non-Christians have read Genesis 1 and 2, and Psalm 8, many times, citing these passages in Bible discussions, sermons, lectures, and other gatherings. But these foundational texts have sparked deep theological reflection and debate for centuries, especially around the relationship between science and faith. While the passages are frequently revisited in Christian (and interfaith) contexts, there is no single consensus on their interpretation. This is largely due to differences in methods of interpreting Scripture, theological traditions, views on the authority of science and Scripture, and cultural and historical contexts. The rift in Christian beliefs widens when discussing the relationship between nature and God, humankind's place in the universe, and the power of God in relation to creation.

Science-faith debates have revealed significant differences in the interpretation of "creation" among scientists, theologians, and philosophers. For instance, some scientists argue that plants, animals, birds, and humans have a common ancestor—that they all developed from simple organisms over a very long period. Others believe that God instantaneously created individual plant, bird, and animal species through His creative word. Several views exist between these two extremes, one of which posits that evolution is God's tool for the creation of living things. Thus, certain religious views about the creation of the world and its organisms conflict with the scientific view of evolution.

The inadequate understanding or diversity of perceptions regarding the term "creation" has led to misconceptions that undermine humanity's role in the created order. This debate has tragically divided and polarized the Church, diverting its attention from the God-given mission of living as God's image-bearers, exercising stewardship over His creation and proclaiming the message of reconciliation to the world. Similarly, there has been a tendency to alienate science and ignore the implications of its growing understanding of the physical and biological world.

As both a Christian and a scientist, I have found myself in difficult situations when people attempt to force me to choose between one identity or the other. Some fellow believers insist that scientists should focus on environmental issues while Christians concentrate on saving souls and preparing them for heaven. As far as they are concerned, there is no direct link between faith and the environment.

Contradictory views about creation, especially between literal interpretations and symbolic understandings, have created significant tension within the Church. These divisions have robbed the Church of a deeper understanding of creation and the associated creative power. The resulting theological divides have, at times, distracted the Church from the profound and transformational implications of God's creative power and the deep understanding of creation itself. When these views are polarized, the Church risks losing sight of the deeper theological truths in the creation story. Instead of a broader and richer reflection on God's creative power, we often find ourselves caught in an either/or debate, either God created the world as described in Genesis literally, or the entire account is symbolic and doesn't point to any concrete truths about the world or the Creator. This limiting view prevents Christians from fully embracing the mystery and grandeur of God's creative power.

Rather than focusing on who God is as Creator and how creation reflects His goodness and power, the debate often centres on how the universe came into being and which view "wins." Unfortunately, in doing so, the Church may miss the opportunity to integrate the insights of modern science with the rich theological understanding of God's ongoing creation. The creative power of God becomes disconnected from our lived experience of creation, from our environmental responsibility to the beauty of the world, to the theological truths science reveals, such as order, complexity, and interconnectedness.

Analysis of God's creative activity should lead to specific tasks that reflect the enormity of the power needed to bring creation into being and sustain it. We can never fully grasp the extent of God's power if we do not understand what it is meant to accomplish.

The diversity of views about creation has raised many questions: What does it mean to create? Who creates, God, humanity, or both? What is the nature of the universe God created? What are the implications of divine power for the universe God created?

This chapter aims to explain what constitutes creation and the place of humankind within it, establishing the relationship between the power of God and His creation. It encourages believers to reflect on their God-given vocation as earth-keepers and people-keepers, as they exercise the authority and power entrusted to them by God.

Misconceptions About Creation

There are several misconceptions about nature that negatively affect our perception of the nature and power of God, as well as the relationships between God and humans, God and non-human creation, and between humans and non-human creation. Some of the key misconceptions are summarized below.

Misconception 1: There is no Clear Relationship Between Faith and Nature.

Perhaps our language confuses us when we talk about "creation" and "environment" as if they are distinct concepts. Many Christians recite verses, compose songs, and prepare sermons on creation, yet unconsciously consider creation and nature as separate entities. For example, how do we relate the use of electricity, water, paper, food, cars, clothes, wood, computers, printers, and other goods to God's creation and to the environment? God created the universe primarily to glorify and praise Him and to reveal His invisible attributes, His nature and divine power. Yet, as His stewards, we are often complicit in the destruction and degradation of nature.

Created in the image of God as His representatives on earth, He has mandated us to rule over His earthly creation. But many Christians ignorantly, indifferently, or arrogantly resist God's call to care for creation. The false division between creation and the environment in the created order has compromised the Christian vocation and the Church's mission. Many theologians, scientists, philosophers, and Christians agree that there is a strong relationship between faith and nature.

Misconception 2: Humankind, Created in the Image of God, is Separate from Creation.

Some believers exclude humans from the concept of creation. They use the term "creation" to describe non-human creation, while assigning humans a status that sets them apart. Even the Hebrews, at times, viewed God as the God of history rather than the God of nature, the idea of humanity as part of nature likely seemed almost pagan to them.

Today, many people view nature as a resource, and the notion that we are also part of creation often eludes us. Some speak of creation, but their views are not reflected in their values and practices. As a result, humanity's dual role of earth-keeping and people-keeping has been compromised, with many Christians and Church organizations focusing only on people-keeping.

When we listen to discussions about environmental issues, including climate change, biodiversity loss, pollution, and land degradation, we may think that these concerns do not directly involve us. In many cases, we participate in the destruction of God's creation in the comfort of our homes through the waste of water, electricity, food, paper, and other resources.

Harris (2006) observes that the central question of the gospel has been reconstructed as, "What is more important for people, their eternal salvation, or their well-being in the present?" He further argues that "by extension, this question has served to starve Christian environmental initiatives in recent years, as the polarity between the needs of people and the needs of the wider creation has set them in opposition or ranked them in importance." Are earth-keeping and people-keeping not integrated? Is our failure to care for creation, alongside people-keeping, due to ignorance or resistance to our God-given mandate? The view that humankind is separate from nature is, therefore, not entirely true.

Misconception 3: The Earth Was Created Solely for Humanity.

Some Christians and non-Christians believe that the earth exists primarily to satisfy human needs, viewing it merely as a resource for exploitation. This perception often ignores, or reflects ignorance of, the fact that all creation is valuable in its own right and has a God-given purpose in the universe, independent of human use.

The belief that humans are inherently superior to all non-human creation, and therefore free to use the earth's resources as they wish, has led to overharvesting, overconsumption, pollution, and widespread environmental degradation. Sadly, even the body of Christ, tasked with earth-keeping, is often complicit in the misuse of creation. This anthropocentric view of creation is challenged in both Christian theology and the scientific community.

Misconception 4: Environmental and Social Justice are Solely the Responsibility of Governments and Environmental Organizations.

Many people assume that ensuring environmental justice and social justice is the domain of governments and specialized institutions. According to the United States Environmental Protection Agency, environmental justice is defined as the *fair treatment and meaningful involvement of all people regardless of race, colour, faith, national origin, or income with respect to the development, implementation, and enforcement of environmental laws, regulations, and policies*. Social justice, on the other hand, refers to equal access to wealth, opportunities, and privileges within society.

Environmental injustice often disproportionately affects marginalized communities. For example, polluting industries are frequently located in areas inhabited by low-income populations, exposing them to serious environmental health risks. In tropical regions, illegal logging destroys water catchment areas, reducing water availability for communities without access to piped water.

Professor Robert Bullard notes that *whether by conscious design or institutional neglect, communities of colour in urban ghettos, in rural 'poverty pockets', or on economically impoverished Native-American reservations face some of the worst environmental devastation in the nation.* A striking case of environmental injustice is the ongoing conflict in Nigeria's Niger Delta. Foreign oil corporations have profited enormously from petroleum extraction, while local ethnic groups like the Ogoni and Ijaw have suffered displacement, poverty, underdevelopment, and environmental degradation (Iniaghe et al., 2013). Oil spills, obsolete pipelines, and deforestation have caused widespread damage, affecting land, water, and mangrove ecosystems.

Similarly, in Ecuador, Texaco (now Chevron) became embroiled in a legal conflict with indigenous communities in the Lago Agrio region. These people were displaced and left to deal with pollution and deteriorating living conditions caused by oil drilling operations.

Excessive hunting and exploitation of wildlife to meet the demands of affluent groups also deplete biodiversity, degrade ecosystems, and rob local communities of their livelihoods. In many regions, the discharge of untreated industrial effluent into water bodies destroys aquatic life and poisons essential natural resources.

These practices not only destroy God's creation but also harm resource-dependent communities, particularly the poor. God, who loves both human and non-human creation, grieves over the abuse of His handiwork.

Therefore, the idea that only governments or environmental organizations are responsible for ensuring environmental and social justice is incomplete. Believers are called to be faithful stewards of God's creation. Environmental stewardship is a core part of the Christian vocation. Ignoring this role undermines the Church's mission to be salt and light in the world.

Misconception 5: God Created the Universe from Pre-existent Material (creation ex materia)

This view holds that God did not create the universe out of nothing, but instead shaped it from eternally existing matter. Rooted in Aristotelian physics, this idea suggests that matter and energy are eternal and uncreated, existing alongside God. In this view, the universe has no beginning or end but exists in a *steady state*, having always been as it is.

Proponents of the steady-state theory argue that matter is continuously created *ex nihilo* (out of nothing) to maintain a constant density as the universe expands. In the 19th century, Hermann von Helmholtz's articulation of the law of conservation of matter and energy seemed to reinforce the idea that the universe was eternal, since matter and energy can neither be created nor destroyed, some concluded that the universe must always have existed.

However, both scientific and theological evidence challenges this belief. Theologically, the doctrine of creation *ex nihilo*, that God created all things from nothing, is central to Christian orthodoxy (cf. Gen. 1:1, Heb. 11:3). Scientifically, the Big Bang theory implies a definite beginning to space, time, and matter, suggesting that the universe had an origin. These insights together discredit the view that the universe is eternally self-sustaining and uncreated.

Misconception 6: God Created the Universe from Himself (creation ex deo)

Another theological misunderstanding is the belief that God created the universe from His own substance, known as creation *ex deo* ('from God'). Advocates of this idea argue that, if God alone existed before creation and "nothing comes from nothing," then the universe must have been formed from God's own being.

For instance, Aftab (2012) claims: *If God created the universe out of nothing and before that the only existence was God... then God must have created the universe out of His own being.* Similarly, theologian George MacDonald is cited by William Raeper as teaching that *men and women were born out of the heart of God, not ex nihilo as traditionally held by the church...* (Raeper, 1987:243).

This view leans toward pantheism, the belief that God and creation are one and the same. Richard (source unspecified) outlines four philosophical tenets of this theory:

1. All reality is one, and that single reality is God.
2. There is no absolute distinction between Creator and creation.
3. The cosmos is either an illusion from God or an emanation of God's being.
4. The true human *self* is God.

However, this idea has largely been rejected by mainstream Christian theology.

Scripture clearly teaches that God is distinct from His creation (cf. Isa. 45:5–12; John 1:1–3; Col. 1:16). While humans are made in the image of God (Gen. 1:27), we do not share His divine essence. Creation is dependent on God, but it is not an extension of God's being.

Misconception 7: God Created the Universe Out of Pre-existent Material (creation ex materia)

Some secular materialists and naturalists claim that the universe was formed from eternal, pre-existing matter. They argue that finite realities such as space, time, and energy are derived from material that has always existed. This view implies that matter is uncreated and eternal, thus rejecting the necessity of a divine Creator. Kenneth Richard outlines four key features of this belief:

1. Matter exists eternally in some form.
2. There is no supernatural Creator.
3. Human beings are entirely physical and mortal.
4. Humanity evolved purely through naturalistic processes and is different from animals only in degree, not in kind.

According to this view, the universe is a closed, self-sustaining system that does not require divine intervention or origin. However, this contradicts both scientific and theological evidence. Theologically, Scripture teaches that God created the universe *ex nihilo*, out of nothing (Genesis 1:1; Hebrews 11:3). Scientifically, the Big Bang and the Second Law of Thermodynamics suggest a beginning to space, time, and matter, undermining the idea of eternal material.

Misconception 8: Nature is Autonomous and Independent of God's Providential Control.

Another common belief is that the universe, once created, functions independently of God's ongoing involvement. According to this view, nature operates under fixed physical laws and internal mechanisms, requiring no divine interaction after its initial creation.

This idea resembles the deistic view of God as a watchmaker, who winds up the universe like a clock and then steps away, allowing it to run on its own. While this model acknowledges a Creator, it denies God's active, providential governance of creation.

However, this contradicts the biblical witness. Scripture affirms that God is continually sustaining and governing all things: In Him all things hold together (Col. 1:17); He gives life to everything (Neh. 9:6). Natural processes, from rainfall to the movement of celestial bodies, are not independent phenomena, but expressions of God's ongoing care and providence.

Misconception 9: God's Power is Only Evidenced in the Supernatural

Some people assume that God's power is only displayed in miraculous or supernatural acts, those that defy natural laws or human explanation. This leads to a false division between "divine" acts (e.g., resurrection, parting of the Red Sea) and "natural" events (e.g., sunrise, childbirth), as though God is present only when the natural order is suspended.

However, this view promotes a "God of the gaps" theology, where divine action is seen only in areas that science cannot yet explain. This minimizes God's role in the regular, everyday operations of the universe.

The Bible paints a different picture. God is equally at work in both the extraordinary and the ordinary. The rain that falls, the crops that grow, and even human reasoning and learning are all possible because of God's sustaining power (cf. Psalm 104, Acts 17:28, James 1:17). God's power is not limited to the miraculous, it permeates every aspect of life, whether seen or unseen.

Misconceptions about how God created and governs the universe distort our understanding of His nature and power. Whether through the mistaken belief in eternal matter, the independence of natural processes, or the confinement of divine activity to miracles, these views undermine the biblical portrait of a God who is both transcendent and immanently involved in all of creation.

Misconception 10: Creation is an Enemy to be Subdued or a Resource to be Exploited for Human Leisure.

This misconception is rooted in a dual distortion: first, the belief that human dominion over creation, as described in Genesis, permits aggressive exploitation; second, the false ideology of human superiority - whether racial, cultural, or national - that has historically justified violence against both people and the environment.

The idea that creation exists solely for human use has led to widespread environmental destruction and justified systems of oppression. Throughout history, this belief was often paired with a sense of racial superiority, especially during colonialism. For example:

- European colonization of the Americas contributed to the death of up to 90% of the indigenous population over 500 years.
- The Spanish conquest of the Americas resulted in the deaths of an estimated eight million people.
- Genocidal campaigns and systemic violence occurred in the Caribbean, Australia (e.g., against Tasmanian Aboriginal people), and many other regions.
- The Holocaust in Nazi Germany saw the extermination of six million Jews.
- Colonizers often exploited indigenous populations as forced labour, particularly on plantations in the Americas, Africa, and Asia.

This ideology extended to nature itself. Colonial powers often viewed land as a commodity to be conquered and stripped for profit. One stark example: after the American Civil War, approximately 20,000 hunters were commissioned to kill 10 million bison, devastating the food supply and culture of Native American communities (Peterson, 2017).

Such acts - genocide, slavery, and resource exploitation - are tragic legacies of a distorted understanding of dominion. This form of domination is contrary to the biblical call to be stewards of creation. In Genesis, dominion is not about domination but about representing God's loving care and governance over His creation.

God, who is righteous and just, grieves over both environmental and social injustices. When believers neglect their role as caretakers of creation, they not only degrade the natural world but also harm the vulnerable - often the poor - who depend most directly on these resources for their survival. These people too are made in the image of God.

More troubling still is the failure to recognize that environmental abuse is a form of resistance against the Creator Himself. God is actively sustaining creation at every moment (Colossians 1:17; Hebrews 1:3). To recklessly exploit or destroy what God upholds is not just careless—it is spiritually defiant.

We must ask: if God invests divine power and purpose into sustaining creation, how can we, as His representatives, justify trashing it without consequence?

What is creation?
The Significance of the Doctrine of Creation

The doctrine of creation has long been a major subject of discussion among both Christians and non-Christians. Several compelling reasons explain its prominence in theological, philosophical, and scientific debates. Creation - and the true, potentially comprehensible record it has left on earth - serves numerous purposes:

- It reinforces the notion of God's necessary existence as the only being who cannot be created (Craig, 2004).
- It offers insight into God's character and reveals humanity's creaturely responsibility.
- It forms the foundation for humanity's mandate to have dominion over the earth (Gen. 1:26–27) and legitimizes scientific and technological activity in fulfilling this mandate (Tappeiner, 1977).
- It affirms humanity's absolute dependence on God as Creator.
- It provides ultimate meaning to human existence, which is to glorify and praise God.
- It proclaims the reality of the Creator God in contrast to the world's false gods and idols.
- It testifies to God's direct involvement in the creation and ongoing sustenance of the physical universe.

- It preserves a true and potentially understandable record of creation.
- It reveals the truth of God's general revelation through nature.
- It upholds the trustworthiness of God's character.
- It discloses God's invisible attributes, His eternal power and divine nature, to His creatures (cf. Romans 1:20).
- It affirms the significance of both natural and human history (Miller, 1993).
- It communicates God's transcendence, immanence, power, and authority.
- It emphasizes the vastness of the universe and humanity's relative smallness and dependence.
- It highlights God's grace in making us His image-bearers and inviting us into fellowship with Him.
- It demonstrates the constancy of creation as a pledge of God's faithfulness.
- It underscores God's absolute sovereignty over creation.
- It reveals purposeful divine activity in both living and non-living things.
- It bridges the God of religious faith and the God of physical reality.
- It affirms the physical and moral structure of the universe, accessible to both scientific inquiry and personal experience.
- It shows that everything in the universe depends moment by moment on the sustaining power of God.
- It rejects the notion that humanity is the result of meaningless processes in an impersonal cosmos, affirming instead that humans are made in the image of God.
- It asserts that God created the universe freely and independently.
- It helps us recognize that God's mode of existence as Creator is fundamentally distinct from our own as created beings.

These remarkable truths about creation have drawn the attention of theologians, scientists, philosophers, and artists alike. However, confusion still exists, especially in the use of the term *creation*, within both Christian and non-Christian communities. This confusion arises from differences in worldview, philosophy, science, and even language.

The verb *create* is somewhat alien to human language, and we often use it imprecisely. Many people apply the term broadly, describing things like mobile phones, laptops, poems, songs, cars, chemicals, architectural designs, or church anthems as "creations." But are these truly *creatures* in the strict theological sense?

This section aims to clarify the meaning of *creation* by exploring its definitions across scientific, artistic, and biblical contexts. It will distinguish between *creation* and *mediated creation* and outline the key tenets of the biblical account of creation.

Creation Defined

There is no universally agreed-upon definition of the term *creation*. Different knowledge domains, such as theology, science, and art, have developed their own definitions based on contextual and disciplinary interpretations. In everyday usage, the term *creation*, refers to the act of bringing something into being or the result of such an act, a product of creation. Consider the selected definitions below:

- *Creation* is: the act or process of creating; something that has been brought into existence or created, especially a product of human intelligence or imagination; the whole universe, including the world and all things in it; an unusual or striking garment or hat; God's act of bringing the universe into being; and the universe as thus brought into being by God (Collins English Dictionary, 2012).
- *Creation* is that which God has created, the world and all that is in it (Online Etymology Dictionary, 2010).
- *Creation* is: 1) the act of creating, especially the act of bringing the world into ordered existence; 2) the act of making, inventing, or producing, such as the act of investing with a new rank or office, or the first representation of a dramatic role; and 3) something that is created, such as the world; creatures singly or in a group; an original work of art; and a new, usually striking article of clothing (Merriam-Webster Dictionary, 2018).

The variety of definitions above reveals five salient features:

- Creation as the act of bringing something into existence.
- Creation as a product of a creative activity.
- Creation as the act of bringing something into being out of nothing.
- Creation as making, inventing, ordering, restructuring, and arranging things into new products.
- Creation as an original work of art.

Collectively, these definitions imply that God created the universe and everything in it, and that everything (except God) is a creation. While this interpretation of the creation account appears valid, there may be concerns with this view, as we shall explore later. According to Hearn (1996), definitions of the term *creation* broadly fall into three categories, summarized below:

a) Creation in a Scientific Sense:

Scientific discussions of creation have contrasted the views of scientists who believe that the universe had a definite beginning, as a super-dense concentration of matter, with those who argue that the universe has always existed in a steady state. However, overwhelming scientific evidence supports the idea that the universe had a beginning. The Big Bang theory, now widely accepted, points to a finite time when space, matter, energy, time, physical laws, and life began. Scientists propose that life originated when inorganic material became alive, and that creative evolution has brought about all forms of life, plants, animals, birds, and humans. Based on this understanding, Hearn argues that *creation clearly involves nothing more than the appearance of something new, either matter itself or a new arrangement of matter* (Hearn, 1996). Again, this definition qualifies the universe and everything in it as creation.

b) Creation in the Artistic or Inventive Sense:

Human creativity, in artistic or inventive contexts, is often used to recognize innovation. Scientists, students, musicians, architects, poets, and others whose works are deemed exceptional are often described as creative. In this context, creation refers to producing, inventing, and rearranging existing matter. This implies that God's creatures, humans, can also create. But can humans create in the same way that God does?

Hearn argues that humans do not truly create, instead, they arrange. A scientist does not create the laws of the universe; rather, he discovers and describes them. While acknowledging that poetry and music have been generated by electronic computers as models of human creative processes, he contends that the mere appearance of a new arrangement of matter does not necessarily imply a true creative act has taken place.

Creation in this context is a purposive act involving "creative effort" on the part of the inventor or artist, the essence of which lies either in art or science. This involves the random scanning of stored experiential data for possible new relationships, and the selection of arrangements most suited to the creator's purpose. Hubbard (1969) asserts that: *At best man conserves, rearranges, combines... God alone creates.*

Creation in a Biblical Sense:

Our understanding of what creation is has evolved over time. There was a time when God's people believed the habitable world was surrounded by chaotic waters that would engulf it if not held back. While they believed in God, the Hebrews often resisted the idea that humanity was simply part of nature.

Today, the belief that God created the universe out of nothing (*ex nihilo*) is a widely held Christian doctrine. We affirm belief in:
- The God of History, who created the world (Jer. 27:4–7; 32:16–25),
- The absolute sovereignty of God over His creation,
- The created world of nature as God's handiwork, but never to be worshipped (Genesis 2:7; Isa. 29:15–16).

Thus, the biblical account of creation emphasizes that God created the universe from nothing and that it has a definite beginning. Creation is defined as the sovereign act of God alone, by which He, of His own free will and in an ordered sequence, brought into existence all things, visible and invisible, *ex nihilo*, from the depth of His being as pneuma, by the Word of God, through the agency of the Spirit, for the manifestation of His glory and the benefit of humanity. It was declared to be very good.

This definition emphasizes the following key points:

a) *An act of God alone* – Reflects the orthodox Christian view that creation is not a cooperative act nor the result of pre-existing matter or beings.

b) *Of His own free will* – God was not compelled to create; creation is an expression of divine freedom and love.

c) *In an ordered sequence of actions* – Aligns with the Genesis narrative, portraying a purposeful, step-by-step unfolding of creation. (Note: This phrase may require careful handling when seeking harmony between theological and scientific perspectives.)

d) *Ex nihilo (out of nothing)* – A central tenet of classical Christian theology, distinguishing the biblical view from ancient creation myths involving pre-existing chaos. Affirmed by early Church creeds and councils.

e) *From the depth of His being as pneuma* – A poetic and theological phrase. "Pneuma" (Spirit or breath) has rich biblical significance (e.g., Gen. 1:2; John 4:24), though it may require unpacking for non-theological audiences.

f) *By the Word of God, through the agency of the Spirit* – Emphasizes Trinitarian involvement in creation (cf. John 1:1–3; Gen. 1:2; Psa. 33:6).

g) *By the word of the LORD the heavens were made, and by the breath of His mouth all their host* (Psa. 33:6).

h) *For the manifestation of His glory* – Creation reflects and reveals God's glory (e.g., Psa. 19:1; Rom. 1:20).

i) *For the benefit of humanity* – Expresses God's relational intent and generosity in creating a world to be inhabited and enjoyed.

j) *And all very good* – Reflects God's affirmation and delight in the goodness of His creation (Gen. 1:31).

This theological definition of creation implies that God the Father created the universe through Jesus Christ by the Holy Spirit. Creation is an expression of God's mind, character, and power, meant for His glorification and praise. A theological definition of creation, suitable for a Christian philosophy of science, must emphasize the purposive activity of God in bringing into existence that which never existed.

Tenets of Biblical Creation Account

There are unique characteristics of creation that qualify them as creative acts—whether they bring matter, energy, space, and time into existence or are products of God's ongoing creative activity. These are summarized below.

God's Work of Creation: "Out of Nothing" and "Mediated"

The universe itself was created *ex nihilo*—out of nothing—while everything within it was created *mediately*, using pre-existing materials. According to Augustine, in the beginning, God called into being all created substances and forms. The book of Genesis uses the special Hebrew verb bārā' for "create," a verb used exclusively with God as its subject, signifying a uniquely divine creative action.

The author of Hebrews affirms this understanding: *By faith we understand that the universe was created by the word of God, so that what is seen was not made out of things that are visible* (Heb. 11:3). Davis (1998) adds: *The word 'create' is used exclusively of divine action and implies a creative work that is beyond human power.* This type of creation—bringing into existence what previously did not exist—is unique to God. Genesis 1 underscores that by God's command, the universe came into being from nothing. A similar creative act is referred to in Amos 4:13, in which God "creates the wind."

Biblical Examples of Different Creative Acts

The concept of creation out of nothing is sometimes easier to grasp than other types of divine creative work. Consider the following scriptures:

- *So, God created mankind in his own image* (Gen. 1:27, NIV).
- *Then the LORD God formed a man from the dust of the ground and breathed into his nostrils the breath of life* (Gen. 2:7, NIV).
- *He who forms the mountains, who creates the wind…* (Amos 4:13, NIV).
- *You are worthy, our Lord and God, to receive glory and honour and power, for you created all things…* (Rev. 4:11, NIV).

- *When you hide your face, they are terrified; when you take away their breath, they die... When you send your Spirit, they are created* (Psa. 104:29–30, NIV).
- *For you created my inmost being; you knit me together in my mother's womb* (Psa. 139:13, NIV).

These examples raise theological questions:

- Is humanity created *ex nihilo*, or formed from pre-existing material?
- Does this contradict the principle of *creation ex nihilo*?
- Do humans also create within nature, and if so, how does that relate to divine creation?

Explaining the Apparent Tension

God did not speak humanity into existence as He did the universe; instead, He formed man from dust and breathed life into him. While this might seem inconsistent with *creation ex nihilo*, it reflects a different mode of creation, not a contradiction. The initial act of creation (*bārā*) brought the universe into existence. From there, God's creative acts continued mediately using the created materials.

Tracy (2013) distinguishes between what God does directly, without intermediaries, and what He does indirectly, through created causes. God may endow creatures with causal powers, enabling them to induce changes. Thus, while only God creates in the absolute sense, He allows mediated creation to occur through His creatures.

At best, humanity can conserve, rearrange, or combine existing substances to make something new. Tracy further argues that when a creature brings about an effect, when an artist composes music, a technologist invents a machine, or an architect designs a building, this action can still be attributed to God in two ways:

- God acts directly in and through the creature, sustaining its being.
- God acts indirectly through the creature's intentional actions, such that the work can be described as a divine act as well.

From Chaos to Order

In Genesis 1:2, we read that *"The earth was without form and void"*—described in Hebrew as *tōhu vabōhu*, meaning formless and empty. What God initially created was a chaotic, unstructured mass. He then ordered it through His divine artistry. In this sense, humans—made in God's image—can be seen as sub-creators, reflecting God's creativity by forming and ordering creation.

The key features of a creative acts are summarized below:

- The universe was created *ex nihilo* by God alone.
- Subsequent creation occurred mediately, often using pre-existing materials.
- Humanity participates in creativity but does not create in the absolute sense.
- Biblical creation involves both direct and indirect divine action.
- The distinction between formless creation and structured order explains how human creative acts mirror divine work without equalling it.

Humans fashion, arrange, mould, and make things that are often beautiful. This capacity is, in part, what Genesis 1:26–27 means when it says that Adam was created "in the image of God." We, too, "create" - in the sense of composing poetry, music, literature, or designing architectural wonders - but not in the same way that God does.

Human creativity is relative and derivative, not absolute. Yet, in the creative act, humans sometimes experience profound insights into the structure of created reality. These insights arise from a holistic mode of perception, associated with the depths of human being. Still, to create in the absolute sense is an act reserved exclusively for God. God is the source of all created reality, though He has given the physical universe a role in its own development.

George Murphy describes this as *mediated creation ex nihilo*, God is the sole creator, but the material world has been produced mediately, often through natural processes and secondary causes. Similarly, the apostle Paul writes: *Continue to work out your salvation with fear and trembling, for it is God who works in you to will and to act according to His good purpose* (Philip. 2:12–13).

This demonstrates that while the Creator remains sovereign, He gives His creation the freedom to participate in the fulfilment of His will, all while providentially sustaining it.

Gisela Kreglinger (2014:84), citing George MacDonald, emphasizes the fundamental distinction between divine and human creativity. MacDonald argues that when a poet uses the term "create," it is used figuratively, not literally. He insists that God alone brings things into existence from nothing, and that mankind is part of that creation—not co-creators in the absolute sense.

Life comes from God alone, not from any latent potential within matter itself. Genesis affirms this: *Then God said, 'Let the land produce vegetation...* (Gen. 1:11); *Let the waters teem with living creatures...* (Gen. 1:20); *Let the land produce living creatures...* (Gen. 1:24). Though the materials (earth and water) already existed, it was God who commanded life into existence. This demonstrates that the potential for life was only realized at God's command. In this sense, redemption itself is a kind of mediated creation, we are made into a "new creation" (2 Corinthians 5:17), not from nothing, but through divine transformation.

Martin Luther, in his explanation of the First Article of the Creed (*I believe in God the Father Almighty, Maker of heaven and earth*), affirms this understanding of divine providence: *I believe that God made me and all creatures; that He has given me my body and soul, eyes, ears, and all my members, my reason, and all my senses, and still preserves them... All this He does out of pure, fatherly, divine goodness and mercy, without any merit or worthiness in me.* This creative activity is not direct creation out of nothing but rather a mediated process: food comes from the farmer, the store, and photosynthesis, through a whole chain of created structures and laws. God's ongoing creative activity is mediated through these natural intermediaries, making it possible to describe the universe at one level in terms of creatures, while affirming God as the ultimate source.

Between the beginning of the universe and its end, the creative voice of God is not silent. It resounds moment by moment, providing grass for cattle, prey for young lions, salmon for bears, browse for giraffes, bread for humans. These provisions are expressions of divine generosity, mediated through the processes of nature.

Creation Ex Nihilo: A Foundational Doctrine

The doctrine that the universe was created *ex nihilo*, out of nothing, is foundational to biblical theology. Before this concept emerged, ancient myths typically portrayed gods shaping a pre-existing cosmos. In contrast, the Hebrew tradition, and the religious thought that followed, introduced the radical idea of absolute creation.

All three Abrahamic faiths - Judaism, Christianity, and Islam - affirm that God brought the universe into being from nothing, not from chaos, energy, or divine essence, but by His sovereign word. This origin is not merely temporal, but ontological, the universe depends entirely on God for its existence.

In contemporary cosmological language, "nothing" may refer to a state without classical space and time, a realm of unrestrained quantum gravity, where matter, energy, time, and space have no coherent meaning. As physicist Alexander Vilenkin (quoted in Murphy, 1987) explains, such a state defies classical understanding, but it does not imply that *something* existed before creation. Rather, it is a true nothingness, incomprehensible to our space-time conditioned minds. Some sceptical alternatives have been proposed:

1. That the universe existed eternally.
2. That it was formed from pre-existing matter.
3. That God created it from His essence or energy.
4. That it arose from divine love.
5. That God used "nothing" as a kind of raw material.

However, these views fall short of the biblical teaching. Scripture insists that God brought the universe into existence from nothing, through the power of His will and word. Thus:

- Humans are creative in a relative, not absolute, sense, our creativity reflects, but does not replicate, divine creation.
- God alone creates *ex nihilo*; human creativity is derivative and mediated.

- The doctrine of *creation ex nihilo* affirms God's sovereign freedom and the universe's complete dependence on Him.
- God's mediated creative activity continues through nature, providence, and even human action.
- The biblical view of creation offers a unique ontological starting point, distinguishing it from mythological or speculative alternatives.

The Universe Has an Absolute Beginning

The **biblical account of creation** affirms that the universe has an **absolute beginning.** The opening statement of Scripture, *In the beginning God created the heavens and the earth* (Gen. 1:1), implies a definite starting point when the universe came into existence. Theologians, Church Fathers, scientists, and believers have consistently affirmed that the universe is **not eternal** but had a **finite beginning.**

The **Church Fathers** firmly upheld the doctrine of *creatio ex nihilo*, creation out of nothing, in direct opposition to the prevailing Hellenistic belief in the **eternity of matter.** In **Aristotelian physics**, *prime matter* was believed to be eternal and uncreated, like God Himself. In the 19th century, physicist Hermann Helmholtz reinforced this view with the **law of conservation of matter and energy**, which states that matter-energy cannot be created or destroyed. This seemed to support the idea of an **eternally existing universe**.

However, modern science has provided **compelling evidence** that the universe began to exist. The **Big Bang theory** describes a moment when all space, time, matter, energy, and the physical laws themselves came into existence. According to Christian apologist **William Lane Craig**, two key scientific findings support the idea of an **absolute beginning**:

1. *The Expansion of the Universe:* As time progresses, galaxies are observed to move away from one another, like buttons on an inflating balloon. If the universe had existed forever, this expansion would likely have ceased. The ongoing expansion suggests a point of origin.
2. *The Second Law of Thermodynamics*: This law states that a closed system tends toward a state of equilibrium over time. If the universe were eternal,

it should already have reached this state, a "heat death." But it hasn't. The universe is still dynamically active, indicating a finite age.

By tracing the universe back through its expansion, scientists have proposed a **singularity**, a point of infinite density in the finite past, where all distances shrink to zero. Most cosmologists agree that this singularity marks the **beginning of the universe**, where **matter, energy, space, and time** came into existence. As Craig concludes, this aligns with the doctrine of *creation ex nihilo* and echoes the message of Genesis 1:1. Both **science and theology** now affirm that the universe has an **absolute beginning**.

Creation displays functional integrity

The universe God created exhibits **functional integrity**, the ability to fulfil its purpose using the internal resources and laws God established. Though the earth was initially *"formless and empty"* (Gen. 1:2), it contained the "right stuff" to support complex physical structures and life.

According to **Howard Van Till** (2002), the universe was endowed with a full set of **resources, formational capabilities, and potentialities** needed to actualize every structure and organism in its history. The earth, from the beginning, possessed the **dynamic capacities** to bring forth the full array of life forms conceived in the mind of God. The original creation lacked nothing required to accomplish God's intended outcomes.

Before creation unfolded in time, all creatures existed **in the mind of God** and **potentially** within the created, formable substances of the world. These creaturely forms existed not actually, but as **potentials** embedded in the formless matter, what Van Till (1996) calls "**seed principles**." These principles were divinely implanted in creation from the beginning.

In this view, each kind of living thing - plants, animals, birds, and humans - carried within itself the **invisible potential** for development and diversification. God made all things together in an act of unified creation, planting within them the elements needed for their full expression in time. The creatures, including not only humans and heavenly bodies but also all biological forms, **existed in potency** within creation before they were fully realized.

At the **appointed time**, these created beings received their proper **form and function**, emerging visibly from the **hidden causes** placed in them. Thus, the *formless and void* earth was not a chaotic mess, but **ordered potential**, pre-programmed by God to produce the variety of creation at His command.

Reflecting on this idea, **Basil the Great** notes: *...of all this nothing was yet produced; the earth was in travail with it in virtue of the power she had received from the Creator. But she was waiting upon the appointed time and the divine order to bring it forth.* If **God is the sole author** of the universe, He also implanted the **formational capabilities** within all species and systems. The material world is thus not passive but **active and responsive** to God's creative word.

Everything That Exists Originates from God

Everything that exists, **except God Himself**, originates from His creative will and power. The Lord freely chose to speak, and the universe came into being. Outside of God's **creative word**, nothing could come into existence. The doctrine of **creation ex nihilo** confirms that the universe is not self-originating, eternal, or a product of necessity. It is a **contingent reality**, grounded entirely in the **free decision** of a personal Creator.

The Universe Has an Absolute Beginning

Science tells us that the universe originated at a singularity, a finite point in the past where matter, energy, space, and time came into existence. Nothing existed before this singularity in the physical sense. However, science cannot determine what, if anything, existed before this point, because it lacks the tools to explore beyond the boundaries of space-time. While science is adept at predicting future events based on known laws and conditions, it cannot explain the ultimate origin of the universe.

In contrast, the Bible affirms that only God existed before creation, and that He is the source of everything. Creation reflects the collaborative work of God the Father, His Word (the Son), and the Holy Spirit, revealing that the depth of

God's being is the source of His creative activity. As John 1:3 declares: *All things were made by him; and without him was not anything made that was made.*

The Initial Universe Was Not in its Final Form

Genesis 1:2 states that *"the earth was without form and void, and darkness was over the surface of the deep."* This description suggests that the initial creation did not yet possess the structure, life forms, or conditions God intended. The earth, as first created, was not yet complete. It was an unstructured and empty mass, submerged under water and covered in darkness.

Some interpret this state as chaotic, but not in the sense of disorderly or failed creation. Rather, it is an indication of potential—a raw material awaiting the ordering Word of God. Was this dark and formless state a mistake, or a limitation of divine power? Certainly not. The initial creation was a deliberate and sovereign act, the greatest event eternity had witnessed, intended to unfold in stages according to God's will.

God's act of creation reveals His generosity, love, order, intelligence, and sovereignty. He could have created the universe fully formed in a single moment, but instead chose a process, allowing His creation to participate in the unfolding of His will. Though He remains the sole source of creative power, God has gifted the universe with the capacity for development.

Creation as a Dynamic Process

God created the universe in a state of potential, endowing it with the ability to transform from unformed matter into a cosmos full of life and beauty. This reveals a divine principle of process—God involves His creation in shaping its ultimate form. This principle is also evident in Christian redemption, a form of mediate creation. As Paul writes: *If anyone is in Christ, he is a new creation* (2 Cor. 5:17). Yet, though declared righteous, the Christian is not perfected immediately. Instead, believers are told to *work out your salvation with fear and trembling, for it is God who works in you* (Phil. 2:12–13). Just as creation unfolds, so too does spiritual transformation.

God's decision to bring creation into existence in an unfinished state is not a flaw but a gracious invitation for creation to participate in its own fulfilment—under His providential guidance.

Humanity: Created in the Image of God

To be made in the image of God (*imago Dei*) includes several dimensions: rationality, moral awareness, spiritual capacity, creativity, and responsibility for stewardship. As Provan (2006) suggests, humans reflect God in ways other creatures do not, through reason, personality, free will, self-awareness, and intelligence.

Humans were created to mirror God's nature, live in relationship with Him, and exercise rule over creation in fellowship with their Creator. These relational and functional attributes point to our divine origin and purpose.

Though physically formed from the dust like other creatures (Gen. 2:7), what sets humanity apart is the breath of God—the spiritual essence imparted by the Creator. This soul or spirit is the seat of consciousness, will, emotion, and moral reasoning, and it grants us the capacity for eternal relationship with God.

Being made in God's image also means we are intrinsically religious beings, created for covenant fellowship with God. Our purpose is to glorify and enjoy Him, reflecting His character in the world.

Humanity as Image Bearers and Stewards of Creation

Like the Godhead, humans were created for fellowship and to perceive creation in ways that reflect God's own view. God loves His creation and actively cares for it. In creating humans in His image and likeness, He entrusted them with a similar vocation of love, stewardship, and care. After forming Adam, God tested his competence by assigning him a key task of stewardship—naming the animals (Gen. 2:19-20). This was not merely about taxonomy but signified understanding, responsibility, and authority.

Understanding the language of *image* and *likeness* is essential for grasping both our nature and our vocation. It implies that humans are representatives or viceroys of God on earth. Out of all creation, we have been chosen as stewards. As image-bearers, we hold a special status that connects us both to God and to non-human creation. This dual kinship forms the basis for a dominion that is not exploitative but grounded in sacrificial service, reflecting the character of God Himself.

Our ability to fulfil this divine commission is based on our dual nature: we are materially united with the natural world and spiritually receptive to the divine. Genesis 1 and 2 present this dynamic beautifully—we are both part of nature (formed from the dust) and apart from it (bearing God's breath). Likewise, we possess both a ruling and serving nature. As integrated beings—physical and spiritual—we are capable of imaging God to the rest of creation, both in authority and humility (Gen. 1:26–27).

Philosopher Georg Kühlewind (1986) suggested that human consciousness, like all of creation, consists fundamentally of word-structure, a personal, knowing substance. In this sense, we can interpret creation as a text, meant to be read, understood, and engaged. This "worded" nature of reality underpins humanity's calling to scientific inquiry, technology, worship, and praise, all ways of participating in and revealing God's glory.

However, sin has marred the image of God in humanity, distorting our ability to rule, serve, and recognize God's revelation in creation. Yet, through the death and resurrection of Jesus Christ, we have been redeemed, and our capacity as rulers and stewards has been restored. In Christ, we become a new creation (2 Cor. 5:17), and our renewed perception of creation reflects our identity as citizens of God's Kingdom under the reign of Christ.

The Old Testament models kingship as benevolent leadership, defending the oppressed and showing compassion to the afflicted (Psa. 72:2–4, 12–14). Christ is the ultimate model of divine authority exercised through humility and servanthood (Philip. 2:5–8). His leadership redefines dominion as self-giving love, and this becomes the blueprint for Christian stewardship.

If we truly understand our position as God's image-bearers, then the Church, often silent on environmental matters, can become a powerful force for ecological stewardship. This vision also offers a theological foundation for the environmental movement, supplying a moral and spiritual ethic rooted in God's creative purpose.

Creation as the coordinated work of the Spirit and the Word

The Word and Wisdom of God brought structure, order, and purpose to creation. The Genesis narrative shows that God's spoken commands follow the mysterious and almighty work of the Holy Spirit, who hovers over the formless, void earth (Gen. 1:2).

The imagery of the Spirit *hovering* has often been likened to a bird brooding over its young, which is rich in theological significance. According to *Encyclopaedia Britannica*, birds brood by spreading their feathers and warming their young, providing nurture and safety. In a similar way, the Holy Spirit brooded over the waters, not passively, but preparing and preserving the raw material of creation, awaiting the Father's Word to give it form and life.

This maternal metaphor portrays the Holy Spirit as nurturing creation, readying it for the Father's creative commands. The formless earth was pregnant with potential, and the Spirit was intimately involved in shaping and animating what was to come.

Thus, creation is not a solitary act but a majestic and mysterious collaboration between Father, Son (Word), and Spirit. Each Person of the Trinity is active: the Father wills, the Son speaks, and the Spirit prepares and enlivens. The initial earth was not chaotic in a negative sense, but rather rich with possibility, a womb of creation awaiting the unfolding of God's perfect will.

The performative power of God's Word and Spirit in creation

Each time God issued a creative command, *Let there be...*, the Spirit of God, brooding over the earth, energized creation to bring into being the object of the divine decree. This image captures the creative energy, presence, anticipation, and movement that characterize divine action. God's thought, will, and Word took effect because the One who thinks, wills, and speaks is also the One who acts—the principal executor of all creative activity. This reveals the performative power of both the Word and the Spirit.

The Word is the outward expression of the inward life of God. Thus, creation becomes like a poem, a wisely structured manifestation of God's inner being, written to reveal His glory to humanity.

The Word imprints creation with a textual order, a structure that can be observed, classified, analysed, and shaped into meaningful realities. When humans pursue knowledge, especially through deep reflection or scientific discovery, they are participating in a process where insight into the nature of created reality emerges from within, revealing creation's coherence and God's wisdom.

As Tappeiner (1977) observes, the history of art and science offers numerous examples of the dynamic interplay between the Spirit and the Word at work in human creativity. The Holy Spirit provides depth, vitality, and inspiration, while the Word gives form, articulation, and clarity. It is the Spirit who inspires insight, and the Word that gives it intelligible expression.

The Book of Nature as Divine Revelation

God's creative activity has produced not just a world, but a Book of Nature—a form of self-revelation. He authored it in a language that His image-bearers are equipped to understand. In nature, God progressively unveils the eternal riches of His wisdom, beauty, and glory.

Theologians throughout history - Augustine, Aquinas, Calvin, and in more recent times, Alister McGrath and John Polkinghorne - have spoken of two books: the Book of Nature and the Book of Scripture. Nature is not just the backdrop of human life, but a living text, authored by God for His creatures to read, interpret, and respond to with reverence and stewardship.

Creation as a Personal and Purposeful Act of God

Creation is not an unconscious overflow of divine abundance. It is a deeply personal act, proceeding from God's self-determined will and grounded in His essence. Only a personal Being speaks and brings creatures into existence by command.

God was not compelled by any lack or necessity to create. Some sceptics suggest that God created because He was lonely or needed something to love. But such views are inconsistent with classical Christian doctrine. God is perfect, complete, and self-sufficient, eternally satisfied within the communion of the Trinity: Father, Son, and Holy Spirit. He is the same with or without creation.

Creation, then, is not deficiency driven. It is the free, generous, and loving act of a God who delights to share His life and glory. In contrast, all of creation, including humanity, utterly depends on God for its origin, purpose, and continued existence.

Creation is Not Random but Purposeful

The universe is not the result of random, unguided processes. It is intended, designed, and directed toward a goal. It has an origin, a direction, and a destiny—all rooted in God's wise and loving character. Because God is good and purposeful, creation reflects order, intelligibility, beauty, and the potential for flourishing.

Since God created through personal commands, everything that exists carries a divine purpose. The ultimate goal of creation, redemption, and consummation is the full manifestation of God's glory. This is affirmed throughout Scripture: *All the earth shall be filled with the glory of the Lord* (Numb. 14:21); *The earth will be filled with the knowledge of the glory of the Lord as the waters cover the sea* (Hab. 2:14); and *Whether you eat or drink or whatever you do, do it all for the glory of God* (1 Cor. 10:31). These texts challenge the sacred-secular divide. Every moment - every decision, task, relationship, or meal - can be aligned with God's purpose and become an act of worship. We are invited to live intentionally, joyfully, and purposefully under God's reign, glorifying Him in all things.

The Glory of God in All of Life

The word *glory* refers to God's weight, worth, radiance, and beauty. To glorify God means to make much of Him, to reflect His greatness in how we live, love, work, and worship. Glorification is not confined to worship services or private devotions; it extends into every sphere of life.

When we eat with gratitude, work with integrity, speak with love, and rest in trust, we declare that God is worthy of all. Even the mundane moments of life can become acts of worship that magnify His glory.

Everything God Does is Purpose-Driven

Everything God does is purposeful and intentional. This is clearly illustrated in the divine decision recorded in Genesis 1:26 (KJV): *And God said, Let us make man in our image, after our likeness: and let them have dominion over the fish of the sea, and over the fowl of the air, and over the cattle, and over all the earth, and over every creeping thing that creeps upon the earth.* This verse reflects a deliberate act of the triune God and introduces humanity's cultural mandate, to develop, protect, and cultivate creation in harmony with God's will. It is a royal commission, not to dominate but to exercise dominion with servant leadership, wisdom, and care as stewards of God's creation.

Dominion is not about power or exploitation, but rather a partnership with God in the ongoing care and cultivation of His world. Since humans are given authority over sea creatures, birds, land animals, and the earth itself, this dominion implies a comprehensive and relational responsibility, one that informs Christian perspectives on environmental stewardship, science, agriculture, justice, and vocation.

Creation as Purposeful Design

Every creative act of God has a specific, intentional purpose. From galaxies to grains of sand, creation reveals intelligent design, intricate order, and relational significance. Even the seemingly mundane serves a place in the broader tapestry of divine intention.

Modern science increasingly affirms that nature displays purpose. Purpose shapes the structure and function of things; it distinguishes between creatures, and it often governs the form and behaviour of biological systems. For example:
- A bird builds a nest to protect and raise its young.
- A whale stores fat for insulation, buoyancy, and energy during migration.

- Tree roots absorb nutrients and anchor the tree.
- A chick's neck muscles are uniquely developed to help it hatch.
- Migrating birds fly in V formations to conserve energy through aerodynamic advantage.
- Some birds engage in complex courtship rituals to ensure species-specific mating.
- Armadillos give birth to identical quadruplets to prevent inbreeding.

Each of these examples illustrates inherent design and function, a hallmark of purposeful creation.

Humanity as Purposeful Image-Bearers

Human beings reflect this same principle. Each body part has a distinct function: the nose is designed for breathing; the eyes for seeing; the ears for hearing; the mouth for eating and speaking; and the tongue for tasting. This purposeful design reflects the character of the Creator. Just as a wise person rarely acts without a reason, so God, infinitely wise, does nothing without purpose. In humanity, God's image-bearers, we see the convergence of intentional design and moral vocation: to live purposefully in alignment with His will, reflecting His wisdom in all we do.

God is Immanent in Creation

Thomas Aquinas once remarked, *"When a builder departs, the house still remains standing... But God is directly, by Himself, the cause of the very existence and communicates existence just as the sun communicates light to the air and to whatever else is illuminated by the sun."* In contrast to a human builder who walks away after construction, God is not an absent architect. He is not only the Creator but also the continuous cause of existence itself.

Just as light flows continuously from the sun, our existence flows from God moment by moment. Creatures receive existence, but they do not possess it independently. Aquinas emphasized this truth when he said, *Creatures do not merely receive existence once from God, but receive it continually, as long as they exist.* Without God's sustaining presence, all things would cease to exist.

Scripture affirms this idea of continual creation (*creatio continua*). God brought everything into being and sustains all things by the Word of His power (Heb. 1:3). He gives life to all creatures and maintains their functional state: *When you hide your face, they are terrified; when you take away their breath, they die and return to the dust. When you send your Spirit, they are created, and you renew the face of the earth* (Psa. 104:29–30). This ongoing divine activity is also seen in passages such as Acts 17:28 (*In him we live and move and have our being*) and Colossians 1:17 (*In him all things hold together*).

Paul, in encouraging the Philippians, wrote: *Work out your salvation with fear and trembling, for it is God which worketh in you both to will and to do of his good pleasure* (Phil. 2:12–13 KJV). God is continually at work in us, not just initiating life but sustaining and shaping it. As theologian David Wilcox wisely observed: *Anyone who is a fully biblical theist must consider ordinary processes controlled by natural law to be as completely and deliberately the wonderful acts of God as any miracle, equally contingent upon His free and unhindered will.*

Too often, we treat God's involvement as visible only in the supernatural, thereby falling into a "God of the gaps" mentality, invoking divine action only where science cannot yet explain. However, God is both transcendent and immanent: above creation, yet fully present within it.

God's Creation is Inherently Good

Because God is good, His creation is intrinsically good. This includes both its physical and spiritual dimensions. In the Genesis account, God repeatedly evaluated His creative work and declared it "good" (Gen. 1:4, 10, 12, 18, 21, 25). This is not a casual observation but a divine judgment of alignment with His will and purpose. When Scripture says, *"God saw that it was good,"* it can be understood in several ways:

- It was fit for its intended purpose.
- It was perfectly aligned with God's eternal wisdom.
- It was suitable for human well-being and flourishing.
- It was beautiful and pleasing to God.

Each aspect of creation, regardless of human opinion or utilitarian value, was good in its own right. God's declaration of goodness stands independent of our preferences. What He calls good may seem offensive or unpleasant to us, but His evaluation is final and fully informed. Every creature, even those we fear or dislike, reflects some dimension of the Creator's wisdom and purpose.

Humans have long judged the value of creatures based on the benefits they provide to us. This human-centeredness, or anthropocentrism, has compromised our God-given role to rule and serve creation faithfully. It has also contributed to the lack of environmental activism within the evangelical community.

The authors of *Earth keeping: Christian Stewardship of Natural Resources* emphasize that Genesis 1 clearly presents creation's goodness as intrinsic, found in the things themselves, not merely in their usefulness to humans. Humanity does not even appear until the final part of the chapter. To reduce the value of creation to its utility for the only creature made in God's image is to miss the deeper theological meaning of the text. Genesis 1 celebrates the vibrant, ordered, and flourishing complexity of life, a world pulsing with God-given worth long before humanity sets foot on it. Modern scientific discoveries about the cosmos and earth deepen our appreciation for God's care for the non-human universe.

After completing His creative work, *God saw all that He had made, and it was very good* (Gen. 1:31). While each day's work was declared "good," the culmination, all creatures and systems interacting in harmony, was declared "very good." Humans, made in God's image, are part of this very good creation. This affirms the interconnectedness and communal harmony of all creation.

The Genesis story presents a cosmos that sings, abundant, intricate, teeming with life and form. Even before humans arrive, the world is filled with birds, fish, and stars (Gen. 1:20–21), all called "good." This supports the idea that non-human creation glorifies God in its own way. Psalms 148 and Job 38–39 reinforce this: mountains, seas, stars, and wild animals all join in a cosmic chorus of praise.

Because creation is good, it is worth preserving, nurturing, and even redeeming. This doctrine grounds a theology of environmental stewardship, human dignity, and even artistic expression. It also affirms the goodness of the material world, countering dualistic ideas that see matter, the body, or nature as evil or inferior. Environmental degradation is a symptom of a groaning earth, and Christians are called not to exploit or trash it, but to strive for its renewal and flourishing.

Thus, creation is inherently good because it flows from the good nature of God. Its diversity and beauty reflect God's wisdom, love, and order. This goodness calls us not only to wonder and gratitude, but to a sacred responsibility to care for, enjoy, and live faithfully within what God has made.

Creation is Corrupted

While creation was originally "very good" (Gen. 1:31), it has since been wounded by sin, not just humanity, but the whole created order. Genesis 3 describes the rupture of harmony: sin enters the world through human disobedience, severing the relationship between God, humanity, and creation. As a result, the serpent, the woman, the man, and even the ground itself is cursed.

This was not just a personal or moral failure, it was a cosmic fracture. God entrusted humanity with the responsibility of stewarding creation according to His wisdom and purposes. But through rebellion, our ability to govern creation rightly was distorted and corrupted.

Cut off from God, our spiritual perception of God and creation was darkened. The flesh (our fallen human nature) began to define our identity, while our spirit, once oriented toward God, was disoriented and disconnected from the Holy Spirit. This spiritual condition denied us access to the divine wisdom, counsel, and power needed to live righteously and care for the earth.

In this fallen state, humanity ceased to be a steward and became, instead, an agent of creation's corruption and decay. As Paul writes in Romans 8:20–22, *The creation was subjected to frustration... in hope that the creation itself will be liberated from its bondage to decay and brought into the glorious freedom of the children of God.* Creation now groans, waiting for its liberation, which is tied to the redemption of humanity.

By design, God intends to bless creation through humanity. This implies that non-human creation depends on humanity to provide them with their much-needed care to fulfil their purpose, although God is still involved. God has chosen to bless and care for creation through humanity, who are called to steward it. Though creation ultimately depends on God, He has entrusted humans with a vital role in its flourishing.

Creation is corrupted but not worthless. But it is no longer functioning fully as it was meant to. Diseases, death, decay, and ecological disorder or environmental crises are signs of a world out of alignment with its original purpose. Yet its goodness remains, like beauty in a shattered mirror. And God has not abandoned it. Creation may be corrupted, but it is also redeemed, cherished, and destined for renewal.

Through Jesus, God is not only saving people, but He is also reconciling to himself all things, whether on earth or in heaven (Col. 1:20) and making all things new (Rev. 21:5). However, creation is frustrated by human disobedience which is distorting its harmony and subjecting it to decay. Paul captures this when he writes that *.. creation waits in eager expectation for the sons of God to be revealed. For creation was subjected to frustration, not by its own choice, but by the will of the one who subjected it, in hope that the creation itself will be liberated from its bondage to decay and brought into the glorious freedom of the children of God* (Rom. 8:19-21 NIV). The fate of non-human creation is tied to that of humanity. But God has not abandoned His world; through Christ, creation groans with hope, awaiting the full restoration of all things.

Salvation of Humanity implicitly means liberation of non-human creation

The salvation of humanity is inseparably tied to the liberation of non-human creation. God's redemptive work in Christ isn't limited to saving human souls, it encompasses the renewal of all creation. *For God loved the world the world that he gave his one and only Son, that whoever believes in him shall not perish but have eternal life* (John 3:16 NIV). God sacrificed His Son as a penalty for the sin of humanity. Through the crucifixion, death and resurrection of Jesus Christ,

God forgave and washed away our sins, adopted us as His sons and daughters, and clothed us with His righteousness.

The good news is that the corrupted nature of humanity was nailed to the cross with Jesus Christ, and His death and resurrection have produced a new creature in those that believe in Him. Therefore, if anyone is in Christ, He is a new creation; the old is gone, the new has come (2 Cor. 2:17 NIV). Salvation does not only reconcile humanity to God but also restores him as His representative (viceroy) in creation.

As a new creation in Christ, we have a responsibility to fulfil the Great Commission (preach the gospel, baptize the converts, and disciple the followers) and to care for the needy in our midst. Salvation through Christ, which involves grafting us on Christ as the rootstock, enables us to enjoy the union and communion with Him. But this demands that we have His mind and acquire His nature.

We must treat other creatures the way He does. Consider the relationship of Christ to creation: *Christ is the firstborn over all creation. For by him all things were created....; all things were created by Him and for Him*" (Col. 1:15-16). The author of Hebrew also says, The Son is the radiance of God's glory and the exact representation of his being, sustaining all things by His powerful word (Heb. 1:3). Jesus Christ did not just create all things; he united with creation and sustains all things by the Word of His power. As His disciples, he expects us to love creation as He does and to work with Him to hold it together. If we viewed creation the way our Lord does, the Church would not struggle to embrace environmental stewardship. As members of the body of Christ we learn and do what He shows us. Creation suffers because of human sin and its liberation is linked to our salvation. As we are redeemed and restored, so is creation.

Consummation and New Heavens and New Earth

The Consummation is the final and glorious act of God's redemptive plan: the renewal of all creation in the New Heavens and New Earth. It is not the escape from the world, but the fulfilment of its purpose, where God dwells with His people, creation is healed, and all things are made new in Christ. It is the last chapter of the biblical narrative of creation, fall, redemption, and consummation. Grounded in both Old and New Testaments, consummation, does not imply abandonment of the Old, but it's renewal and resurrection. Creation will not be discarded; it will be transformed.

Consummation reminds us that: there will be no more death, mourning or pain; full reconciliation between God, people and creation is guaranteed; God will dwell with humanity in unveiled intimacy; and a redeemed creation will retain continuity with the old, but in a gloriously transformed state.

Christians, a new creation in Christ, await the second coming of the Lord when He will take them to heaven and their eventual return to rule with Christ in the new earth. Revealing this mystery to the Corinthian saints, Paul describes what is to happen at the second coming of the Lord Jesus Christ: Listen, I tell you a mystery: We will not all sleep, but we will all be changed – in a flash, in the twinkling of an eye at the last trumpet (1 Cor. 15).

When the trumpet sounds, signalling the return of the Lord, believers dead in Christ will rise with bodies that are imperishable and immortal. Those who will not have died, will also acquire imperishable and immortal bodies in a twinkling of the eye. Humanity will be mediately created into beings with glorified bodies like Jesus Christ. The Lord will take to heaven a glorified bride for the earthly corrupted bodies will have no place in the new heaven and earth.

While in a trance (Rev. 21), John received a revelation of a new heaven and a new earth, which replaced the old. And out of heaven rolled out the Holy City, New Jerusalem, the citadel of God on earth. The recreated universe, humanity, and non-human creation will have new relationships: creation will praise and glorify God, humanity will obediently rule over and serve creation, and God will love and cherish His creation.

Living in view of the consummation entails hope which calls us to: live faithfully now, knowing history has a destination; care for creation, since God values it enough to redeem it; proclaim the gospel, because God is drawing all things into His kingdom; and worship with joy, anticipating the day when faith becomes sight.

CHAPTER 7
Manifestations of His Power

Creation reveals the power of God. It is the first canvas upon which His power is displayed. God brings the universe into being out of nothing (*ex nihilo*) by the sheer force of His will and Word (Ps. 33:6, 9; Jer. 10:12). The act of creation is one of the clearest demonstrations of God's limitless power, not merely in His ability to make, but in His capacity to speak things into being, sustain them, and give them purpose. This power is not chaotic or random; it is creative, purposeful, and wise.

Have you ever watched a compelling National Geographic documentary or a science film that transported you to remote parts of the natural world? How often do we associate such breathtaking wonders with the world described in Genesis 1? We often fail to grasp the full theological significance of God's eternal and infinite power in relation to creation, including ourselves.

Some argue that discussing God's creative power and the process of creation is not relevant to the "more important" work of the Kingdom. Others dismiss creation care or scientific inquiry as distractions from spiritual concerns, relegating them to scientists, as though science exists apart from faith or divine purpose.

Additionally, many believers hesitate to engage with nature due to contentious science-faith debates. Even those with a sound understanding of creation sometimes pay only lip service to the Creator. Tragically, our failure to integrate faith and science has led many scientists to feel alienated from the Church.

Scientists sitting in pews often wonder why their vocation is not recognized as a calling to explore God's self-revelation through nature. Scientific discovery reveals the magnificence of God's handiwork, enriching our worship and glorifying God. It also equips humanity to fulfil its original calling: to steward and serve creation.

A holistic understanding of God's infinite power must include His revelation through both the Book of Scripture and the Book of Works, also known as the

Book of Nature. Christ's personal revelation through His life and ministry further completes this triad of divine self-disclosure. Ignoring God's self-revelation through creation is a serious theological omission.

As God's image-bearers, we cannot fully represent Him unless we recognize and embrace the manifestation of His eternal power and divine nature embedded in the natural world. The only way to know anyone, including God, is by knowing what they have said and done.

This chapter explores the relationship between God's power and creation, and its profound implications for humanity.

God's Power Hidden in Creation

In God's grand scheme, creation is foundational to the revelation of His essence and power. As Paul declares, *"Since the creation of the world God's invisible qualities, his eternal power and divine nature, have been clearly seen, being understood from what has been made, so that people are without excuse"* (Rom. 1:20). God conceived and created a world capable of communicating His invisible attributes. Through the beauty, order, and complexity of creation, God's eternal power and divine nature are made visible. Nature is an open book that reveals these attributes, testifying daily to the glory of its Creator and inviting all people to behold, to wonder, and to worship.

The visible creation displays the invisible qualities of God. Paul emphasizes that divine attributes, though unseen, are clearly perceived in the things God has made. Just as we cannot see the wind but can observe its effects, we cannot see God's essence directly, but we see His fingerprints on the natural world. Nature is both *open*, accessible to all people across time and culture, and a *book*, communicating truth, beauty, and meaning. Even those without access to Scripture can discern through creation that there is a Creator, a moral order, and a purpose.

Paul reminds every disciple of Christ to read the *textbook* of nature to understand God's eternal power and essence. We must discern the *Logos*-structure embedded in the natural world, for it contains data and meaning about God's character. Though nature is not divine, it carries a comprehensive commentary on God's power. When God sought to impress His transcendence, power, and authority upon Job (Job 38–41), He pointed him to the created universe. Solitude in the natural world can reveal aspects of God in a way not easily accessible elsewhere.

God's power is evident in the vastness and order of the cosmos. From galaxies and stars to ecosystems and DNA, creation reveals His greatness, wisdom, and creativity:

- Vastness reveals God's majesty.
- Order and structure reflect divine wisdom.
- Beauty and intricacy express His goodness and artistry.

God's creative power did not cease after the initial act of creation. As Hebrews 1:3 tells us, *"He upholds the universe by the word of his power."* Every sunrise, every breath, and every heartbeat continues by His sustaining will. The God who created by His power also redeems by His power. The resurrection of Jesus is not only a triumph over death but a new act of creation, a preview of the new heavens and new earth to come.

God's power is uniquely displayed in creation, where He brings light from darkness, life from nothing, and order from chaos. His creative power is not just a historical act but a present, sustaining force that reveals His majesty, wisdom, and love, a power that forms the cosmos and transforms hearts.

As Van Till (1996) insightfully notes, the universe was brought into being in a less-than-fully-formed state yet endowed with all the capacities necessary for transformation in accordance with God's will. The world did not lack anything required to become what God intended. At creation, God, by His infinite power, endowed all things with the potential to actualize the marvellous array of forms He had in mind. The formless and void earth was endowed with this power and awaited God's appointed time and divine order to give birth to His creative purposes.

Everything God created was given a kind of *power budget*, reserves to assume a specific form aligned with the Creator's intention. In envisioning the universe and its environment, God also established the divine energy necessary to bring all things into being, to transform the formless into form, and to sustain creation. This divine power supply was ordained before creation began.

Creation as Expression of Infinite Power

The doctrine of creation *ex nihilo* underscores a vital theological truth: God alone is eternally and infinitely powerful. While some philosophical traditions assert that "from nothing, nothing comes," and therefore reject the idea of creation from nothing as absurd, Christian theology proclaims that this very impossibility is what showcases God's incomparable omnipotence. The creation of an intelligent, ordered universe from absolute nothingness is not only possible for God—it is the supreme expression of limitless divine power.

From the vastness of the cosmos to the intricate design of a flower, creation reveals the overflow of a God who is infinite in power, wisdom, and life. God created the universe *ex nihilo*, without pre-existent matter, without assistance, and without compulsion. This type of creation is not merely impressive; it is uniquely divine. It affirms God's self-sufficiency (He needs nothing), supreme freedom (He creates by choice), and absolute power (He brings being from non-being).

Only an infinitely powerful being can bridge the absolute gap between nothing and something. The scale of creation itself justifies the necessity of immeasurable power. There is no middle ground between non-being and being; thus, the force required to bridge this ontological divide is beyond measure. The sheer scope and complexity of the universe reflect the vastness of its Creator (Ps. 147:5; Isa. 40:26). From galaxies and gravity to cells and atoms, creation manifests power that is creative, sustaining, intelligent, intentional, and infinite.

Importantly, this infinite power in creation is echoed in the work of redemption. As Paul writes in 2 Corinthians 4:6, *For God, who said, 'Let light shine out of darkness,' made his light shine in our hearts...* and in Ephesians 1:19–20, he speaks of *the immeasurable greatness of His power* displayed in the resurrection of Jesus. The original creation and the new creation in Christ are twin displays of divine omnipotence, one physical, the other spiritual, both miraculous and transformative.

Creation is power wrapped in beauty and wisdom. God's power is not chaotic or brute, it is guided by divine wisdom and love. As theologians have long observed, the power of a creator is revealed both by the substance of what is made and the way it is made. Creating a complex machine from parts is remarkable; creating the entire universe from *nothing* is infinitely more profound.

Thomas Aquinas affirms this truth: *...a greater power is required in the agent insofar as the potency is more remote from the act.* In other words, the further a thing is from existence (potency), the greater the power needed to bring it into being (act). Before creation, there was no potential, nothing existed. Therefore, only infinite power could make the leap from non-being to being.

This can be illustrated in everyday analogies. A Masai herdsman knows that producing a calf from a bull and cow takes a certain kind of power. But producing a calf from nothing at all would require a radically greater kind of power, one that crosses the infinite chasm between nothing and something. Likewise, raising the dead or transforming fallen creation also involves immense divine power, for the distance between death and glorified life is vast. Paul captures this in Ephesians 1:19–20, calling it *the immeasurable greatness of His power.*

Our human attempts to measure power pale in comparison. Most things are measurable because they have limits. We might measure a person's height or a machine's output. But the power required to bring the universe into existence has no boundaries and therefore defies human measurement. Infinite power is the only adequate explanation for the existence of anything at all.

The universe stretches out across unimaginable distances, populated by billions of galaxies, stars, and planets. God exerts His creative power over expanses that light takes billions of years to traverse. Only a limitless, immeasurable power could create and sustain such a universe.

As Isaiah reminds us: *Who has measured the waters in the hollow of his hand, or with the breadth of his hand marked off the heavens? Who has held the dust of the earth in a basket, or weighed the mountains on the scales...?* (Isa. 40:12, NIV). We marvel when humans lift impressive weights. For example, Mateusz Kieliszkowski, the 2018 World's Strongest Man, lifted 1,041 lbs (472.2 kg) to win the title in Manila. Such feats impress us because they push the limits of human capacity. Yet even this is infinitesimally small compared to the power of God. God's power is not merely additive, it is in a category all its own: infinite, immeasurable, and divine.

Scientists affirm that the universe is finite, constrained by the dimensions of space and time. However, since what is finite cannot contain or account for the infinite power required to explain its own existence, it follows that an infinite Being must exist, one whose power is immeasurable. Nature itself holds the evidence: it bears the marks of this infinite power and reveals the divine nature of its Creator.

Humans and God's Power

Humans are created by God's power, sustained by it daily, and invited to share in it through a relationship with Him. Though fragile in ourselves, we reflect God's strength when we live in dependence and obedience. His power is not only the source of our existence, but also the hope of our transformation, from dust to glory. The theme of humanity and God's power lies at the intersection of creation, dependence, vocation, weakness, and glory.

As we image God and seek to rule over and serve creation, we must cultivate a holistic understanding: of God as revealed in creation; of physical structures, biological organisms, and their environments; and of how to relate rightly to God, one another, and the rest of creation. This understanding draws from the Book of Scripture, the Book of Nature, and the self-revelation of Christ.

Humanity exists solely because of God's power (Gen. 2:7). We are formed from dust, yet animated by God's breath. This means we are both fragile and infinitely valued, formed by His will and continually sustained by His infinite power. We depend on Him moment by moment for life, breath, and purpose.

His power is made perfect in human weakness (2 Cor. 12:9). One of the most beautiful paradoxes in Scripture is that we don't need to be powerful in ourselves. God often chooses the weak, the humble, and the overlooked to display His strength. Our limitations become the very stage on which God's power is revealed.

Through union with Christ, humans share in God's power. Believers participate in God's life and strength (Eph. 1:19). The same power that created the world, raised Jesus from the dead, and sustains the universe is now at work in us, transforming our lives, empowering us to live in holiness, and preparing us for glory. God entrusts this power to humanity as stewards. When we submit to Him, His power flows as a channel of His grace.

No one created in God's image can experience a deficit of divine power, so long as they fear God and obey His commands. As His representatives on earth, we have access to immeasurable divine power for life and stewardship. Your energy reserves are always sufficient for your God-given mission, but only if you stay plugged into God's power source. God knows that His power drives our words and actions; without it, we cannot function spiritually.

When I first visited a mining town in Zambia, I had the opportunity to meet miners who spent much of their week underground. One striking insight I gained was that many of the tunnels where they extracted minerals were naturally flooded. To keep these areas dry, massive surface water pumps ran continuously, day and night, pumping water out of the mine. The company even had standby pumps ready to take over at a moment's notice in case any pump failed.

As expected, each of the pumps required a continuous and reliable supply of power. In case of power failure, standby heavy-duty generators would automatically kick in to bridge any gaps in the grid's electricity supply. Learning that a naturally flooded underground mine could be kept dry year after year by a network of steadily powered pumps was an amazing experience.

How often do we pause to reflect on the immeasurable power of God that sustains all of creation? God created all things with built-in "power generators," connected ultimately to Him as the true and eternal source. In the physical realm,

He has provided both biological and physical power systems to maintain life within the broader ecosystem. For instance, human and animal cells contain mitochondria, cellular structures that generate energy to power bodily functions. Yet even these systems are interdependent, relying on energy from other living organisms.

The sun, too, is a divinely established powerhouse, supplying energy to sustain life on Earth, including vital processes in plants, animals, and humans. If the sun were to stop delivering energy, Earth's average surface temperature would drop dramatically, by about 14°C, and plants would cease to produce food. This would break the flow of energy through the food chain (plants → herbivores → carnivores), including humans, who rely on both plants and animals for nourishment.

Some scientists argue that once creatures were endowed with internal power-generation capabilities by the Creator, the system could thereafter run on its own, without further divine intervention. They use this argument to support the idea that humans evolved from a single-celled organism over a long process of natural development. Although this work does not engage directly with the creation-versus-evolution debate, this perspective has serious implications for understanding God's providential role.

To suggest that the evolutionary process could unfold entirely without the involvement of an infinitely powerful Being is a controversial claim. Unfortunately, this view has led some believers to downplay God's ongoing power in natural processes like sunrise and sunset, eating, walking, or breathing. These daily functions are often taken for granted, until they go wrong, at which point we suddenly recognize our dependence on divine intervention.

We are frequently tempted to divide life's functions into two categories: those that run "naturally" by physical or biological mechanisms, and those that require direct divine power. But this distinction is artificial. God's power is continually necessary, not only for miraculous events but also for our ongoing existence.

Failure to recognize this reality can lead us to unplug from the source of divine power. This self-inflicted "power deficit" will eventually deprive us of the life and godliness that God freely provides to those who abide in Him.

Our position as image bearers in creation adds a profound dimension to our humanity. We are both biological and spiritual beings. Because of this dual nature, biologically and physically generated power cannot sustain our spiritual lives. This is why we cannot please God through our own strength or wisdom. We need the power of the Holy Spirit to accomplish the good works that God has prepared for us.

By creating us in His image, God granted us access to immense power, to commune with Him, and to manage His creation. Consider the scale and complexity of plants, animals, microorganisms, and ecosystems, and yet God gave humanity the authority and capacity to oversee them. This monumental task required a divine power source, and humanity originally had access to it.

In the Garden of Eden, humankind had the capacity to speak with God. They were equipped with all the power they needed to cultivate and care for creation. This power, however, was conditional. It depended on their reverence for God and their obedience to His commands, including the prohibition against the tree of the knowledge of good and evil. Their disobedience brought grave consequences.

After the fall, humans experienced spiritual death, and their relationships with God and creation were broken. This severed their access to divine power. Yet, in His mercy, the Creator continued to grant power for specific purposes when needed. Most importantly, God initiated a plan of redemption.

Through the crucifixion, death, and resurrection of Jesus, God made divine power once again accessible to humanity. On the day of Pentecost, the disciples were filled with the Holy Spirit and received power (Acts 1:8). That same power is available to us today, if we remain in Christ.

God's mercy provided immeasurable power for the redemption of humanity: from Christ's miraculous birth to His ministry, death, resurrection, and ascension. Your salvation and sanctification are acts and processes empowered by God and should never be underestimated.

God loves you and me so deeply that He supplied all the power needed to redeem us and sustain our souls. As John writes, *"He came to His own, and His own received Him not. But as many as received Him, to them gave He power to become the sons of God, even to them that believe on His name"* (John 1:11–12, KJV). Jesus, the eternal Word, entered His creation, but was largely rejected, particularly by His covenant people, Israel. Still, to all who believed, He gave the right (Greek: *exousia*) to become children of God. This is a divine gift, an authoritative transformation. To become sons and daughters of God by grace means entering a new identity (beloved, adopted), a new family (God's people), and a new inheritance (eternal life, fellowship, and glory). It is the gracious power of God that turns outsiders into insiders, enemies into heirs, and sinners into sons and daughters.

Your allocation of divine power is sufficient for your life and your calling. *"His divine power has given us everything we need for life and godliness through our knowledge of Him who called us by His own glory and goodness"* (2 Peter 1:3). God has provided you with everything necessary for sustaining life and fulfilling your mission on earth.

This same power continues to sustain believers as they walk the paths of righteousness, and it will one day glorify our bodies, making them incorruptible and immortal at Christ's return. God's power is shaping a new creation: a new heaven and earth, a New Jerusalem, and a renewed people engaged in a new way of life, worshiping God and loving one another. This means that our lives are being rescued from formlessness and restored into the image of our Creator, in alignment with His sovereign purpose (Hubbard, 1969).

While God's infinite power is readily available to all whom He has saved and placed in the custody of Christ, many Christians do not see themselves as stewards of creation, let alone seek to access His divine power to fulfil their God-given missions on earth.

God's Word and Its Creative Power

The Word of God is not mere communication, but a dynamic, living force that creates, sustains, transforms, and redeems. God doesn't build creation with tools, He speaks it into being. Every element of creation arises from a divine command.

His Word has the power to call forth reality from nothing. This shows that God's Word is not passive, it accomplishes exactly what God intends. Creation, therefore, is not just a work of power, but also a work of divine communication.

The essence of God and His eternal power are intertwined. When He speaks, His words carry both the design conceived in His mind and the creative power to bring it into being. When God issues a command (*fiat*), His infinite power manifests creation. There is power in His Word, and this is why God never wastes words. The Word spoken through your mouth, when aligned with God's will, carries immense potential, resources, and capabilities. Therefore, it should never be uttered carelessly. God's creative Word is living, personal, and incarnate.

The Word is the eternal Son of God, Jesus Christ, the agent of creation and of new creation. The Word and the Holy Spirit work in unity to bring forth existence. God speaks the Word, and the Spirit gives it life. Together, they demonstrate that creation is a Trinitarian act, flowing from the Father, through the Son, and in the power of the Holy Spirit. This same Word continues to create and sustain. God's Word never fails; it brings fruit, order, and life. It also creates spiritually: it re-creates hearts and lives. When people hear the gospel, the same creative Word that shaped the universe is at work, awakening faith, bringing new birth, and shaping new creations.

Every word God speaks is purposeful and must fulfil its mission: *So, shall my word be that goes forth out of my mouth: it shall not return unto me void, but it shall accomplish that which I please, and it shall prosper in the thing for which I sent it* (Isa. 55:11, NKJV). This verse affirms that God's Word has a 100% success rate, it always achieves its intended purpose. As image-bearers of God, we are called to reflect this purposeful speech. When the Godhead dwells in us and we fear Him and obey His commands, our words are empowered by the Spirit. However, sin corrupts speech, draining it of divine creative potential. When spoken from a heart clouded by sin, our words lack the Spirit's activation to bring about the intended outcomes.

King Solomon reminds us: *Death and life are in the power of the tongue: and they that love it shall eat the fruit thereof"* (Prov. 18:21, NKJV). This aligns with James's teaching (Jam. 3:3–12), emphasizing the need to tame the tongue, which can either build or destroy depending on how it is used.

In Genesis 1, God spoke the universe into existence. Initially, the earth was formless and void, with darkness over the deep. But God's voice brought order, filling the void with physical structures and biological organisms that He had conceived in His mind. God's commands shaped the chaos: He brought light (Gen. 1:3), separated land and sea (Gen. 1:9), created vegetation, animals, and humans (Gen. 1:11, 24), and filled the waters with living creatures. He also established the sun, moon, and stars, and with them, the rhythms of days, seasons, and years. Through His Word, God also ordained the mathematical and physical laws that govern the cosmos.

God epitomized His work of creation by forming man from the dust of the earth and breathing into his nostrils the breath of life. He also created a helpmate for Adam from his rib. These acts of creation were power-intensive, showcasing the immense creative force of God. Through His Word, God not only made the world, He also remakes it, bringing new life to human hearts and hope to a broken world.

God's Power Sustains All Creation

God created the earth as a vast ecosystem, comprising both living and non-living things, processes that maintain the ecosystem's life and productivity, and an environment to sustain life. The Creator holds all things together by the word of His power (Heb. 1:3). Beyond just creating the world, God continually sustains the physical structures and biological organisms (animals, plants, birds, and humans) and their environment, ensuring they remain functional and productive to praise and glorify Him. He maintains the beauty, goodness, and purposeful nature of His creatures. His infinite power formed each species with the ability to reproduce after its kind, ensuring continuity and preventing extinction.

Even after the earth was corrupted and God decided to cleanse it through the flood, He preserved "seeds" of humanity and all bird and animal species. Noah and his family gathered breeding pairs of every species and kept them in the Ark during the flood. Noah had to account for every species, and God provided him with everything he needed to successfully preserve them.

God's divine power also facilitates the actualization of blessings. He began with a couple in the Garden of Eden, and breeding pairs of birds, marine creatures, and animals. Each breeding pair had to be fertile to produce offspring, and subsequent generations needed to reproduce in large numbers. This divine blessing ensured the continuity of species and the production of healthy populations to fill the earth. God's hidden hand is always at work to sustain earthly creatures. He is intimately involved with creation, sustaining the sparrow, the deer in the forest, the oceans, and every one of us. No human being can fully observe what goes on moment-by-moment between a mother and her offspring during pregnancy. It is only through the power of God that the processes of gestation are sustained.

God invests immensely in His creation to ensure there are enough humans and animals to fill the earth, birds to populate the sky, and marine life to fill the seas, all according to the carrying capacities of their respective habitats. The various living creatures and their environments are equipped with the power to reproduce not just after their kind, but also to produce enough offspring to sustainably fill their habitats.

In addition to being fruitful and multiplying, animals, birds, marine life, and humans were also blessed to fill the earth. A significant aspect of filling the earth involves the dispersal of living things. God has equipped many species with the ability to migrate from crowded areas to less populated ones, preventing competition for resources. For instance, Europeans travelled thousands of kilometres to settle in the Americas. Similarly, many bird and marine species possess the resources, potential, and abilities to travel long distances and relocate to new environments.

As God's image-bearers in creation, we are blessed with the capacity to have dominion over the rest of creation on earth. This dominion is not as military rulers using force to maintain order, but as kings who love, protect, provide for, and rescue their subjects from injustice.

Luther expounds this in his explanation of The First Article of the Creed: "I believe in God the Father Almighty, Maker of heaven and earth: I believe that God made me and all creatures, that He gave me my body and soul, eyes, ears, and all my limbs, my reason, and all my senses, and still preserves them; He provides me richly and daily with all that I need to support this body and life, protects me from all danger, and guards me from all evil; and all this out of pure, fatherly, divine goodness and mercy, without any merit or worthiness in me." Regardless of your situation, God is committed to sustaining your full cycle of life moment-by-moment. You may not physically feel His presence or divine power, but He is working tirelessly, behind the scenes, to ensure that you do not prematurely depart from the earth.

The very fabric of creation reflects relationships, interdependence, and harmony. From ecosystems in the natural world to the bonds between people, all of creation speaks to a divine design rooted in unity and connection. Nature constantly teaches us this: trees share nutrients through root systems, bees and flowers exist in mutual dependence, and oceans, skies, and land work in rhythms that support life. Even the Trinity itself - Father, Son, and Holy Spirit - serves as the ultimate model of community: three persons, perfectly united in love and purpose. Creation reflects this divine relationship.

God has designed living things in nature to thrive in community. Hayley Kinsey states that trees are stronger in numbers. They have a secret underground network, which scientists have dubbed the *wood wide web*, the fibre optic broadband of the natural world: fungi. These fungi have thin filaments that can cover large areas of ground and connect trees whose roots do not touch. The filaments transmit signals that allow trees to warn each other about dangers like pests or drought. When trees communicate and share resources, they benefit from being warned about threats in the area and from receiving nutrients from other trees when they are struggling. Without healthy, connected trees around, an individual tree is left to fend for itself and is more likely to succumb to attack or thirst.

At every level of existence in God's world, there is a form of organic unity. Living things, including humans, are relational and tend to form groups based on shared characteristics, values, and other complementary attributes. In our world, there are many relational groups comprising individuals in human, animal, plant, or bird populations. Arveson (1987) analysed social relationships within groups and identified three key relational characteristics:

- Unity (U): Relatedness, sharing the same substance, oneness (John 17:20-23; Phil. 2:1-5; 1 Peter 3:8; Ps. 133:1; Eph. 4:13)
- Diversity (D): Difference, variety, contrast, distinction, or individuality (Eph. 4:7-12; 1 Cor. 7:17; Rom. 14:1-7)
- Equality (E): Parity, co-importance, mutuality, impartiality, interdependence, or fairness (2 Cor. 8:14; Gal. 3:28; 1 Cor. 11:11-12)

A complete relationship, according to Arveson, is one where all three characteristics (unity, diversity, and equality) are fully operational. A social relational group that fits the UDE model is a community. Arveson defines a UDE relationship as a plurality of members forming one whole, composed of diverse individuals who all share equally in their importance.

A UDE community is a group of variously-functioning but equally needed individuals with agreement on a common purpose. Examples of communities include cells in a body, organs of the body, a colony of ants, a swarm of bees' a colony of flamingos, a colony of penguins, a herd of elephants, a pride of lions, and plant communities.

Biologists have also found that profound relationships exist in living things, which are termed as "organic unity". The basic building unit of a human body, or any higher plant or animal is a cell. And each cell, as a self-contained unit, generates its own energy and can reproduce itself. But there are different types of cells, all working together to perform a needed function. For example, cells forming the heart cooperate to circulate blood to all parts of the body.

The triune God is the author of the concept of community and the UDE relationship is evident in Him, His Word and all His works. He is a perfect community in which unity, diversity and equality are operating simultaneously and eternally as one relationship. Biblical thinking is relational and less focused on personal relationships (Arveson, 1987).

Every creature has inbuilt potential and capacity to relate to other individuals that share the same relational UDE characteristics. God created the world, which consists of a great diversity of communities modelled after His principles. Humans, formed in the image of God, also organically develop communities (i.e. married couple; family; home Church; local Church, and the universal Church) to glorify and praise God.

The Old Testament view of community is vividly displayed by Israelites who accepted the unity of all humans because of their common creation. The organic nature of the house of Israel, centred on family relationships, extends to other generations providing a time-related dimension to the community.

A UDE community (Unity, Diversity, and Equality) is a group of individuals with various functions but equal importance, working together in agreement toward a common purpose. Examples of such communities include cells in a body, organs of the body, a colony of ants, a swarm of bees, a colony of flamingos, a colony of penguins, a herd of elephants, a pride of lions, and plant communities.

Biologists have discovered that profound relationships exist within living organisms, often referred to as "organic unity." The basic building block of any higher plant, animal, or human body is the cell. Each cell, as a self-contained unit, generates its own energy and can reproduce itself. However, there are different types of cells, all working together to perform essential functions. For example, cells forming the heart cooperate to circulate blood throughout the body.

The triune God is the author of the concept of community, and the UDE relationship is evident in Him, His Word, and all His works. God Himself is a perfect community, in which unity, diversity, and equality are operating simultaneously and eternally as one relationship. Biblical thinking is inherently relational, focusing not just on personal relationships but also on a broader communal understanding (Arveson, 1987).

Every creature is endowed with the potential and capacity to relate to other individuals who share the same relational UDE characteristics. God created the world, a world filled with diverse communities modelled after His principles. Humans, formed in the image of God, also organically form communities (e.g., married couples, families, house churches, local churches, and the universal Church) to glorify and praise God.

The Old Testament view of community is vividly displayed through the Israelites, who accepted the unity of all humans due to their common creation. The organic nature of the house of Israel, cantered on family relationships, extends across generations, providing a time-related dimension to the community.

The Church is a community comprising the followers of Christ. In Paul's letter to the Ephesians (Eph. 4), he asserts that our physical bodies gather and organize themselves into spiritual bodies, churches. At the highest level is the global body, the universal Church. Efforts to foster unity among Christian churches worldwide are intended to reinforce this broader community.

Paul's theology carries the concepts of the unity of humanity from the beginning of creation to the New Testament Church. He employs the large group personality to extend the principle of solidarity, including the doctrine of redemption. The UDE relational model of a fully biblical community is not merely abstract; it is a practical goal that can be realized in everyday life.

According to Arveson, Paul discusses the Church/body relationships in 1 Corinthians 12, establishing the basis for these relationships: all share the same Spirit, Lord, and God; the common purpose is the *common good*; there is a variety of gifts apportioned individually as the Spirit wills (v. 11); and the essential equality or co-importance of all parts is affirmed. God even ensures that the "inferior" parts of the body are given greater honour so that the members may care for one another equally.

In 1 Cor. 12:26, Paul makes an analogy to the physical body: *If one member suffers, all suffer together; if one member is honoured, all rejoice together.* A community exists when every member of the body commits fully to contributing to the common cause. How connected are you in the body of Christ?

The author of Hebrews reaffirms this in Hebrews 10:25: *Let us not give up meeting together, as some are in the habit of doing, but let us encourage one another, and all the more as you see the Day approaching"* (NIV). Any child of God seeking to fulfil his or her God-given mission must ensure they belong to a strong local church, house church/cell/Bible study group, or other related groups. This was one of the main drivers of personal and corporate growth in the early Church.

Every community based on God's principles requires God's divine power to exist and fully express the UDE (Unity, Diversity, and Equality) relational characteristics. Depending on the nature of the community, biological and/or spiritual power must hold together the relational components. For example, lung cells need energy for a human being or an animal to breathe in and out. The supernatural power of God keeps the lungs functional, allowing them to observe natural laws.

The Church was birthed after the disciples received the power of the Holy Spirit on the day of Pentecost (Acts 1:8). The activities and processes involved in building and sustaining the Church, such as preaching the gospel, baptizing the saved, teaching the Word of God, and other aspects of discipleship, are entirely dependent on the work of the Holy Spirit. Even Jesus, the Son of God, needed to be filled with the Holy Spirit to teach and carry out the work the Father sent Him to accomplish.

Our Heavenly Father understands that we can't achieve anything without the Holy Spirit. It was for this reason that He instructed His disciples to wait in Jerusalem for the baptism of the Holy Spirit: *Do not leave Jerusalem, but wait for the gift my Father promised, which you have heard me speak about* (Acts 1:4).

Paul prayed that the eyes of the hearts of the Ephesian saints would be enlightened so they could know the incredible greatness of God's power for those who believe in Christ (Eph. 1:18-19 NIV). Describing the power accessible to believers through the indwelling of the Holy Spirit, Paul wrote: *And what is the exceeding greatness of His power toward us who believe, according to the working of His mighty power which He worked in Christ when He raised Him from the dead and seated Him at His right hand in the heavenly places* (Eph. 1:19-20). No matter how complex a community may be, any member who exercises this power will accomplish everything God has assigned to them.

God's Power Makes Creatures Beautiful (Aesthetic Beauty)

There is something deeply moving about the way beauty shows up in nature, from the tiniest insect wing to the grandest mountain range. Many people see that beauty as a reflection of God's power and creativity, each creature, plant, and landscape carrying a piece of divine intention. Think about the symmetry of a butterfly's wings, the way trees bend toward the light, the size and grace of a whale, or even galaxies swirling in space. It's as if nature itself is art, and God is the artist.

By His divine power, our Creator conceived, created, and sustains creation, adorning it with aesthetic beauty. God takes pride in creating things that are good and beautiful. According to Genesis 2:9, the Lord made all kinds of trees to grow out of the ground, trees that were pleasing to the eye and good for food. The planets orbiting our sun in our galaxy, along with countless others, display their created beauty for God's pleasure and glory alone. A bewildering array of plants and animals have come into being and passed into extinction during the long history of life on earth. These creations were good and pleasing to God in their own right. Our Creator also populated the land, air, and sea with a wide diversity of beautiful organisms, animals, birds, and plants. Humans, too, contribute to the intricately crafted and beautifully decorated masterpiece of God's creation.

The Kew Royal Botanic Gardens in London (UK) attract people from all over the world to admire the beauty of plants. In my local city, the Cambridge University Botanic Garden is another iconic place where people enjoy the beauty of a landscape adorned with a variety of unique plants. It's no surprise that people rent these places for special lifetime events to capture the scenic beauty of the landscape.

Maria Luisa Cohen, writing on the subject *Botanic Gardens: A Tribute to the Role of Beauty in the Conservation of Our Plant Heritage*, said, "Gardens and gardening have not only given humanity centuries of pleasure, but also have a strong aesthetic element, without which they wouldn't attract a wider public." The Earth Council and Green Cross International (1999) recognized the necessity of a shared vision of basic values, which includes the preservation of the Earth's vitality, diversity, and beauty. Beauty and diversity are completely interwoven. When God designed the Garden of Eden, He ensured that there was adequate animal and plant diversity with a measure of beauty that satisfied the inhabitants of the Garden, Adam and Eve.

Humans have an affinity for beauty, just like their Creator. But they were not the only ones who enjoyed the flamboyant display of nature in the Garden. In the cool of the day, God visited the Garden, which provided a very beautiful setting for His conversations with Adam. Engrained with beauty, diversity was a very valuable incentive for preserving creatures in the Garden, because their loss would result in the loss of beauty. Equally pleasant were the inanimate creatures of God, landforms, rock outcrops, oceans, rivers, waterfalls, springs, mountains, and lakes, that enhance natural beauty.

In God's wisdom, the diversity of races, languages, and ethnic groups enriches the beauty of His creation. God looks at humans - whether black, white, brown, or any other shade - as fearfully and wonderfully made in His image and likeness.

The historical account of the Garden of Eden paints a picture of a beautiful artifact of scenic beauty. God personally planted different plants - trees, shrubs, herbs, grasses, and vines - in the Garden, which was nourished by four amazing rivers. God-fearing and law-abiding humanity had the potential to produce beautiful landscapes that looked absolutely awe-inspiring. The Garden, with its Manager Adam, was a very beautiful piece of work displaying our Creator's artistry. If God appreciated its beauty, the image-bearers must have enjoyed this rare and magnificent environment.

I have never had the privilege of seeing this Garden, but I can only imagine how it might have looked, based on what I've seen in botanical gardens and natural landscapes. While those can never be compared to the Garden God planted, the earth is still full of breathtaking natural features that portray God's perception of beauty.

Despite the fall of man and the curse upon his land, the beauty God designed in the natural world still manifests and is there for all to see. There are major wonders of the world that serve as centres of attraction. Natural wonders, such as the Great Barrier Reef (Australia), the Grand Canyon, Victoria Falls (Zambia), the Harbor at Rio de Janeiro (Brazil), Mount Everest (Nepal), the Northern Lights (Canada, Iceland), and Paricutin Volcano (Mexico), are just a small selection of the marvellous works of God.

The large number of tourists flocking to these natural features suggests that humanity has an instinct for beauty, a trait that can be traced back to God. This appreciation for natural beauty is also expressed through architectural designs, which utilize the gifts that God has deposited in us.

Nations, cities, towns, and villages are endowed with both man-made and natural features that appeal to our innermost appreciation for beauty. While some human-initiated wonders glorify God, others reflect the ego of man. However, it is not surprising that people are willing to pay huge sums of money to see plants, animals, birds, butterflies, and other wonders of the world. All these things glorify God and express the beauty of His creation.

As we appreciate both natural and man-made wonders, we must remind ourselves that these are the handiwork of God. You might be wondering if breathtaking engineering structures have anything to do with God. Yes, they do. It is also important to emphasize that humans themselves are a wonder. David said, *"I praise you because I am fearfully and wonderfully made. Your works are wonderful, I know that full well"* (Psalm 139:14). After reflecting on the awesome works of God, David examined himself, appreciated his beauty, and concluded that he was fearfully and wonderfully made. Was there any need for David to appreciate his beauty? After all, people knew he was handsome, with a fine complexion and bright eyes. However, his description goes deeper than merely appreciating his physical appearance. In fact, the basis for his conclusion was what God did when forming him in his mother's womb.

David is grateful that God created his innermost being and knitted him together in his mother's womb (Psalm 139:13-14). He testifies that his soul knew the works of God that brought him into being. Taking a leaf from David, it is not sinful to reflect on what God has done in your life and to glorify Him for His wonderful works. Consider yourself a priceless wonder.

Psalm 104 talks extensively about this kind of beauty: *"How many are your works, Lord! In wisdom you made them all; the earth is full of your creatures"* (Psalm 104:24). It's a reminder that the elegance and design we see in creation aren't random, they're intentional, purposeful, and full of meaning. However, sin distorts our perception of natural beauty and drives us to damage beautiful creatures with impunity. Imagine how beautiful the different types of fish in the ocean are, and yet countries, companies, and even individuals dump toxic waste into these water bodies. Humans are recklessly hunting rhinos, elephants, and big cats, despite numerous warnings that the populations of these animals are decreasing at a rapid rate. The infinite power of God is still effective, but human beings must take responsibility for maintaining the beauty of God's creation.

God's Incredible Power Preserves Diversity in Creation

God's power doesn't just create diversity; it actively sustains it. From ecosystems that balance themselves to species that evolve to fill their unique niches, there's a divine harmony at work. It's not chaotic, it's intentional, vibrant, and interconnected. You see it everywhere: the sheer variety of flowers, some blooming in deserts, others in rainforests; coral reefs packed with thousands of species, each playing a role; birds migrating with astonishing precision across the globe; and seeds designed to grow only under certain conditions, yet perfectly suited for where they are planted. Creation is like a living symphony, and God is the conductor, ensuring each note plays at the right time. Even when ecosystems are fragile, there's still resilience and diversity—proof of divine care in the design.

God's immeasurable power maintains healthy populations of different life forms (biodiversity), which glorify and praise Him, revealing the invisible qualities of our Creator. According to the Convention on Biological Diversity (CBD), a healthy diversity of life provides several essential services, including: (1) Ecosystem services, protection of water resources, nutrient storage and cycling, pollution breakdown and absorption, contribution to climate stability, maintenance of ecosystems, and recovery from environmental disasters; (2) Benefits from living things, such as food, medicinal resources, pharmaceutical drugs, wood products, ornamental plants, breeding stocks, and diversity in genes, species, and ecosystems; and (3) Social benefits, such as research, education, recreation, tourism, and cultural values. Humanity, as a subset of nature, also exhibits great diversity.

When God looks at human beings, He sees different races, tribes, ethnic groups, and other forms of cultural diversity, fearfully and wonderfully woven together to reflect His image. If we were to look at each other through God's eyes, we would see a rich diversity of humanity. It is the failure to understand God's perspective of humanity that leads to segregation and abuse of others.

At the end of His work of creation, God evaluated everything He had made, including the diversity of life, and saw that it was very good: *"God saw all that He had made, and it was very good"* (Gen. 1:31 NIV). Individual acts of creation produced good things, but the diversity of creation, woven together, was very good.

When works of creation are assessed as part of a complete system of interacting individuals, they appear more beautiful than when evaluated separately. The more diverse the elements of the system, the more colourful and beautiful it becomes.

Think about a family. The Lord God looked at the lonely man and said, *"It is not good that the man should be alone; I will make him a helper suitable for him"* (Gen. 2:18 KJV). When a man and woman marry, diversity is introduced. When the couple has children, the diversity increases. God has designed His systems so that the greater the diversity, the stronger, more stable, resilient, and productive they are.

The Convention for Biological Diversity found that at least 40 percent of the world's economy and 80 percent of the needs of the poor are derived from biological resources. In addition, the richer the diversity of life, the greater the opportunity for medical discoveries, economic development, and adaptive responses to new challenges such as climate change (Convention on Biological Diversity, 2014). Imagine, for a moment, that God gave you the assignment to create and sustain an earth with the diversity He conceived from the beginning. What resources would you require to do this task? Keeping a highly diverse world functional is a costly endeavour in terms of energy use.

Consider this: every individual needs energy to breathe, move, eat, drink, utilize food and water, excrete waste, and reproduce. Add to this the energy needed to fuel interactions between individuals within a species and across species in an ecosystem. Finally, think about the energy required by humans to manage ecosystems and ensure the functional integrity of a diverse creation. And yet, God has an energy budget and reserves enough to sustain the diversity of His creation.

God's Powered Creation Expresses the Mind of God

Creation is like God's handwriting in the world, a living message revealing His mind, heart, and presence. The power behind it isn't just raw force, it is wisdom, love, and purpose. It speaks to a deep truth that creation is not merely a product of divine strength, but of divine intelligence, intention, and artistry. Think about this: the precision of the laws of physics and mathematics -gravity, time, light - all point to an ordered, intelligent mind. The interdependence in ecosystems shows thoughtfulness and design, not randomness. Even the beauty in things that don't have to be beautiful, like the pattern on a seashell or the sound of birdsong, feels like a reflection of God's joy, personality, and even imagination.

Before bringing the universe into being, all physical structures and life forms, including creaturely processes, were conceptualized in the mind of God. Everything that was, that is, and that is yet to come originates from what the Creator thinks. As a spiritual being, the causal realm is spiritual. Everything you see in the natural world started as a seed, a divine thought. According to Parsley (2014), White asserts:

Before the seed, there comes the thought of bloom. Before His creative activity and processes, God conceived a blueprint of the universe and everything within it, according to the purpose and will for which He created them.

The seed in the mind of our Creator contained the blueprint for all creation, capable of coming into existence in God's time. The mind of God is like a womb that conceives and gives birth to an offspring. Quizzing Job, God asked: *Out of whose womb came the ice? And the hoary frost of heaven, who hath gendered it?* (Job 38:29 KJV). A womb is both a physical and spiritual organ that brings forth life and broods it until it is ready to be born at the end of the gestation period. All creation existed as ideas of potential physical structures and life forms that were conceived, nurtured, and fully developed, awaiting the great voice of God and His creative power to bring them into being.

The acts and processes of creation in Genesis 1 reveal God's blueprint of the universe and all things contained in it. Our Creator brought them into being by the word of His power. The mind of God also contained a variety of seeds, such as: blessings, the ability to be fruitful, multiply, replenish the earth, subdue it, and have dominion over creation on earth (Gen. 1:28); success and prosperity (Josh. 1:8); salvation through Jesus Christ (John 3:16); and the baptism of the Holy Spirit (Acts 1:8).

As God's image-bearers, we have the capacity to conceive things in our finite minds because the mind of God birthed in us divine inspiration, empowerment, potential assignments, promises, gifts, abilities, and purpose. Humans carry the seeds and power of God, and when they speak what is conceived in their minds through Jesus Christ and the Holy Spirit, things happen.

Saint Peter said, *"His divine power has given to us all things that pertain to life and godliness, through the knowledge of Him who has called us by glory and virtue"* (2 Pet. 1:3). The mind of our Creator conceived all things that pertain to our natural life and godly life and has downloaded them into our minds. But we need to bring them into being by God's immeasurable power that is at work in us. The Holy Spirit in us empowers us to translate God's mind into our reality.

Our minds are equipped with resources, capabilities, and potentialities to conceive, incubate, and develop ideas to: please, glorify, and praise God; fulfil the great commission; care for God's creation; and assist the needy in communities. His power budget and reserves are more than adequate for these tasks.

God's Powered Creation as the Basis for Scientific Innovation

The created order bears the marks of divine character (Logos, structure) and is therefore knowable to man. The created works of the rational and intelligent God are orderly and comprehensible to those creatures in whom He invested His image, and this is foundational to the practice of science. Albert Einstein said: *The most incomprehensible thing is that it is comprehensible.* God created a world that is rational, intelligent, uniform, and orderly, and it is accessible to reason. Professor John Polkinghorne also explained that *What attracts young men and women to study the physical world and holds them to it despite the weariness and frustration in research, is the marvellous way in which the world is open to our understanding.* It is possible to understand rational sequences that lead to the divine works of creation without assuming continual divine intervention. Scientists believe that the world exists to be observed. Without this divine work, science would be impossible, and the universe could only be understood based on direct revelation.

The orderliness of creation bears witness to the Creator's sense of order, coherence, and harmony. There are beliefs about the intelligibility, orderliness, and uniformity of creation, presumptions that underpin the scientific enterprise, but these cannot be established from within science itself. The fact that science can provide a partial understanding of the world offers empirical support for the theological assertion of the rationality of the world. Creation contains a reliable record of its history, documenting God's creative activity and how the universe was and is. Progressive change through time, whether in cosmology, geology, or biology, is the overwhelming conclusion from reading the creation record.

A true and potentially understandable record of creation affirms the meaning of both natural history and human history. God created a formless and void earth to set the stage for all other creatures. The earth is like an artist's blank canvas, ready to be filled with the vibrant masterpiece of creation. Isn't it amazing that our scientific theories are rooted in the formed earth and heavens?

As a scientist, I have been keen to understand the basis of different theories, and after reading several of them, I must accept the truth that humans must work with substances whose origin they cannot explain using scientific principles. All scientific inquiries ultimately reach a limit at the beginning of the universe, according to the Big Bang theory.

During the early years of my secondary education, I learned that matter can neither be created nor destroyed. All processes that transform matter from one state to another never result in its destruction or creation but simply change its form. This theory presupposes that matter has always existed. However, the Big Bang theory, which explains how the heating and cooling of the universe led to the formation of stars and galaxies, reaffirms that the universe had an absolute beginning. It further demonstrates that God created human beings, who have the capabilities and potential to read the text divinely written into creation. Like a library, creation contains immeasurable quantities of data, which scientists must access and interpret to explain how things work in the natural world.

Nature speaks a language using symbols that humanity can understand. The data and information in nature provide how God displays, in time, the rich text He has eternally embedded in it. But what keeps the world intelligible, uniform, and orderly, making it knowable? What maintains the natural data and information in a state accessible to humanity? What sustains the energy flows in ecosystems? The word of God's power sustains all creatures (Heb. 1:3). The Lord holds all things together to express their intelligence, uniformity, and orderliness.

God's Power Sustains Creation's Ability to Praise Him

Creation is not just made by God, it is alive in response to Him. The birds do not just sing, they praise. The waves do not just crash, they worship. The stars don't just shine, they declare His glory. Psalm 19:1 reaffirms this: *The heavens declare the glory of God; the skies proclaim the work of His hands.* Jesus echoed this when He said: *If they keep quiet, the stones will cry out.* Creation is wired to praise, and God, in His power and grace, sustains that expression. Even in brokenness, even under human misuse, creation still finds a way to glorify Him.

Can you imagine? The rivers run with joy, the mountains lift their voices, the trees clap their hands, in a song not by choice. Built into their being, from the first light of days, is a whisper, a shout, an unending praise. Not by their might but sustained from above. They live, they move, they breathe out His love. All this is sustained by the power of His Word.

In many parts of Africa, chiefs and kings have specially trained people who shower them with praise. In 2003, I had the privilege of attending the Ncwala ceremony of the Ngoni people in eastern Zambia. I was mesmerized by the elaborate rituals of giving praise to Chief Mpezeni. An elderly man, specially schooled in Ngoni tradition, performed certain ritualistic acts to praise the chief.

The man praising the chief was so skilled that he convinced the people there was nobody as important as the chief at that moment. He employed a variety of techniques: dancing around the king, blowing a horn, singing and declaring praises, and bowing before him. In addition to this man, singing groups from various sub-chiefdoms also performed. The artistry of this praise was so captivating that people lost track of time and distance as they accompanied the chief from his palace to the celebration venue. But where did humanity get this practice of showering each other with praise?

The universe and everything in it were created to praise and glorify God. If God were to take you to a vantage point where you could observe everything happening in heaven and on earth, you would see angels and heavenly hosts feeding God with philharmonic praise. Look at the earth, and you'll witness a great diversity of creatures offering praise to their Maker in diverse ways. Soaking this in would permanently change your perception of praise.

Both human and non-human creation on earth praise God. David, conversing with the Lord, said: *All the earth worships and sings praises to you; they sing praises to your name* (Psalm 66:4). The land, seas, air, and everything they harbour have the power and ability to praise God. Can you imagine a rock, a snake, a vulture, a hippo, a butterfly, or a mole praising the name of the Lord? Yet they do. Whether we acknowledge it or not, everything around us praises the name and Word of the Lord.

Humans are created to offer sensational praise to their Maker. Speaking through the prophet Isaiah, God said: *The people whom I have formed for myself, that they might declare praise* (Isa. 43:21). David also wrote: *From the lips of children and infants you have ordained praise* (Psa. 8:2). God delights in a human species endowed with the ability and creativity to praise Him in diverse ways, with their bodies, hearts, souls, and minds.

David understood his inherent capacity to praise God and did his best to honour his Maker. He expressed his conviction when he said, *Praise the LORD, O my soul. I will praise the LORD all my life; I will sing praise to my God as long as I live* (Psa. 146:1–2, NIV). His soul was wholly committed to praise. He never allowed anyone or anything to interfere with his devotion to offer quality, heartfelt worship. David praised God with his whole heart, publicly, emotionally, and sometimes even in an undignified manner (as when he danced before the Lord in 2 Samuel 6:14). Does David challenge your attitude toward praise?

David praised God in every season. Whether hiding in a cave or reigning from a throne, David found a reason to praise. Just read through the Psalms. he praises through fear, heartbreak, betrayal, and victory. He shows us that praise is a choice rooted in trust, not circumstance. His praise was also honest. David didn't sugarcoat his struggles, his psalms are raw, emotional, and real. Yet even in lament, he often ended with praise. God desires authenticity in our praise, not perfection.

David made praise a lifestyle. It became part of his daily rhythm, in the morning, at noon, and in the night. He built his life around worship. Is praise a reaction for us, or is it a rhythm? Praise can be our daily heartbeat. We should never be coerced to praise God. David understood this so well that he wrote psalms of praise, called all creation to worship, and praised God so freely that his own wife accused him of disgracing himself. But that unfiltered praise pleased God. David was simply expressing his true nature as a creature of God. Nothing should hinder us from praising our Creator. Is it any wonder that, despite his flaws, David was a man after God's own heart?

Even non-human creation is endowed with the ability to praise God. Our Creator said: *The mountains and hills will burst into song, and all the trees of the field will clap their hands* (Isaiah 55:12, NIV). As a child, I climbed many hills, but it never occurred to me that they were praising God. Worse still, there were times when we cut down trees for fun, not realizing that we were silencing part of God's choir.

In Psalm 148, David calls upon the heavenly hosts and all inhabitants of the earth - land, sea, and air - to praise God, including non-living things. He also wrote: *Let everything that has breath praise the Lord* (Psa. 150:6, NIV). No exceptions, no conditions, everything that breathes, from the smallest insect to the grandest whale, is called to offer God every form of praise, from a whispered prayer to a thunderous song.

The heavens, skies, land, and seas, and all their hosts, are summoned to praise God. *The heavens declare the glory of God; the skies proclaim the work of his hands. Day after day they pour forth speech; night after night they reveal knowledge. There is no speech or language where their voice is not heard. Their voice goes out into all the earth, their words to the ends of the world* (Psa. 19:1–4). Creation has a language, a form of praise, that, while not always intelligible to us, is real and constant. Scientists have even discovered that plants can communicate across distances. Human languages are complex, but the languages of non-human creation are perhaps even more intricate. Yet each element of creation speaks a perfect, authentic language of praise to its Creator.

It's humbling to realize that creation around us is continually praising God, though we often fail to recognize it. This communication between God and creation is deep and mysterious, and because it lies beyond human comprehension, some believers diminish or ignore it. But our inability to understand it doesn't silence creation's voice. In fact, we bear a responsibility to steward creation, so it continues to offer quality praise to its Maker.

Praise flows from a deep recognition of who God is and what He has done. We cannot generate meaningful praise unless we come to know God through the Book of Nature, the Scriptures, and the life and words of Jesus Christ. As we draw from these deep wells, our praise becomes grounded in divine truth and wisdom. Praise is the outward expression of our inner communion with God.

One of David's secrets to a vibrant life of praise was his sensitivity to God's creative activity and sustaining power. Praise, for David, was a declaration of God's handiwork. Look at his psalms: every mention of praise is followed by a reason. For example, *Praise him for his acts of power; praise him for his surpassing greatness* (Psa. 150:2); *Praise the LORD… For the LORD takes delight in his people; he crowns the humble with salvation* (Psa. 149:1–4); and *Let them praise the name of the LORD, for he commanded, and they were created* (Psa. 148:5). These verses show us that we are surrounded by reasons to praise God throughout the day.

Praise takes many forms, depending on the creature involved, singing, dancing, playing instruments, painting, or writing. Some Christians say they can't sing, confusing the spiritual gift of singing with the general ability to sing. Yet even those who think their voice is not "good enough" still sing during church services. Why use that "bad" voice in church but not when you're alone? God doesn't measure your praise by vocal quality, He looks at the heart. Even the croakiest voice contains praise that pleases God. We have no excuse not to sing.

God expects us to praise Him both privately and communally. By God's grace, I've sung in choirs and quartets throughout my life. One key lesson from those experiences is that when individual singers know their parts well, the harmony touches people deeply. More importantly, it delights God.

Praise is a constant reminder of God's generosity, grace, and love. God remains God whether we praise Him or not, but praise is a spiritually life-sustaining activity. It keeps us aligned with our Creator. Scripture says: *God inhabits the praises of His people* (Psa. 22:3). When God is enthroned in our praise, He acts as He wills, some are healed, others overwhelmed with joy, and others experience His peace. We must learn to see our ability to praise as a sacred gift from God.

High-quality praise is often costly. Like an orchestra preparing for a concert, musicians must devote time and energy to rehearsals. The same goes for choir members, instrumentalists, and soloists. It requires discipline, sacrifice, and commitment. Yet all this effort is ultimately a gracious response to God's greatness.

The created order has built-in capacity, resources, and potential to offer God quality praise. Every part of creation, living and non-living, has been endowed with unique features to glorify its Creator. Diversity in creation means diversity in expression, in timing, and in continuity of praise. When all creation praises God, it forms a grand symphony, a harmonious chorus unlike anything heard before.

God not only designed all creation to praise Him, He also ensured it had all it needed to do so. He calculated the cost of praise even before creating the universe. This echoes the truth Peter affirms: *His divine power has given us everything we need for life and godliness through our knowledge of him who called us by his own glory and goodness* (2 Pet. 1:3). God's power created and sustains all things, including our capacity to praise His name and Word.

God's Power Shaped the Earth Through Purposeful Processes

The earth, powered by God, came into being through divinely guided processes. The Almighty could have created the universe and everything in it with a single command, but He chose instead to do it in stages, through a series of intentional creative acts. God first created the universe, then brought structure to the shapeless earth and filled it with both visible and invisible creatures in a deliberate sequence.

We do not know exactly how God created the universe from nothing. But Scripture shows that His commands triggered creative activity that transformed a formless and empty earth into a "very good" finished creation. A closer look at the creation narrative reveals that it unfolds through a purposeful and logical process.

Genesis 1 outlines God's creative commands: bringing light into existence; forming the sky; separating dry land from seas; producing vegetation; creating lights in the sky (sun, moon, and stars); filling water bodies with living things; populating the sky with birds; producing animals from the land; and finally, making humanity in His image. These might appear to be one-step events, but are they really?

Genesis 2 offers more detailed accounts, especially regarding humanity's creation. In making man, God took the dust of the earth, moistened it, and moulded it into a human form, then breathed into the man's nostrils the breath of life, and he became a living being. This act involved a logical sequence of steps.

In creating woman, the LORD God caused the man to fall into a deep sleep. While he was sleeping, He took one of the man's ribs and closed the place with flesh. Then, from that rib, God made a woman (Gen. 2:21–22). This delicate, well-structured process shows God's intentional design for this creative act. We see processes like this in everyday life too, don't we?

As a child, I often watched my mother bake a cake. She would consult a small piece of paper, a recipe, as she carefully mixed flour, sugar, eggs, and other ingredients, always in the same order. Later, I realized that nearly everything in life has a process: recipes for dishes and beverages, research methods, wound-dressing procedures, and pharmaceutical manufacturing.

Consider the bull elephant: it is the product of a process, mating between mature elephants, conception, gestation, birth, and nurturing. Birds, reptiles, insects, plants, and aquatic creatures each have unique processes for reproduction, nourishment, waste elimination, and adaptation to their environments.

Another powerful example is found in Ezekiel's vision of the dry bones (Ezek. 37:1–10). The hand of the LORD transported the prophet to a valley filled with very dry bones. God then commanded Ezekiel to do something seemingly impossible: to prophesy life into those bones. The LORD said: *"Prophesy to these bones and say to them, 'Dry bones, hear the word of the LORD! This is what the Sovereign LORD says to these bones: I will make breath enter you, and you will come to life. I will attach tendons to you, make flesh come upon you and cover you with skin; I will put breath in you, and you will come to life. Then you will know that I am the LORD'"* (Ezek. 37:4–6).

Could God have instantly turned dry bones into living humans? Absolutely. But instead, He revealed a step-by-step process to illustrate His redemptive power over Israel. The transformation involved a sequence: rattling bones, tendons forming, flesh covering them, and finally, breath entering the bodies. Once again, God used a process to carry out His purpose. These examples highlight three key aspects of God's creative work:

- The universe was not created in a finished state, the formless, empty earth served as raw material for the rest of creation.
- Creation was the result of a divine, logical process, carried out through phases.
- All creative acts followed a clear and ordered sequence, revealing God's methodical approach.

God has embedded processes into creation to make the earth habitable for human and non-human life. For instance:

- Weathering of rocks produces soil that supports plant growth.
- Fallen leaves decompose and release nutrients.
- The water cycle provides rainfall.
- The sun's energy maintains a liveable temperature.

Whenever these natural processes are disrupted, the consequences can be catastrophic.

Scientists dedicate immense resources to studying and describing these processes. Medical doctors investigate life-sustaining bodily functions, use diagnostics to detect abnormalities, and prescribe treatments to restore health. Soil scientists study formation and nutrient cycles. Ornithologists examine birds' reproductive and behavioural patterns. Cosmologists explore how the universe began. Every scientific discipline depends on process.

Humanity may forfeit the benefits of the processes God has embedded in nature when their activities modify, interrupt, or diminish the effectiveness of this vital feature of the created order. For example, clearing forests for agriculture reduces plant diversity and disrupts key ecological processes such as removing carbon dioxide from the atmosphere, stabilizing soil temperature, and preventing erosion by binding soil particles together.

On a larger scale, human interference with major ecological processes has contributed to global warming, pollution (of air, water, and soil), eutrophication, biodiversity loss, land degradation, and many other harmful effects. In our "microwave" age, we often try to bypass or accelerate natural processes to save time or increase profits, but the long-term results have frequently been disastrous.

Processes are an integral part of God's creative work and the ongoing sustenance of His world. These processes are often complex and require divine power to actualize. Yet the LORD has graciously supplied sufficient power for every process in the universe to function at its full capacity. God sustains natural processes when they operate in accordance with both physical/mathematical laws and spiritual principles.

God Powers Food Production Systems for Creation

God's power has established and sustains diverse food production systems to support the growth and development of all living things and to enhance their productivity. As Psalm 145:16 (NKJV) affirms: *You open Your hand and satisfy the desire of every living thing.* Every creature receives its portion of food from its Creator, through systems that vary depending on the species involved.

God has designed a complex, process-driven food chain to provide nourishment according to each creature's biological structure and feeding behaviour. Living things are broadly grouped into several categories within this system:

1. Plants, which manufacture their own food using sunlight, water, and carbon dioxide through the process of photosynthesis.
2. Certain plants and fungi, which produce food using energy from non-light sources (e.g., through chemosynthesis).
3. Herbivores, such as cattle, sheep, goats, duikers, zebras, horses, elephants, and many insects, which feed primarily on plants.
4. Carnivores, including lions, cheetahs, tigers, eagles, and sharks, which feed on other animals.
5. Omnivores, such as humans, which consume both plants and animals.

These groupings reflect the wisdom and purpose with which God designed creation. The food chain is a delicate web of interdependence, requiring all organisms to harvest their food in balanced proportions to maintain productive ecosystems.

When one category in this system is disrupted, for example, through the overharvesting of carnivores, the result is imbalance. Without predators, herbivore populations can grow unchecked, leading to overgrazing or excessive browsing. This can devastate plant communities, reduce biodiversity, and even threaten the survival of the ecosystem.

God has embedded self-regulating mechanisms into ecosystems to manage such interactions. However, when human actions disrupt these systems - by overharvesting, polluting, or mismanaging resources - these processes can break down, triggering ecological crises. Stewarding these natural processes wisely is part of our calling to care for God's creation.

The food chain consists of complex processes that produce various food substances to meet the needs of different organisms. As organisms feed within ecosystems, energy flows from one level of the food chain to another. While food systems may appear simple on the surface, they are highly complex in operation and require a well-established energy base to be sustained.

The LORD God, who created all living things and their food production systems, is actively involved in sustaining their functions. As the psalmist declared: *He makes grass grow for the cattle, and plants for man to cultivate, bringing forth food from the earth* (Psa. 104:14). God provides all the necessary conditions for grass to grow so that the cattle may have food.

God also provides for predators. Appreciating God's providence, David wrote: *You bring darkness, it becomes night, and all the beasts of the forest prowl. The lions roar for their prey and seek their food from God* (Psa. 104:20–21). Predators depend on God to guide them as they hunt. It took me some time to understand that when a lion kills a zebra or wildebeest, it is not cruelty, it is simply receiving the providential care of the Lord. Every living creature depends on God for food.

The psalmist helps us see that even our agricultural systems are undergirded by

God's divine power. Who gives us the knowledge and skill to till the land and plant the seed? Who waters the land and maintains the right temperature for the seed to germinate? Who instructs the seed to sprout and provides the energy it needs to grow? God sustains all these processes by the word of His power (Heb. 1:3).

Ultimately, the power of God sustains all food production systems, whether in the wild or managed by human hands. Truly, God's immeasurable power both created and continues to sustain the universe and everything in it.

CHAPTER 8
Manifestations of the Power of God

Whatever God has created requires some form of power to function. We cannot fully understand how the power of God operates without considering the rebellion led by Lucifer. The Bible clearly teaches that angels were created to serve God and to offer Him worship. God meticulously designed them for this unique purpose and endowed them with the corresponding power to carry it out.

Lucifer was created with exceptional beauty and musical ability. According to tradition and biblical imagery (cf. Ezek. 28:12–17), the praise he offered was beyond comparison, more beautiful than the sound of the most advanced musical instruments ever invented. However, he became proud of his ability and convinced that he deserved the same praise, honour, and glory that belonged to God alone.

This shift in ideology, from giving praise to desiring it, violated his original purpose. As a result, Lucifer's position in heaven became untenable, and he was cast out of God's presence. Although he lost access to God's power to replicate His kingdom, God still permitted him to operate according to his now-corrupted nature. The power Satan now exercises is based on rebellion against God and always results in opposition to God's will.

From this rebellion, we see the existence of two distinct kinds of power: the power of God and the power of Satan. Each functions through its own hierarchy. God - the Father, Son, and Holy Spirit - is the source of all power. No one can control or regulate His power, and He gives it as He wills. God's angels operate under His authority and by His power.

Satan, on the other hand, leads fallen angels, referred to in Scripture as principalities, powers, rulers of darkness, and spiritual forces in heavenly places (Eph. 6:12). The power they possess is not original; it is derivative. Since God created Lucifer, even the power Satan uses ultimately originated from God. But it is now misapplied, twisted from its original purpose.

Unlike God, Satan cannot create. He cannot bring into being humans, animals, plants, or inanimate objects. His role is more like that of a virus: unable to function on its own, it must hijack the mechanisms of a living host. Likewise, Satan corrupts God's good creation when it comes under his influence. That's why Jesus described him as a thief, a murderer, and a destroyer (John 10:10). He cannot originate anything good; he can only distort what already exists.

The creation account in Genesis affirms God's power to bring forth life and order. Everything He created, living and non-living, was declared good. Humanity, made in God's image, was given authority through divine power to steward the earth and care for all living things. But Satan used his power of rebellion to influence Adam and Eve, thereby corrupting humanity's relationship with God and the rest of creation.

Since then, two powers have been at work in the world: God's eternal, life-giving power and Satan's corrupted, rebellious power. Through Jesus Christ, however, God has made a way for humanity to be restored and to walk again in His original power. The spiritual, social, and environmental state of the world often reflects which of these powers is operating.

When Satan's influence dominates, relationships shift from a God–man–creation triangle to a Satan–man–creation triangle. This shift brings serious spiritual, cultural, economic, and ecological consequences. The "ecology of power", whether divine or corrupted, affects how families, organizations, nations, and ecosystems function.

Without the power of God at work in the human heart, people begin to view others - and the rest of creation - as objects to exploit. Consciences become numb. Violence, deception, injustice, biodiversity loss, environmental degradation, and resource-driven conflicts are, in many cases, symptoms of corrupted power at work in human systems.

The devil has convinced many that economic welfare overrides every other aspect of life. Under this ideology, God's creation is increasingly viewed as nothing more than a tool for generating wealth. Is it not troubling that people willingly pursue economic gain even when it results in polluted rivers, irreparably degraded land, the destruction of freshwater and marine life, or the denial of a decent life to others? What could possibly justify human trafficking, the exploitation of children, drug trafficking, the commercialization of sex, and other evils so prevalent in our societies today? What would lead a nation that once feared God and built its institutions on His Word to remove the Bible and religious education from its schools? These are hallmarks of the power of rebellion, a rebellion that Satan has subtly and systematically injected into the fabric of society.

But is the battle lost? Absolutely not. Believers are still in the fight, because we have access to the incredibly great power of God, a power strong enough to overturn the schemes of Satan and redeem what has been corrupted.

As Simon Peter reminded the early church: *"By His divine power, God has given us everything we need for life and godliness"* (2 Peter 1:3). Our ability to do God's will and live in holiness does not come from human strength, it flows from a divine power that originates in God Himself. However, to use this power effectively, we must first understand what it is and how it can be applied in our daily lives.

Expressions of the Power of God
Power to Conceive Ideas

The power to conceive ideas can be seen as a gift of creativity and intellectual capacity granted by God. This ability allows humans to imagine, create, and problem-solve, all of which reflect the image of God in them. It is part of the divine creativity that God has endowed mankind with. Just as God spoke the universe into existence, humans are also given the ability to form thoughts, envision possibilities, and create solutions that reflect His image. This power, rooted in the mind and spirit, allows individuals to innovate, design, and shape the world around them in ways that fulfil God's purposes.

The power to conceive is not merely a function of intellect but a profound gift that aligns with God's will for human flourishing and stewardship of creation. This idea ties into God's image in humanity, highlighting how creativity, wisdom, and innovation are all reflections of God's nature. God's power to give and sustain these abilities allows humans to engage with the world in ways that are both purposeful and aligned with His divine plan.

The art of conceiving ideas originates from God. Before anything comes into existence, it is first identified and visualized in the mind. Allen (1992) stated that, *the mind is the master power that moulds and makes*. Whatever has existed, exists now, or will exist in the natural world began as a seed, a divine thought, in the mind of God. Created in the image of God, our finite minds have the power to conceive things within the created order. There are several examples in the Bible where God's children were asked to use their power of conception to align with His planned activities:

a) God asked Abram whether he was able to number the stars in the sky as a representation of the number of descendants he would have. Then He took him outside and said, *Look up at the sky and count the stars, if indeed you can count them. Then He said to him, So shall your offspring be* (Gen. 15:5). Abraham was being asked to see with the eyes of his mind and count his descendants by the stars in the sky. God wanted Abraham to spiritually envision the multitude of his descendants, even before he had his first son, Isaac.

a) Moses sent twelve spies into the land of Canaan to help the Israelites conceive what their land of inheritance looked like. Ten of the spies reported that the land was inhabited by giants who made them feel like grasshoppers in comparison. As a result, the Israelites began to see giants in their minds and became reluctant to possess the land. However, Joshua and Caleb encouraged the people to see a land flowing with milk and honey and to conceive victory over its inhabitants because the LORD had promised to give it to them.

a) Jacob transferred sheep and goats from Laban's herd to his own by using a visual strategy involving striped branches. After agreeing that his wages would be the streaked, speckled, and spotted animals from Laban's flock, Jacob devised a method to increase his share. He placed striped branches (from poplar, almond, and plane trees) in the watering troughs where the animals mated, especially when the stronger females were in heat. As a result, the animals gave birth to streaked and speckled offspring, which belonged to Jacob according to their agreement. The weaker animals were left to Laban, while the stronger ones went to Jacob. In this way, Jacob became exceedingly prosperous (Gen. 30:41–43). The breeding outcome seemed to be influenced by what the animals were looking at during conception, highlighting a mysterious interaction between visual stimulus and reproductive outcome.

a) While teaching His disciples, Jesus said: *You have heard that it was said, Do not commit adultery. But I tell you that anyone who looks at a woman lustfully has already committed adultery with her in his heart* (Matt. 5:27–28). This implies that by imagining the act of sleeping with a woman in one's mind, the individual has already committed the act in a moral and spiritual sense. As Scripture says, *For as he thinks in his heart, so is he* (Prov. 23:7, NKJV).

a) God conceived the natural world; the fall of humanity; the birth, death, and resurrection of Christ; the Church; the ascension of Christ; the return of the Lord Jesus Christ; the marriage of the Lamb; the new heavens and earth; and the New Jerusalem. Some of these events have already taken place. God saw you in your unformed state, and every single day of your life was recorded in His book before any one of them came to be (Psa. 139:16).

a) Finally, we use the power of conception in art, design, visioning, business, career, marriage, and in our walk with the Lord. Every believer needs to use the art of conceiving to translate the mind of God into their life in Christ. Unfortunately, we often go with the flow of circumstances and fail to use the power of conception that God has given us.

Solomon struggled with the thought that God has planted eternity in the human heart, and yet, tragically, people still cannot see the full scope of God's work from beginning to end (Eccles. 3:11). When God instructed the children of Israel to camp by the Red Sea, they perceived both God and Moses as leading them into a trap, boxed in by the sea in front of them, rocky mountains on either side, and the advancing Egyptian army behind them.

The only safe space was heavenward, where God appeared to them in a pillar of cloud. However, the Israelites could not spiritually perceive that they were in a position of strength, one that would reveal the vulnerability of their enemies, enable them to supernaturally cross the Red Sea on dry ground, and build their trust and faith in God to carry them through the wilderness.

Amid his tragic loss and suffering, Job longed for the prosperous years of the past. He was convinced that, in those years, God had taken care of him. Job claimed that God was with him during his years of prosperity (Job 29) but had chosen to abandon him in his time of suffering. What Job did not perceive, however, was that during his suffering, God was preserving his life. God had instructed Satan to spare his life (Job 2:6).

What we perceive as disaster can be divine preparation. If God had given Satan full freedom to do whatever he willed, he probably would have destroyed Job. Fortunately, Job later confessed that in his argument with God, he had spoken of things he did not understand, and he quickly retracted everything he had said (Job 42:3–6). Job had no idea that God would restore his fortunes. In fact, God gave him twice as much wealth in the second half of his life as in the first (Job 42:10–12). How often has God led us through situations we perceived as disastrous, only for us to later realize that we needed those very experiences to move forward in our marriages, families, studies, businesses, ministries, or other areas of life?

Unless we have access to the power of perception, misjudged situations and misunderstood fortunes will continue to haunt us. The good news is that the power to see and perceive rightly is found in Christ, and it is available to us if we walk with Him.

Power to Create

The power to create is one of the most profound aspects of God's nature, as demonstrated throughout Scripture. In Genesis, God's creative power is revealed as He speaks the universe into existence—creating the heavens, the earth, animals, plants, and finally, mankind. This power to create is not just about bringing things into being but about shaping, ordering, and making things function according to His divine purpose. Made in God's image (Gen. 1:26-27), humans were endowed with the ability to create in various forms, whether in art, innovation, relationships, or leadership. God's spirit within us gives us the power to conceive ideas, create solutions, and form relationships that reflect His image and creativity.

Jesus creates new life in the spiritual realm by bringing transformation to individuals through salvation (2 Cor. 5:17). The Holy Spirit empowers believers to create new things spiritually by building the Kingdom of God through evangelism, discipleship, and works of love. Creative potential in every believer comes from God. Just as He created all things in the world, believers have the capacity to make things that can reflect His glory. Like God, we can use our faith and imagination to envision things in our minds (dreams, projects, businesses, relationships) and make them a reality.

God mediately 'creates' by producing or making things using pre-existent materials. As His image-bearers, He has given us the power to 'create' through the Holy Spirit. Often, we view this power as either beyond what we can accomplish or incomprehensible. There are miracles that I would describe as acts of 'creation.' One verified testimony that caught my attention was of a man who literally had no ear. Physicians confirmed that he lacked an ear. After receiving prayer, the man grew a functional ear. Since he originally had no ear, the only explanation for this new ear was that the power of prayer had 'created' it.

Jesus Christ gave sight to a man who was born blind. He had no experience using his sense of sight because his eyes were either underdeveloped, deformed, missing parts, or physically dead. Whatever the case, Jesus gave this individual new, functioning eyes, and the man was able to see. The power of God either created the missing parts, brought to life parts of the eye that were dead, or straightened components that were deformed. In any case, Jesus 'created' or made the eyes.

Jesus Christ assured believers that the Holy Spirit would enable them to 'create' and do even greater things than He did: *I tell you the truth, anyone who has faith in me will do what I have been doing and will do even greater things, because I am going to the Father* (John 14:12). Jesus was preparing His disciples (and all future believers) for the Holy Spirit's empowerment after His ascension, enabling them to continue the mission of spreading the gospel, healing, delivering, and advancing God's Kingdom on earth. He assures them that, through faith in Him, they will continue His work on earth and even do greater things.

The foundation for doing the works of Jesus is faith in Him. This involves trust in His power, His teachings, and His authority. Doing even greater things doesn't necessarily mean that each believer will perform greater miracles than Jesus. Instead, it means that the scope of the work will be greater. For example, after Jesus' resurrection and ascension, His followers would spread the gospel globally, reaching more people than He physically could during His earthly ministry. Similarly, the promise of doing 'greater things' is made possible through the Holy Spirit, who empowers believers to do God's work.

Jesus Christ, the Creator and Sustainer of creation, assures us that we, too, would create and sustain creation, though not in the same context as He did. If He has given us this power to create, yet we are not creating, we need to examine our 'toolkit' to see what tools might be missing or dysfunctional.

Power to Transform

The concept of the power to transform reflects how God's power can change individuals, situations, and even entire nations. The power to transform is not only a function of divine action but is also available to believers through the Holy Spirit, enabling them to live out God's will and purposes in their lives. Key aspects of this power include:

- Transformation through new birth (2 Cor. 5:17): The first transformation that occurs when a person comes to faith in Christ is a new birth, a spiritual transformation. Believers are made into a new creation, and this is only possible through the power of God.

- Renewed mind through the Holy Spirit (Rom. 12:2): Transformation of the believer is a continual process, beginning with the renewing of the mind. This transformation enables a believer to align their thoughts, desires, and actions with God's will.
- The Holy Spirit's role in transformation (Tit. 3:5): The Holy Spirit is the agent of transformation. He is at work in the believer's life to sanctify, guide, and empower for godly living.
- Transformation of lives and circumstances (Philip. 4:13): The power of Christ allows believers to endure challenges, break free from the strongholds of sin, and overcome adversities. God gives them the strength to experience change, both inwardly and outwardly.
- Transformation of relationships and society (Eph. 4:22-24): As individuals are transformed by God's power, their relationships and communities are also affected. This includes transforming how people interact, serve others, and build a society that reflects God's righteousness.
- The goal of transformation (Rom. 8:29): The goal of transformation is to be made into the likeness of Christ through the process of sanctification, where believers grow to reflect Christ more clearly in their character and actions.

The idea that spiritual transformation begins with the new birth is a foundational concept in Christian theology. When a person comes to faith in Christ, they are spiritually reborn, and this transformation is only possible through the power of God. The new birth is a one-time event that marks the believer's entrance into a new life in Christ (John 3:3, 2 Corinthians 5:17). However, transformation is an ongoing process. As the believer grows in their relationship with Christ, there is a continuous renewing of the mind (Romans 12:2), which allows them to increasingly align their thoughts, desires, and actions with God's will. This process, known as sanctification, is the work of the Holy Spirit in the life of the believer, gradually making them more like Christ over time. So, the transformation is both an initial change (the new birth) and a continuous process (the renewing of the mind) throughout a believer's life.

In Romans 12:2, Paul is urging believers to renew their minds and no longer conform to the pattern of the world. The world, in this context, represents the values, behaviours, and desires that are contrary to God's will. Paul is calling the Roman Christians to transform their way of thinking and living, moving away from a lifestyle that reflects worldly influences to one that is centred on Christ.

When Paul speaks about renewing the mind, he is not just talking about a superficial change in thoughts or behaviours. Instead, he is emphasizing a deeper transformation, a change in the fundamental way of thinking, which should reflect the mind of Christ (1 Cor. 2:16). This transformation involves the believer aligning their thoughts, values, and desires with the truth of God's Word and the example of Jesus, allowing the Holy Spirit to guide and empower them.

So, the focus of Paul's admonition is that believers should stop conforming to the world's way of life and, instead, be transformed by a renewed mindset that reflects the character and purposes of Christ. This renewal leads to a life that is holy, pleasing to God, and lived in alignment with His will.

God, the author of transformation, applied this concept in His acts and processes of creation. After creating the universe, He transformed the void and shapeless earth, which was covered with water and darkness, into a structured earth with physical structures and life forms. The result of this transformation was an earth that was very good.

The power to transform is one of the most profound aspects of God's divine intervention in the life of a believer. This power works on the heart, mind, soul, and body, enabling believers to experience the renewing of their spirits and the restoration of God's image in their lives. Personal transformation shifts us from addiction to freedom, from despair to hope, and believers experience inner changes through God's power. As believers grow in Christ, they experience a deeper intimacy with God, characterized by more powerful prayers, greater discernment, and a greater desire to live out the gospel. This transformation can be seen in their attitudes, behaviours, and responses to life's challenges.

In social and cultural transformation, God's transformative power can also affect society at large. This can be through acts of justice, mercy, and love that challenge systems of inequality, poverty, and injustice.

Believers have the power of transformation in their toolkits that God gives to them at salvation. We need it to transform different areas of our lives. It is not enough to simply carry the kit around; we must use it.

Power to Sustain

The power to sustain refers to God's ongoing work in maintaining and preserving creation, as well as providing for and strengthening believers in their daily lives. It is the divine power that upholds all things and ensures that they continue to function according to God's will and purpose. At the conception of the universe and all things in it, in the mind of our Creator, God's divine power was available for their creation and sustenance.

When we create or make something new, there is always a possibility that it could revert to its old self. For example, many people who have believed in Jesus Christ as their Lord and Savior have abandoned their faith and returned to their old sinful life. Somehow, they could not sustain the new status quo.

When God created the universe from nothing, He knew there was a risk it could disappear if the status quo was not maintained. In most cases, we either take things for granted or do not appreciate what it takes to keep something in its desired state. Take, for example, a car. When a driving instructor is teaching someone how to drive, they go through a series of lessons to teach the learner driver how to maintain a car for effective performance. Despite those elaborate maintenance lessons and the emphasis on taking the car to the garage for service and regular mandatory Ministry of Transport automobile checks, vehicle owners still miss or avoid these important responsibilities.

Every created or manufactured product usually consists of different parts, which should be in a fully functional state and properly adjusted to work with other parts it is designed to mesh with. These different parts must hold together for the product to work effectively and efficiently. Similarly, everything God created must hold together for the universe to function according to His standards. Paul affirms this when he declares: *He is before all things, and in Him all things hold together* (Col. 1:17). Without Christ's power that holds all parts of the universe together, its parts would disintegrate.

The author of Hebrews also emphasizes: *The Son is the radiance of God's glory and the exact representation of His being, sustaining all things by His powerful word* (Heb. 1:3, NIV). This assures us that God's power holds our bodies and lives together. If your life seems to be disintegrating, consider checking your spiritual *toolkit*, you may be missing the power needed to maintain yourself and stay in harmony with others.

There are four key aspects of God's power to sustain:

1. God sustains the world: God actively sustains the universe (Heb. 1:3). Every planet, star, creature, and plant is preserved by His power. Without His continuous intervention, creation would cease to exist. Nature's cycles and seasons are upheld by God, who also provides for the needs of all living things (Psa. 104:27–30).
2. God sustains believers: God is the source of spiritual strength (Phil. 4:13). His power enables believers to live out the Christian life and fulfil their divine purpose. Even in weakness or suffering, His grace is sufficient (2 Cor. 12:9), giving believers the strength to persevere.
3. God sustains us through the Holy Spirit: Jesus promised the Holy Spirit would dwell with believers, guiding, teaching, and empowering them (John 14:16–17). The Spirit sustains faith, brings comfort, provides strength, and enables perseverance through life's challenges.
4. God sustains through the Word: Just as our bodies need food, our spirits need the nourishment of God's Word (Matt. 4:4). The Word strengthens, renews, and anchors believers through every season of life.

To live a sustained life:
- We must rely on God - trust in His strength during trials and uncertainties.
- We need daily sustenance - acknowledging Him as the source of both physical and spiritual provision (Matt. 6:11).
- We need empowerment for ministry - God sustains His Church and equips believers to carry out the mission of making disciples and spreading the gospel.

Power to Manage

God's power to manage creation refers to His sovereign authority to rule over the universe, direct events, uphold life, and fulfil His divine purposes. He is not a distant Creator but an active King who governs with wisdom, justice, and mercy. Scripture reminds us:
- God rules over all the earth: *"The Lord has established His throne in heaven, and His kingdom rules over all"* (Psalm 103:19).
- God establishes our steps: *"In their hearts humans plan their course, but the Lord establishes their steps"* (Prov. 16:9).
- God manages all creation: *"He does as He pleases with the powers of heaven and the peoples of the earth"* (Dan. 4:35).

God's management includes: governance – directing all things toward His divine will; preservation, maintaining the integrity of creation; and concurrence – working through the actions of human beings. God is the original source of all management wisdom. Human stewardship reflects His image and purpose. He is the ultimate author of management principles, strategies, and practices. Through His creative and sustaining acts, God has demonstrated perfect management, organizing, ordering, and overseeing creation with precision and purpose.

Genesis 1:26 outlines humanity's divine assignment: *"to rule over the fish in the sea and the birds in the sky, over the livestock and all the wild animals, and over all the creatures that move along the ground."* As His image-bearers, humans are entrusted with the stewardship of creation, to govern wisely and ensure that everything fulfils God's intended purpose.

Though humanity often takes credit for mastering the art of management, every principle and ability in this field ultimately originates from God. It is the Holy Spirit who empowers both the practical and spiritual aspects of management, enabling us to effectively govern what has been entrusted to us.

Every child of God is called to manage a part of His creation. Whether it be in the family, workplace, ministry, business, or elsewhere, God's power equips each of us to govern our unique spheres of influence. When we operate under His authority, He gives us the wisdom and strength to manage well—whether our assignment is small, medium, or large.

Power to Judge

God's power to judge refers to His divine authority to evaluate, discipline, and bring justice according to His perfect righteousness. Unlike human judgment, which is often flawed or limited, God's judgment is always just, holy, and true. He judges motives, actions, and even the secrets of the heart.

Sitting in a courtroom while the judge reads the verdict is one of the most intense and difficult moments in a defendant's life. When a judge takes the bench to preside over a case, silence fills the courtroom, especially when the verdict is announced. The judge has the authority to either convict or acquit the defendant, deciding based on the evidence presented and the law.

Seated in my living room, I watched a TV program documenting the trial of Dr. Larry Nassar, a former USA Gymnastics team doctor who abused 156 female gymnasts at Michigan State University. He molested women and girls between 1997 and 2016 and was sentenced to 40 to 175 years in prison. The sheer scale of the sexual abuse, and the lengthy jail sentence handed down by the federal judge, astonished me.

Regardless of the outcome of a ruling, some parties will believe that justice has been served, while others may argue that justice has been denied. Beyond the emotional stress suffered by the gymnasts, the case also caused significant reputational damage to USA Gymnastics and Michigan State University. The sentence itself highlighted just how much power a judge holds.

However, the Psalmist declares: *But it is God who judges: He brings one down, He exalts another* (Psa. 75:7). For some, taking an oath while holding the Bible is the closest they get to God, and it may be done under duress. Beyond that, they don't perceive any role of God in the trial. For others, God needs to intervene in their favour, and hence they seek Him during the period of the trial. Considering that the judge is God's representative passing judgment over people created in His image, our LORD is actively involved in every detail of the trial.

God provides a perfect model of the power to judge. No one teaches or commissions Him to judge, but He is the author of justice. God is a righteous judge, a God who displays His wrath every day (Psa. 7:11). He is the perfect embodiment of justice, judging with righteousness. His judgment is value-free, fair, seasoned with love, based on perfect knowledge of the case and flawless interpretation of the law, and is motivated by His desire to correct us.

God loves His creation so much that He sacrificed His Son to be judged on behalf of humanity and has withheld judgment to give His people time to access the truth before they are judged. His ultimate desire is to save His creation. However, our God is also a consuming fire (Heb. 12:29) and does not compromise His law or standards. *For the wages of sin is death, but the gift of God is eternal life in Christ Jesus our Lord* (Rom. 6:23, NIV).

God has no alternative judgment to death where sin is concerned. 'Have I any pleasure at all that the wicked should die?' says the Lord God: 'and not that he should turn from his ways and live?' (Ezek. 18:23). When man chooses the way of sin, God reluctantly passes the death verdict. But He rewards believers with the gift of eternal life.

God gave Jesus the power to judge: *And the Father has given Him the power to judge all people because He is the Son of Man* (John 5:27). During His life and ministry on earth, Jesus exercised the power to judge wisely, just as the Father does. God has also delegated this power to humanity.

About 3,000 years ago, the land of Israel was ruled by a succession of 15 judges, rather than kings. During this period between Joshua and King Saul, God provided the Israelites with a model of leadership that was different from the kingdoms around them: they had a judge to preside over their affairs.

There are people officially appointed to judge others. However, every human being exercises some form of judgment, even if it is not on the scale of a courtroom. God understands that we cannot measure up to His standard. As a righteous judge, He cautions us: *Stop judging by mere appearances; instead, judge correctly* (John 7:24). Jesus is urging His listeners to go beyond superficial judgment, not to assess people or situations based only on outward appearances, but to judge with righteous, informed, and spiritual discernment.

At that time, I charged your judges: Hear the disputes between your brothers, and judge fairly between a man and his brother or a foreign resident (Deut. 1:16). God expects us to judge our brothers and sisters according to His standards.

Power to Control

God's power to control refers to His sovereign authority over all aspects of creation. This includes His ability to direct the course of events, sustain creation, and ensure that everything unfolds according to His divine will. His control is not arbitrary or tyrannical; it reflects His wisdom, holiness, and love for His creation. God's power to control is a recurring theme throughout Scripture, showing that nothing happens outside of His will.

God's power to control doesn't mean that humans are mere puppets in His plan. Rather, God's sovereignty is partnered with human free will, and yet, His ultimate plan will be fulfilled. His control over creation is seen in both small details (like the number of hairs on our head) and grand, cosmic events (like the rise and fall of nations). For believers, God's control is both a comfort and a challenge. It reassures us that nothing is beyond His reach, but it also calls us to trust His wisdom and timing, especially when things seem chaotic.

As the Creator and Sustainer of all things, God has given us the power to control the forces of nature and other created beings. The Bible recounts an incident when the wind and the sea wielded their power to create a storm that distressed the disciples. However, Jesus was in the stern, His head on a pillow, sleeping. When He was aroused from His sleep, He commanded the wind to be quiet and said to the sea, *Quiet! Be still!* The wind ceased, and the sea became as smooth as glass. The disciples were amazed that even the wind and the sea obeyed Him (Mark 4:35-39). Jesus had the power to calm natural forces, strong winds and a turbulent sea. Jesus, through whom and for whom all things were created, has control over His creation. It is not surprising, therefore, that He commanded the sea to calm, and it lost its power.

In another situation, Jesus assured His disciples that they would trample on snakes and scorpions, and these creatures would not harm them. They could drink poison (a product of nature), and it would not hurt them. There is power in the name and word of Jesus Christ that can destroy or neutralize the venom of snakes and scorpions.

Jesus also used this metaphor to teach the disciples that created things can inflict pain on humanity. However, the potency of these potentially harmful things is subject to Christ Himself. This is good news for the followers of Jesus because He lives in us and, therefore, can command the storms in our lives to settle, and they will lose their power. If Christ is ruling in us, we can command His creation to perform specific acts, and they will obey.

Children of God Can Control Nature

Children of God can control nature. Elijah was a human being, just like us. He prayed earnestly that it would not rain, and it did not rain on the land for three and a half years (Jam. 5:17). He prayed again, and Israel received rain. God commanded Moses to raise his staff over the Red Sea, and it parted (Exod. 14:21). When the priests stepped into the River Jordan, the water was held back upstream. These events clearly demonstrate that God's power, which is operational in us, can control all created things if used according to His will and pleasure.

From the beginning, God designed us to exercise authority over all creation, and with this responsibility came the power to control the destiny of other creatures. However, after man fell from grace, God withdrew this power because it could easily have been abused, causing further damage to troubled nature.

Therefore, God only provided this power when man had a specific assignment to carry out according to His instructions.

To ensure we do not abuse the power to control created things, we can only access it when we yield ourselves to God and allow the Holy Spirit to direct us according to God's counsel. In Christ Jesus, we carry great power to control principalities, powers, rulers of the dark world, and every name that is named. The level of operation of God's power in us is dependent on our level of submission to the Holy Spirit.

Power to Acquire Resources

God gave the house of Israel the power to acquire resources and earn wealth to fulfil the covenant with their ancestors. As God cautioned the Israelites against the vice of self-confidence, He instructed them never to entertain the thought that their own power and the might of their hands had produced their wealth: *And you say in your heart, 'My power and the might of my hand have gained me this wealth.' But you shall remember the Lord your God, for it is He who gives you the power to get wealth, that He may establish His covenant which He swore to your fathers, as it is this day* (Deut. 8:17-18, NKJV). This passage clearly communicates the importance of remembering that all wealth comes from God and that it is God who empowers us. It serves as a great reminder of humility and dependence on God's provision.

God helped the children of Israel understand that whatever wealth they accumulated had to be traced back to God's power at work in them. What made the children of Israel vulnerable to the perception that they produced wealth with their own power and ability is the fact that they physically processed the resources that God gave them to create wealth.

In our own world, deceived by inventions and our work routine, people often explain success and prosperity in terms of novel ideas, business acumen, efficiency, discipline, good marketing skills, or great engineering works. However, this story is incomplete.

We easily forget that God created the resources and, through the Holy Spirit, gives us the ability to perceive, design, and process things, and the energy to produce them. Regardless of who performs a task, whether a follower of Christ or an unbeliever, God still provides the power to acquire resources because the whole earth belongs to Him.

The House of Israel used God's power to acquire wealth from the Egyptians. God said:

And I will make the Egyptians favourably disposed toward this people, so that when you leave, you will not go empty-handed. Every woman is to ask her neighbour and any woman living in her house for articles of silver and gold and for clothing, which you will put on your sons and daughters. And so, you will plunder the Egyptians (Exod. 3:21). What did God place in the words of every Israelite woman that caused every Egyptian woman to give up her gold, silverware, and clothing? It was the power of God, delegated to the Israelite women, that persuaded the Egyptian women to surrender their possessions.

The Israelite women were slaves who were not qualified to wear the gold and silver of Egyptian mistresses, let alone their clothing. However, the power of God can change circumstances so that what was perceived as exclusively for the mistresses became available to the maids. It would not be out of place to suggest that the Lord compensated the Israelites for their several decades of unpaid labour.

In another instance, God instructed Joshua to lead the house of Israel to inherit the land He promised to give their ancestors. In this context, "land" refers to the earth's surface—both land and water—as well as natural resources in their original state, including mineral deposits, wildlife, and fish.

Land as a Primary Factor of Production

Land is a primary input and factor of production that God gave to the children of Israel, and with it came the ability to create wealth. God, through Joshua, assured the Israelites that they would succeed in taking over the land from its inhabitants and would use its resources to create wealth because of God's presence and His power, if they did not depart from the law.

The Promised Land consisted of several cities occupied by different groups of people, ruled by kings. These cities were fortified to ward off potential enemy invasions. Thus, possessing the land meant fighting, conquering the inhabitants, and taking over their possessions. This was not possible unless the Israelites were empowered to defeat the inhabitants and take possession of the land.

In the New Testament, Peter experienced the power of God operating through him. After Jesus had used Peter's boat to teach the people the Word of God, He instructed Peter to launch out into the deep and let down his nets for a catch (Luke 5:1-11). Peter quickly told Jesus that he and his companions had toiled all night and caught nothing. Nevertheless, at the Lord's command, Peter let down his net.

Peter did not fully understand that God's power could mobilize the fish to respond to his fishing effort. His unbelief is revealed in his partial obedience, he let down 'the net' instead of 'the nets.' At the unusual hour of the day, a large school of fish miraculously filled Peter's net.

As the Lord of the earth, Jesus knew where the fish were in the Sea of Galilee and gave Peter the power to attract and catch the fish that had eluded him the previous night. I believe that Peter didn't spend many hours catching that quantity of fish, and that is what demonstrated what God's power in us can do. God has given you and me the power to acquire the resources we need for life and godliness.

Power to Utilize Resources

God has endowed humanity with the power to utilize resources wisely. From the very beginning, He gave humans dominion over the earth and everything in it. This includes the ability to use natural resources effectively to meet our needs, fulfil our purpose, and bring glory to Him.

In Scripture, we see numerous examples of God empowering individuals to utilize resources in extraordinary ways. For example, Jesus provided Peter the power to catch fish when his own efforts had failed. Likewise, through wisdom and divine guidance, people have been able to acquire wealth, build societies, and create systems that reflect God's provision.

The key is that all resources, whether material, spiritual, or intellectual, ultimately belong to God, and it is through His power that we can use them for good. God's power in us enables us to make wise decisions, cultivate the earth, and manage the resources He has entrusted to us.

God has given us the power to utilize resources and derive satisfaction from the wealth He has given us. King Solomon said: *It is a gift from God to be able to eat and drink and experience the good that comes from every kind of hard work* (Eccl. 2:24; 3:13). He further makes a very sobering observation: *God gives wisdom, knowledge, and joy to those who please Him; but to a sinner, He gives the work of gathering and collecting, that He may give it to him who is good before God* (Eccl. 2:26). God not only provides the strength and resources to work but also allows us to experience the joy of reaping the benefits of our efforts.

God Enriches Both Believers and Unbelievers

God can enrich both believers and unbelievers. During the stage of wealth accumulation, it may be difficult to discern who will ultimately benefit from that wealth. It is often only after the wealth has been created that its true beneficiaries become clear. At that point, God gives power to those who please Him to eat, drink, and enjoy the good that comes from their hard work.

By contrast, God may assign unbelievers the task of gathering and accumulating wealth—only for it to be transferred to those who honour Him. Ultimately, God determines who enjoys the wealth produced on earth. As Scripture declares, *"The earth is the Lord's, and all its fullness, the world and those who dwell therein"* (Psalm 24:1).

Those who ascend the hill of the Lord with clean hands and a pure heart are the ones who receive blessing from the Lord and righteousness from the God of their salvation (Psa. 24:3–5). God's blessing includes the ability to enjoy the fruit of one's labour. If God withholds that ability from His faithful servant, it is either temporary or compensated in another way, in accordance with His perfect will.

When the house of Israel left Egypt, God caused the Egyptian women to look favourably upon the Israelite women. As a result, they gave them their gold, silverware, and clothing. The wealth the Egyptians had accumulated over many years was handed over to the Israelites because God had determined that His people, not their oppressors, would enjoy it. The Israelites, His "firstborn son," inherited what others had stored up. This is both a word of encouragement and a warning.

If we walk in obedience and live to please God, He will give us the power to acquire and enjoy resources. But if we rebel or live in disobedience, we risk becoming those who gather wealth only for it to be handed over to those who honour Him. You and I have been given the power to acquire the resources necessary to fulfil God's purpose for our lives.

Power to Produce, Manufacture, or Construct

Genesis 1:27–28 tells us that God created man in His own image and gave him dominion over the earth. This dominion includes the power to innovate, build, and bring order to creation. Being made in God's image means we reflect His creativity, problem-solving ability, craftsmanship, and the capacity to transform raw materials into useful and valuable products.

God rarely gives His people finished products like cars, tables, planes, or meals. Instead, He gives vision, innovative minds, wisdom, resources, skills, and the ability to create, empowering us to produce finished goods. Throughout Scripture, we see this divine principle at work:

- Noah constructed an ark according to God's specifications, demonstrating obedience, engineering skill, and endurance (Gen. 6:13–22).
- Bezalel and Oholiab were filled with the Spirit of God - with wisdom, understanding, knowledge, and craftsmanship - to construct the tabernacle and its furnishings (Exodus 31:1–6).
- Solomon, through divine wisdom, oversaw the construction of the temple, an architectural and spiritual marvel (1 Kings 6).
- Jesus, a carpenter by trade, worked with His hands, affirming the sacredness of manual labour and creativity (Mark 6:3).

Moses reminded the Israelites of this principle: *Remember the Lord your God, for it is He who gives you the ability to produce wealth...* (Deut. 8:18). This "ability" includes mental capacity, physical strength, creativity, access to resources, and skill to produce goods and services. Whatever we build - whether infrastructure, technology, businesses, ministries, or even relationships - God empowers us to envision, design, develop, and sustain them.

This power is not meant for selfish ambition but for stewardship. We are called to use our skills and creative energy to serve others, improve the world around us, reflect God's glory, and fulfil His purposes on the earth.

Sometimes, I stand by the window and watch cars of all shapes and sizes drive past. Then I think about airplanes, ships, skyscrapers, and cathedrals, built even when science and mathematics were in their infancy. Are these simply the result of human ingenuity, or are they echoes of divine wisdom inherited from God?

God's creative activity is the ultimate model of science and technology, far beyond human imagination. He produces and constructs using methods that the brightest minds cannot fully grasp. What kind of workshop manufactures planets, the sun, the moon, and the stars? What kind of laboratory designs animals, plants, and human beings? Only God, the origin and source of all power to produce, manufacture, and construct.

Power to Give

The power to give is not merely about possessing material wealth, it is a divine capacity granted by God. Giving flows from a heart that recognizes God's ownership of all things and trusts in His ongoing provision. Scripture teaches that God is the ultimate Giver, and those who reflect His character will walk in generosity: *Every good and perfect gift is from above, coming down from the Father of the heavenly lights...* (Jam. 1:17). God gave us life, breath, salvation, and even His Son, the greatest gift of all: *For God so loved the world that He gave His one and only Son...* (John 3:16).

Giving is empowered by grace. In 2 Corinthians 9:7–8, Paul encourages cheerful, grace-filled giving: *Each of you should give what you have decided in your heart to give, not reluctantly or under compulsion, for God loves a cheerful giver. And*

God is able to bless you abundantly… The power to give comes from:
- Gratitude – recognizing what God has done for us;
- Faith – trusting that He will continue to provide;
- Love – reflecting God's heart to meet the needs of others;
- Stewardship – understanding that we are managers, not owners, of what we have.

Scripture is full of powerful examples of generous giving: the widow at Zarephath gave her last meal to Elijah, and God sustained her household (1 Kings 17); and the early church shared their possessions so generously that *"there was no needy person among them"* (Acts 4:34–35). The power to give extends beyond money. It includes *time* – serving others, *talent* – using your gifts for God's glory, *words* – encouragement, teaching, prayer, and resources – financial support, food, clothing, shelter.

As a child, one of my earliest tests came when I was asked to share what little I had. Sometimes adults even asked for my only item, like a treat I had just received. The most difficult times were when we had to give away our entire meal to guests, even when we were hungry. In my culture, hospitality is sacred. Visitors must be offered the best we have, no matter the cost. Though difficult, these moments taught me to give, even when it hurt. It stretched my capacity to be generous.

Jesus once observed offerings at the temple. Many rich people gave large sums, but a poor widow gave just two small copper coins. Jesus praised her: *This poor widow has put more into the treasury than all the others.* Why? Because the rich gave out of their surplus, what they could afford to spare. But the widow gave everything she had to live on. Her small gift carried immeasurable sacrifice and trust. Today, many might praise large donations from the wealthy while ignoring the power of sacrificial giving. But God values the heart behind the gift more than its monetary value.

God's Giving: A Model for Us

God's giving was not impulsive—it involved *spiritual, emotional, relational, and cosmic* effort.

Giving is a process:

- Perceiving the need,
- Desiring to meet it,
- Deciding to give,
- Mobilizing resources,
- Choosing the method,
- Delivering the gift.

Each step demands power and grace. When God gave His Son, He exercised the full weight of divine power. Can humans give like this? Not in their own strength, but God lives in us through Christ, and by His Spirit, He empowers us to give with the same joy and sacrifice.

In Exodus 36:3–5, the Israelites gave so much toward building the sanctuary that Moses had to stop them. These were once slaves, yet through God's enabling, they gave abundantly. The Macedonian believers (2 Corinthians 8:1–5) also gave sacrificially. Though poor and afflicted, they exceeded expectations because *they gave themselves first to the Lord.* When God assigns a task, He releases the grace and resources to accomplish it. But if we pursue ventures outside His will, we may struggle financially, not because God is unfaithful, but because He has not given the power to fund that mission.

At the same time, potential givers must discern God's will. A need does not automatically imply a calling. If God is prompting you to give and you hold back, you may miss the opportunity to be a conduit of His blessing. God's power to give is available to every believer, but it must be aligned with His will, sustained by His grace, and motivated by love. When we give ourselves fully to the Lord, we unlock a divine flow of generosity that reflects His own heart.

The ability to truly know and understand God is not merely the result of human intellect, education, or religious routine, it is a spiritual gift and a power granted by God Himself. God desires to be known. From Genesis to Revelation, He reveals Himself progressively, through creation, the prophets, Scripture, and ultimately, in the person of Jesus Christ. He is not a distant or hidden God, but One who longs for a personal relationship with His creation.

As Jeremiah declares: *Let not the wise boast of their wisdom or the strong boast of their strength or the rich boast of their riches but let the one who boasts boast about this: that they have the understanding to know Me...* (Jer. 9:23–24). Knowing God is a work of the Spirit. Spiritual understanding comes by revelation, not just information. It is the Holy Spirit who gives us the power to know God personally and to grasp the deeper truths of who He is. Without the Spirit, we may study theology yet miss the heart of God. But with the Spirit, even the simplest believer can know Him intimately.

Jesus is the perfect revelation of God. To understand God's character, His love, justice, and grace—we look to Jesus. He said: *Anyone who has seen Me has seen the Father* (John 14:9). Through Christ, we are not only reconciled to God, but we are also granted access to a deeper relationship with Him. The veil that separated us from God's presence has been torn (Matt. 27:51). The power to know God comes through relationship. The more we walk with Him - through prayer, worship, obedience, and meditating on His Word - the more we come to know His voice, His ways, and His heart.

Humanity strives to acquire knowledge to improve life and understand the world. We've built educational and research institutions, produced countless publications, and pursued scientific advancement. Yet knowing God goes beyond intellectual pursuit, it is relational knowledge. It's like how a child knows a parent's voice and love. So, does becoming a Christian automatically mean we know and understand the Lord?

Did you know it's possible to be a Christian and still not truly know God? Some believers don't fully understand what it means to be a disciple of Christ. Even Jesus' own disciples struggled to grasp who He truly was. He told them, *If you had known Me, you would have known My Father also. From now on, you do know Him and have seen Him"* (John 14:7, NKJV). Philip responded, *Lord, show us the Father, and that will be enough for us.* Jesus replied, *Have I been with you so long, and yet you have not known Me, Philip?* (John 14:8–9). Jesus was showing them that He is the visible image of the invisible God (Col. 1:15). To see Jesus is to see the Father.

Now pause and consider this: if the disciples - who walked with Jesus, shared meals with Him, witnessed His miracles, and heard His teachings - still didn't fully know Him or the Father, how many of us today can confidently say we truly know Jesus?

Paul, who wrote 13 New Testament letters, also expressed a deep longing to know Christ more. He wrote, *"I want to know Christ..."* (Philippians 3:10), which may seem surprising given his rich background in Jewish law and Scripture. He had reached the height of religious status (Phil. 3:4–7), yet he realized that knowing about God is not the same as knowing God.

It wasn't until Paul encountered Jesus on the road to Damascus that everything changed. That divine revelation transformed him. He came to understand that righteousness does not come through the flesh, but by grace. From then on, he sought to know Christ above all else.

Throughout Scripture, many great men and women of God expressed the same desire. Moses cried out, *Please, show me Your glory* (Exod. 33:18). Paul declared, *I consider everything a loss because of the surpassing worth of knowing Christ Jesus my Lord, for whose sake I have lost all things* (Philip. 3:8). His heart longed to know Christ—the power of His resurrection and the fellowship of His sufferings (Philip. 3:10).

Paul considered knowing Christ so important that he prayed: *I keep asking that the God of our Lord Jesus Christ, the glorious Father, may give you the Spirit of wisdom and revelation, so that you may know Him better. I pray also that the eyes of your heart may be enlightened in order that you may know the hope to which He has called you, the riches of His glorious inheritance in the saints, and His incomparably great power for us who believe* (Eph. 1:17–19). Paul had the right perspective on what it means to know God. His heart was enlightened, and he understood both the inheritance of the saints and the immeasurable power available to believers in Christ.

The greatest desire of a true Christian is to know God. Everything else is secondary. Yet many believers today claim to know the Lord Jesus Christ - and even other people - without fully grasping what it truly means to "know." Perhaps the issue lies in our understanding of the word *know*.

When the Bible speaks of knowing God, it doesn't refer to mere intellectual knowledge, an academic familiarity with facts about Him. It's not about reciting God's résumé, hearing testimonies of His work in others' lives, or even understanding the gospel message alone. The Greek word often used is *epignosis*, a term that implies full, experiential knowledge gained through personal relationship (see 2 Pet. 1:3–11; Col. 3:9–10).

To know God involves a commitment to discovering who He is, what He says, what He does, to believe in Him, and to follow Him. Jesus said: *My sheep hear My voice, and I know them, and they follow Me* (John 10:27). God knows His sheep, and they, in turn, know and follow His voice.

Over time, sheep learn to recognize the voice of their shepherd. They become familiar with its tone, rhythm, and cadence. Similarly, believers who consistently walk with God learn to recognize His voice and discern His guidance. As the relationship deepens, so does trust.

In the Middle East, shepherds lead their flocks across dry, rugged terrain in search of fresh pasture. In this context, sheep learn to associate the shepherd's voice with provision and protection. They come to know the one who feeds, defends, and cares for them, and they distinguish his voice from all others.

A striking example comes from Judith Fain, a Ph.D. candidate at the University of Durham, who spent several months each year in Israel studying sheep behaviour. One day near Bethlehem, she observed three shepherds meeting on the road with their flocks. As the men talked, their sheep mingled into one large group. Judith watched, fascinated, wondering how they would separate them. But when the shepherds were ready to leave, each one simply called out. Instantly, the sheep divided and followed their own shepherd. They knew his voice.

Every true Christian must be able to recognize and follow the voice of the Lord, even when surrounded by countless other, often deceptive, voices. The Great Shepherd knows His own and keeps them together. But knowing God comes at a cost. It's not something we attain through human effort alone. Unless we receive divine power to know and understand, spiritual truths remain hidden from us.

Consider the two disciples on the road to Emmaus: *Jesus Himself drew near and walked with them. But their eyes were restrained, so that they did not recognize Him* (Luke 24:15–16). They couldn't perceive who He was, not because He wasn't present, but because He intentionally withheld His identity. Similarly, when Peter confessed, *"You are the Christ, the Son of the living God,* Jesus replied, *Blessed are you, Simon Bar-Jonah, for flesh and blood has not revealed this to you, but My Father who is in heaven* (Matt. 16:17 NKJV). Jesus made it clear: true knowledge of God comes only by revelation.

As Jesus also said: *No one knows the Son except the Father, and no one knows the Father except the Son and those to whom the Son chooses to reveal Him"* (Matthew 11:27 NIV). And again: *I am the way and the truth and the life. No one comes to the Father except through Me* (John 14:6 NIV). Knowing God is only possible through Christ, for *in Him are hidden all the treasures of wisdom and knowledge* (Colossians 2:1–3). That's why Paul prayed:*… that the God of our Lord Jesus Christ, the glorious Father, may give you the Spirit of wisdom and revelation so that you may know Him better"* (Eph. 1:17 NIV).

So then, earnestly desire the power to know and understand God—not just for information, but for intimate, life-changing relationship. He promises to draw near to those who draw near to Him (James 4:8). The journey of truly knowing Him begins with a heart surrendered, a mind renewed, and a life yielded to His voice.

The Power to Deliver

Jesus came not only to forgive sin but also to break the power of sin. Many people believe in forgiveness yet still live bound by addictions, shame, fear, and spiritual oppression. But Jesus came to *destroy the works of the devil* (1 John 3:8). Selected biblical examples of deliverance illustrate this power:

- Paul and Silas were imprisoned for preaching the gospel. Yet, as they prayed and praised God at midnight, an earthquake shook the prison, and their chains fell off (Acts 16:25–26).

- The man possessed by Legion (Mark 5) lived in torment and isolation. With a single word, Jesus set him free, and he was restored to his right mind.
- Peter was locked in a cell awaiting execution, but an angel of the Lord appeared, his chains fell off, and he walked out of prison (Acts 12:6–11).

In each case, it was God's power, not human effort, that brought freedom. Deliverance is still available today. The same power that delivered Israel, healed the sick, and broke demonic oppression is active now.

Jesus said, *If the Son sets you free, you will be free indeed* (John 8:36). Freedom is not just a concept, it's a person. True freedom comes through relationship with Christ, who gives us power over:

- Sin – *Sin shall no longer be your master...* (Rom. 6:14)
- Fear – *God has not given us a spirit of fear...* (2 Tim. 1:7)
- Addiction – *The law of the Spirit who gives life has set you free...* (Rom. 8:2)
- Spiritual darkness – *He has delivered us from the domain of darkness...* (Col. 1:13)

We are also agents of deliverance. God gives believers the power to intercede, declare freedom, and help others walk in deliverance. Jesus said: *I have given you authority... to overcome all the power of the enemy; nothing will harm you"* (Luke 10:19). This authority is not about human strength or charisma—it's about being submitted to God, walking in the Spirit, and speaking with His authority.

Modern Bondage and the Need for Deliverance

Many situations or forces can restrain individuals from fulfilling God's plan for their lives. These may include:

- Financial debt
- Marital breakdown
- Abusive relationships
- Slavery or exploitation
- Emotional trauma
- Physical or mental imprisonment

- Spiritual bondage
- Rebellious children
- Substance addiction

These burdens can suppress the righteousness of God in a believer's life. Some Christians may feel so helpless that they begin to believe they're unworthy of living. What worsens such situations is the lie that nothing can change.

There is nothing more discouraging than feeling stuck in a tight, dark place with no room to move. Have you ever felt like problems were closing in from every side, your marriage is failing, your children are rebelling, your boss is making work unbearable, debt is piling up, and you're defaulting on your mortgage? The harder you try, the deeper you seem to sink. Yet there is still hope for deliverance.

In many countries, certain individuals or authorities have the legal power to grant pardons or relief under specific circumstances. For instance:

- In the United States, the President can pardon federal offenses (Article II, Section 2 of the Constitution).
- In France, Israel, Italy, South Africa, Ghana, and Zambia, heads of state hold similar powers.
- In Spain, the King holds the right of pardon; in Iran, it's the Supreme Leader.

In addition, institutions like debt relief agencies, marriage counsellors, anti-slavery organizations, and advocacy groups often hold legal or social authority to help individuals overcome various forms of bondage.

However, behind all these interventions, we must recognize that all true power to deliver comes from God. These earthly authorities operate only under the permission or pattern of the ultimate Deliverer, God Himself.

God, the source of all power, delegated to His Son, Jesus Christ, the authority to liberate humanity and all of creation. Isaiah 61 describes Christ's mission: *The Spirit of the Sovereign Lord is on me, because the Lord has anointed me to proclaim good news to the poor… to bind up the broken-hearted, to proclaim freedom for the captives and release from darkness for the prisoners…* (Isa. 61:1–3).

Jesus came to bring freedom to the spiritually oppressed, healing to the emotionally broken, and liberty to those bound by physical or spiritual chains. His power is irresistible and absolute: *But God raised Him from the dead, freeing Him from the agony of death, because it was impossible for death to keep its hold on Him* (Acts 2:24). We see God's delivering power displayed throughout Scripture:

- When Paul and Silas prayed and sang hymns in prison, a divine earthquake shook the foundations, opened the doors, and loosed every chain (Acts 16:25–34).
- David delivered Israel from the oppression of the Philistines by defeating Goliath (1 Sam. 17).
- In the fire, Shadrach, Meshach, and Abednego were set free from death because Jesus was with them (Dan. 3:25).
- Israel was freed from Pharaoh's grip through the miraculous parting of the Red Sea (Exod. 13–14).

Today, that same power delivers God's people from the schemes of the enemy, Satan, the accuser and deceiver. God has also given you and me the authority to participate in deliverance through the Great Commission: *Heal the sick, raise the dead, cleanse those who have leprosy, drive out demons. Freely you have received; freely give.* (Matt. 10:8)

This divine mandate means we are not only called to proclaim the good news but to set captives free - spiritually, emotionally, and physically - as the Holy Spirit leads. The Church carries within it the power to break chains, cast out demons, speak truth to the oppressed, and bring restoration to broken lives. Therefore:

1. God has the power to deliver from every kind of bondage, physical, emotional, and spiritual.
2. Deliverance requires faith in Christ, who alone breaks every chain.
3. We must walk in obedience, because power without surrender can lead to pride or misuse.
4. Believers are not just recipients but carriers of God's delivering power.

Deliverance is not just a biblical theme, it is a present reality for believers. No matter how deep the pit, God's arm is not too short to save (Isa. 59:1). Jesus is still setting captives free today, through His people. You are empowered in Christ to help others break free.

Power to Restore, Rebuild, and Regenerate

In 2014, the Glasgow School of Art's historic Mackintosh Building was gutted by fire. Because of its significance, the chair of the institution declared on May 23, 2014: *We will rebuild and rebuild well.* Their ambition was to restore the structure to its original glory using traditional craftsmanship, detailed conservation, and modern technology. The project sourced timbers from Massachusetts to match the original materials.

But just as the £35 million restoration neared completion, a second fire in 2018 once again reduced the building to its shell. Despite this devastating setback, the determination to rebuild remained strong, highlighting the human drive to restore what is lost.

Likewise, throughout Scripture, one of the greatest expressions of God's power is His ability to restore what is broken, rebuild what is ruined, and regenerate what is dead. Whether in individual lives, families, nations, or creation itself, God's restorative power is always redemptive and overflowing with grace.

The art of restoration originates with God. In His divine foresight, He anticipated the corruption and decay that would result from sin. Though His creation may be damaged when we violate His principles, God has made provision for its renewal. Whether physical or spiritual, what is broken can be restored to its original purpose.

The Power of Restoration

Every creature of God has been created according to the counsel of His will and is meant to function in alignment with His divine standards. Consequently, the various parts of creation are designed with precision to fulfil specific purposes. When any part becomes defective, its performance is compromised, and it falls short of God's intended standard.

In His Word, God has provided quality assurance and control measures, principles that help diagnose and correct deviations from His plan. When we are united with Christ, we gain access to the power that restores, rebuilds, and regenerates what has been damaged. This is the same power Jesus used to raise Lazarus from the dead, heal the sick, restore sight to the blind, and bring wholeness to those suffering from diverse infirmities.

God Restores What Has Been Lost

There are times when God's people suffer loss, whether it be possessions, resources, or positions. A business may lose its market or capital; individuals may face loss through divorce, rebellious children, job loss, broken relationships, or injustice. God's power is available to restore what has been lost, provided we walk faithfully with Christ and it aligns with His will. God has the power to restore lost years, broken lives, and stolen inheritances.

Job is a classic example of this. He lost everything, his children, livestock, servants (Job 1:6–19), the support of his wife (Job 2:9), the respect of his friends (Job 4–25), and was afflicted with painful boils (Job 2:6–8). Yet, after enduring a period of intense suffering, God restored him, giving him seven more sons and three daughters and doubling his wealth. This demonstrates God's power to restore, showing that no loss is too great for God to redeem.

God pledged to restore to Israel the years that the swarming locusts had eaten: *I will restore to you the years that the swarming locust has eaten…* (Joel 2:25). Imagine the Israelites investing their time and effort to grow crops year after year, only to see them devoured by locusts. The people of Judah had experienced devastation due to their sin and the resulting locust invasion. But God, in His mercy, promised not only forgiveness but full restoration of what had been lost. This passage reveals God's nature as a restorer of wasted time and opportunity, something only He can do.

The Israelites also suffered at the hands of enemies who invaded them and took away the fruit of their labour. However, God not only promised to protect their crops going forward but also to restore what had been lost over the years.

This demonstrates that God has the power to bring back into existence what has been destroyed, deformed, or lost.

God also used this restorative power to reconcile a fallen world to Himself through the death and resurrection of our Lord Jesus Christ. He is preparing for the ultimate restoration of creation, when He unveils the new heavens, the new earth, and the New Jerusalem (Revelation 21). Whatever may be dysfunctional in your life today, seek God's face for the power of restoration, and trust His will above all else.

God Restores Through the Holy Spirit

Restoration happens through the work of the Holy Spirit. He plays a vital role in restoring and regenerating lives. The Spirit brings conviction, cleansing, comfort, and direction. He does not just improve us—He makes us new. This is why Jesus told Nicodemus: *Unless one is born of water and the Spirit, he cannot enter the kingdom of God* (John 3:5 NKJV).

But Jesus is the ultimate restorer. The life and ministry of Jesus demonstrate God's power to restore sight to the blind, dignity to the outcast, life to the dead, and hope to the hopeless. When Jesus rose from the dead, He wasn't just raised—He restored resurrection power to all who believe in Him: *Behold, I make all things new* (Rev. 21:5).

This is the future promise of full restoration, when God will renew all of creation and wipe away every tear. Until then, we carry His power within us to restore broken relationships, rebuild shattered lives, and bring regeneration to those around us.

The power of restoration applies to various areas of our lives, including business, career, marriage, children, fertility, health, employment, mental stability, land productivity, livestock, and more. Through Jesus Christ and the Holy Spirit, God has made this power available to us. We are reminded that restoration brings back what was lost, rebuilding puts broken pieces back together with divine precision, and regeneration creates new life out of what was dead.

Is there an area in your life that needs restoring? Do you feel like something is too broken to rebuild? Are you longing for spiritual renewal? Ask God to release

His restorative power in you. He is not only able but willing to make all things new.

God Rebuilds Broken Foundations

God rebuilds broken foundations. He gave Nehemiah the burden and power to rebuild the walls of Jerusalem that had been broken for many years (Neh. 2). Though opposition came, Nehemiah declared: *The God of heaven will give us success…* (Neh. 2:20). The wall was rebuilt in just 52 days, an extraordinary feat that revealed God's favour and enabling power. Isaiah also prophesied: *They will rebuild the ancient ruins and restore the places long devastated…* (Isa. 61:4). This prophetic word speaks not just to physical rebuilding but also to spiritual and societal restoration. God raises up His people to rebuild cities, repair hearts, and restore worship in places that have long been in ruin.

God Regenerates What is Dead

God regenerates what is dead. Regeneration is the divine act of making something alive again. In the New Testament, this is described as the new birth, being born again by the Spirit of God. *He saved us through the washing of rebirth and renewal by the Holy Spirit* (Tit. 3:5 NIV). Through Jesus Christ, dead hearts are made alive, old natures are transformed, and new creations are formed: *Therefore, if anyone is in Christ, he is a new creation; the old has gone, the new has come!* (2 Cor. 5:17 NIV). No matter how far someone has fallen or how broken their past may be, God's regenerating power can bring about complete renewal, spiritually, emotionally, and relationally.

The Power to Reproduce

As a child, there was nothing more fascinating than finding a bird's nest with eggs or young ones. I was also keen to observe young animals grow and develop. Coming from a traditionally cattle-keeping tribe, it was not unusual to listen to adults sharing their experiences of cattle herding. One story my dad shared with us as a family, which has never escaped my memory, relates to a near disaster when he and his brother brought cubs of a leopard home after mistaking them for puppies. The act brought all activities of the village to a halt as the mother wreaked havoc in the village, despite the elderly men quickly returning the young cubs before their mother got to the village. The leopard's response was expected, as many animal species have a powerful, instinctual drive to protect their young. The leopardess fiercely protected her power to reproduce.

Reproduction is one of the earliest expressions of God's delegated power to humanity. In Genesis 1:28, after creating man and woman, God blessed them and said: *Be fruitful and multiply; fill the earth and subdue it.* He also blessed birds and sea creatures to be fruitful, increase in number, and fill the waters in the seas, and the birds to increase on the earth (Gen. 1:22). This command was not just a blessing, it was also a divine empowerment. God gave humanity the power to reproduce, both biologically and spiritually, ensuring the continuity of life and the fulfilment of His will to fill the earth.

Biological reproduction is a natural function created by God, but it remains a divine mystery and a powerful demonstration of His ability. Every child born is a testament to God's creative power in action. As Psalm 139:13-14 says: *For You formed my inward parts; You covered me in my mother's womb. I will praise You, for I am fearfully and wonderfully made.* Even when circumstances make reproduction difficult or medically impossible, God has often demonstrated His supernatural power. Consider the stories of Sarah, who gave birth to Isaac in her old age (Gen. 21), Hannah, who conceived Samuel after years of barrenness (1 Sam. 1), and Elizabeth, mother of John the Baptist, who conceived in her old age (Luke 1). These examples show that God can override natural limitations, granting the power to reproduce when it aligns with His will.

God expects us to be fruitful in all areas of life. Reproduction is not limited to children or disciples. God also empowers us to be fruitful in our work, relationships, ministries, and ideas. Jesus said in John 15:5: *He who abides in Me, and I in him, bears much fruit; for without Me you can do nothing.* When we are connected to Christ, we bear fruit, evidence of a life that produces goodness, peace, love, creativity, and influence for God's kingdom.

God's power underlies every act of reproduction. While the reproductive processes in plants, animals, birds, insects, reptiles, and humans may appear ordinary or routine, they are ultimately sustained by the power of God. We are often quick to acknowledge God's power in miraculous cases, those that defy human explanation, but the truth is that every reproductive act, whether visible or invisible, natural or supernatural, depends on God's sustaining power.

Take the story of Abraham and Sarah: at 100 and 90 years old, respectively, they gave birth to Isaac, a feat that completely defied biology and human experience. If their bodies had functioned only according to natural law, this birth would have been impossible. God's power to reproduce was clearly at work.

In the house of Jacob, we also see divine intervention in reproduction: *When the Lord saw that Leah was not loved, He opened her womb, but Rachel was barren* (Gen. 29:31, NIV). Similarly, God shut Hannah's womb (1 Sam. 1:6) and later opened it in His perfect timing. These examples remind us that God alone has the power to open or close wombs, and His decisions are based on divine wisdom, timing, and purpose.

Perhaps the greatest example of supernatural reproduction is the virgin birth of Jesus Christ. Though it surpasses our understanding, we believe that Mary conceived by the Holy Spirit, and from there, the natural processes of gestation and birth unfolded as they do in any pregnancy. This underscores once again that reproduction, whether miraculous or mundane, is ultimately driven by the will and power of God. But reproduction is not confined to biology alone.

All living things are designed to reproduce. Even without conscious thought or emotional connection, animals instinctively continue their species. As long as they are not disturbed or stressed, they will naturally reproduce. This instinct, too, is embedded by God.

The concept of reproduction extends to other areas of life:
- An artist who sketches a bird is reproducing its image.
- A sculptor mirrors human likeness through crafted stone or clay.
- A teacher reproduces knowledge in their students.

- A mentor imparts wisdom to a younger professional.
- Bezaleel and Aholiab, appointed in Exodus 35:34, were not only filled with creative skill but were also empowered by God to teach others, effectively reproducing their skills in others.

Every living thing and every human calling contains within it the God-given potential to reproduce, biologically, intellectually, creatively, professionally, and spiritually. But the ability to pass on life, wisdom, character, or craft is ultimately sustained by the power of God.

Whether we are raising children, mentoring others, creating art, or building legacies, let us remember: *It is God who gives seed to the sower and bread for food* (2 Cor. 9:10). He gives the seed and empowers the harvest.

The power to reproduce is a divine gift that encompasses physical fruitfulness (biological children), spiritual fruitfulness (making disciples and spreading the Gospel), and productive fruitfulness (using gifts and opportunities for God's glory). This power comes from God and must be exercised in alignment with His will, for His glory and the advancement of His kingdom.

The Power to Receive Divine Revelation

One evening, I sat in the living room and watched a documentary on works of art. The narrator asked a professional artist to explain why he thought the drawing deserved a place in that prestigious art gallery. As a layman, I didn't see anything special about the drawing. But as the artist began to analyse the features of the drawing and decode the information, I realized that the drawing contained valuable information, artistically written but hidden to the ordinary eye.

By analysing the piece of art, the artist explained when it was drawn, the message it communicated to the audience, and the cultural setting in which it was produced. By the end of the program, my perception of art had completely changed. The documentary did not just reveal my naivety; it taught me that things are not always as they appear.

We live in a world where meaning is veiled, and truth concealed from the common eye. In our world, we brush shoulders with many things of which we have very little understanding, until someone skilled or knowledgeable reveals them to us. The individual equipped with tools to read the natural or spiritual world has the power to receive revelation.

The Lord God, who created the world, is omniscient, and His desire is that creation knows Him. He has revealed Himself through Scripture, the works of creation, and through His Son. Yet the world does not know Him. Even some believers have a very vague knowledge of our Creator because they do not have the power to receive divine revelation.

As the boy Samuel ministered before the Lord under Eli (1 Sam. 3:1), God called him twice in his sleep. Twice, Samuel went to Eli to ask if he was calling him. But Eli, on both occasions, said, *"I did not call you. Go back and lie down* (1 Sam. 3:5-6). The Bible records: *Now Samuel did not yet know the LORD; the word of the LORD had not yet been revealed to him"* (1 Sam. 3:7). Samuel did not recognize the voice of the LORD because He had not yet revealed Himself to the boy. Samuel lacked the power to receive the revelation of God.

When Jesus walked with two of His disciples on the road to Emmaus, which was seven miles from Jerusalem, He kept them from recognizing Him. They spent time with Him discussing the events of the time - His death and the events surrounding His resurrection - but they did not realize they were chatting with their Master until He chose to reveal Himself to them. However, *when He was at the table with them, He took bread, gave thanks, broke it, and began to give it to them. Then their eyes were opened, and they recognized Him, and He disappeared from their sight* (Luke 24:30 NIV). Unless the Lord reveals Himself to us, we cannot recognize Him.

Many Christians are still struggling in their walk with God because they don't yet know Him, and His Word has not yet been revealed to them. When we lack the power to hear the voice of God, we may mistake it for the voice of man, just as Samuel did. Anytime God wants to commune with us, we need that power to receive His revelation.

Saint John, while on the island of Patmos, was in the Spirit and received the revelation of Jesus Christ and the events relating to His kingdom, judgment, the establishment of the new heavens and earth, and the New Jerusalem. Another event that has intrigued me is the revelation of Jesus Christ to Saul of Tarsus on the road to Damascus. While the flashlight from heaven surrounded Saul, he conversed with Jesus. *And the men who journeyed with him stood speechless, hearing a voice but seeing no one* (Acts 9:7). Jesus revealed Himself to Saul.

When God was about to destroy Sodom and Gomorrah, He said to Himself, "Will I hide this from my servant Abraham?" The servant of God never made a formal request to God for information regarding His plans for the two cities, and yet God felt the urge to reveal it to Abraham.

Other divine revelations include: the birth of the Lord Jesus Christ to the shepherds in the wilderness; Agabus' prophecy that Paul would be arrested in Jerusalem and handed over to the Gentiles; and the angelic visitation in a dream, which warned Joseph and Mary of Herod's intention to kill baby Jesus. When the Spirit of the Sovereign Lord is upon you, He will reveal things that would normally be inaccessible to our human nature.

God is not silent, He speaks. But not everyone hears, understands, or receives what He reveals. The ability to receive divine revelation is not simply a matter of intellect, theology, or education. It is a spiritual capacity granted by God Himself. Revelation is not achieved, it is received, and this reception requires God-given power.

Throughout Scripture, we see that God reveals Himself in various ways, through creation (Rom. 1:20), through His Word (2 Tim. 3:16), through the prophets (Heb. 1:1), and most fully through Jesus Christ (John 1:18, Heb. 1:2). Yet not everyone comprehends these revelations. Why? Because divine understanding must be spiritually discerned (1 Cor. 2:14). Revelation is a work of the Holy Spirit. Jesus told His disciples: *But the Helper, the Holy Spirit, will teach you all things and bring to your remembrance all that I have said to you* (John 14:26 ESV).

The Holy Spirit illuminates the truth, makes it personal, and enables us to grasp its meaning. Paul explains this beautifully: *What no eye has seen, what no ear* has heard, and what no human mind has conceived, the things God has prepared for those who love him, these are the things God has revealed to us by his Spirit (1 Cor. 2:9-10 NIV). Without the Holy Spirit, we can read the Bible and still miss the voice of God.

Revelation is by God's initiative. Even Peter, who confessed Jesus as the Christ, the Son of the Living God, did so not by his own insight, but by divine disclosure. Jesus responded: *Blessed are you, Simon son of Jonah, for this was not revealed to you by flesh and blood, but by my Father in heaven* (Matt. 16:17 NIV). But revelation requires humility and hunger. Divine revelation is not reserved for the elite or intellectual. God delights in revealing Himself to the humble and hungry. Jesus said: *I praise you, Father, because you have hidden these things from the wise and learned and revealed them to little children* (Matt. 11:25 NIV). If we want to receive revelation, we must come like children, with open hearts, uncluttered minds, and a deep hunger for truth. Revelation is relational, those who walk closely with God tend to hear Him more clearly (Matt. 11:25 NIV).

As a Christian:
- Ask for revelation – *Call to me and I will answer you and tell you great and unsearchable things you do not know* (Jeremiah 33:3).
- Abide in God's Word – Revelation often comes through Scripture as the Spirit brings it to life (Psa. 119:105).
- Yield to the Holy Spirit – He is the revealer of truth (John 16:13).
- Obey what has already been revealed – God often gives more revelation to those who are faithful with what they've received.

The Power of Discernment

The divine power of discernment, from the Greek word *diakrisis*, refers to an individual's ability to distinguish, judge, or appraise a person, statement, situation, or environment. In a corrupt and morally confused world, the ability to differentiate between the influence of God and Satan, good and evil, or the works of the flesh and the Spirit, is an essential component of Christian living.

In Christianity, there is no single definitive meaning for "discernment."

Broadly, it can refer to:
- The process of determining God's will in each situation or for one's life,
- The ability to perceive the true nature of a person or event,
- Or an inner search for clarity regarding one's vocation, be it marriage, singleness, consecrated life, or ministry.

God demonstrates perfect discernment from the beginning. Before creating the heavens and the earth, God foresaw all that would happen, from the fall of man to the redemption and restoration of creation. In His perfect discernment: He excluded the names of beast-worshippers from the Book of Life (Rev. 17:8); chose believers in Christ to be holy (Eph. 1:4); promised eternal life (Tit. 1:2); foreordained Christ as Redeemer (1 Pet. 1:20); and prepared a kingdom inheritance for His faithful (Matt. 25:34). Having foreseen every stage of human history, God implemented redemptive measures long before sin entered the world.

Today, the Church urgently needs believers who are gifted with discernment to protect the body of Christ from deception and spiritual danger. As Jesus warned: *For false Christs and false prophets will appear and perform great signs and wonders to deceive, if possible, even the elect* (Matt. 24:24 NIV). While God performs great miracles, Satan also counterfeits the supernatural to mislead. The challenge is real: how do we distinguish a true servant of God from a manipulative imposter?

Several tragic examples from recent history demonstrate the abuse of authority in some churches:
- In South Africa (2016), a pastor sprayed congregants with insecticide ("Doom"), claiming it cured illnesses.
- In Zimbabwe, a prophet gave congregants water polluted with sewage, after praying over it.
- Another South African preacher gave congregants rat poison, claiming believers were immortal, resulting in deaths and hospitalizations.

These disturbing acts emphasize the spiritual vulnerability of many, especially where there is poor discipleship and weak scriptural grounding. They also highlight the urgent need for the Church to exercise the spiritual gift of discernment.

Discernment acts as a spiritual security system. When deception or corruption enters the Church - whether through false teaching or immoral leadership - believers with the gift of discernment are prompted by the Spirit to raise alarm and protect the flock. Scripture is full of examples: Elisha discerned Gehazi's lie and judged him accordingly (2 Kings 5), and Peter, filled with the Spirit, exposed Ananias and Sapphira's deceit (Acts 5). Mature believers who walk closely with God can sense in their spirit the presence of pride, manipulation, heresy, or occult influence. But immature or uninformed believers are vulnerable to deception.

We are called to pursue and pray for discernment. Paul lists discernment of spirits among the spiritual gifts (1 Cor. 12:10). He also prays: *And this I pray, that your love may abound still more… in knowledge and all discernment* (Phil. 1:9 NKJV). Believers must actively seek the power of discernment—both to safeguard their faith and to help others remain rooted in the truth.

As we grow in our walk with Christ, let us seek and cultivate the power of discernment. It helps us recognize God's voice amidst the noise, test what is truly of God (1 John 4:1), and live wisely in a spiritually deceptive world. *But solid food is for the mature, who because of practice have their senses trained to discern good and evil* (Heb. 5:14 NASB).

Power to Defend

I had just left the scene for an hour to assess the stock of books in my field at the Cambridge Central Council Library, and it was gone. My precious, sturdy mountain bike had mysteriously disappeared. For a couple of minutes, I stood at the very spot where I had chained it to the railings. It had vanished into thin air.

Still in denial, I walked along the fence where other bikes remained chained. Then I returned to the spot once more, hoping for a miracle. But it finally sank in, my bike was gone. Someone who "borrows" with no intention of returning had visited the scene. I had thought my security gadgets were so foolproof that the probability of theft was close to zero. I was wrong. My efforts to protect the bike proved futile.

That incident made me reflect: Can anyone snatch what God has secured? Can anyone take something from the hand of God? The answer is clear: No.

The LORD God, who created the universe, guarantees the security of all that belongs to Him, unless we violate His divine security principles.

God's power to defend is demonstrated vividly in the story of Job. When Satan accused Job of shallow faith, he also admitted something crucial: *Have you not made a hedge around him, his household, and everything he has?* (Job 1:10 NIV). Even the enemy recognized that God's defence system is rock solid.

Throughout Scripture, God's protection is affirmed:

- *No one can snatch them out of my hand* (John 10:28).
- *My God is my rock, in whom I take refuge… He is my shield and the horn of my salvation* (2 Sam. 22:3–4).
- *May your whole spirit, soul and body be kept blameless at the coming of our Lord Jesus Christ* (1 Thess. 5:23).
- *The righteous person may have many troubles, but the Lord delivers him from them all* (Psa. 34:19).
- *Keep me safe, Lord, from the hands of the wicked; protect me from the violent* (Psa. 140:4).
- *In the shadow of your wings I will take refuge until the disaster has passed* (Psa. 57:1).
- *But the Lord is faithful, and he will strengthen you and protect you from the evil one* (2 Thess. 3:3).
- *Do not be afraid… for the Lord your God will be with you wherever you go"* (Josh. 1:9).

From protecting Israel in the wilderness (Deut. 8:15), to shielding Shadrach, Meshach, and Abednego in the furnace (Daniel 3), and defending countless others like David, Daniel, Joseph, and Jacob, God proves time and again that His power to defend is unmatched.

Even Jesus was protected throughout His life. Before He was born, God preserved the Virgin Mary by divine power. *"The Holy Spirit will come upon you, and the power of the Most High will overshadow you"* (Luke 1:35). This word *"overshadow"* echoes the Shekinah glory of God, a divine covering of protection. No sin, no demon, and no human flaw could interfere with the holy child in Mary's womb.

Could Satan have prevented the birth of the Messiah? Impossible. Jehovah built an impenetrable shield around His redemptive plan. God also protected Jesus after birth by warning Joseph in a dream: *Take the child and his mother and escape to Egypt… for Herod is going to search for the child to kill him* (Matt. 2:13 NIV). Divine intervention ensured Jesus survived every attack, until the appointed time of His sacrifice.

In the Garden of Gethsemane, Jesus affirmed His protective role over His disciples: *I have not lost one of those you gave me* (John 18:9 NIV). God defends not just individuals, but purposes, promises, and destinies.

Our Role in God's Defence System

As disciples of Christ, we are not passive. God delegates to us the responsibility to defend what He places under our care. Ephesians 6:10–11 reminds us: *Be strong in the Lord and in His mighty power. Put on the full armour of God, so that you can take your stand against the devil's schemes.* God equips us with:

- Truth to counter lies,
- Righteousness to guard our hearts,
- Faith to extinguish the enemy's flaming arrows,
- Salvation and the Word as weapons for spiritual battle.

We are not left vulnerable. Just as God's power defended His people in the past, His Spirit now empowers us to stand, resist, and overcome.

Whether you need defence against spiritual warfare, personal attacks, emotional battles, or societal injustice, know that God is your shield and your strong tower. He defends not only your body but also your purpose, calling, mind, and spirit. He equips you to defend the faith, protect the vulnerable, and uphold His truth in a world of deception and opposition. *No weapon formed against you shall prosper, And every tongue which rises against you in judgment you shall condemn. This is the heritage of the servants of the Lord, And their righteousness is from Me," says the Lord* (Isa. 54:17 NKJV).

Whatever belongs to God is protected. Whatever He places under your care can be safeguarded through faith, obedience, and spiritual readiness. If man-made chains and locks can be broken, how much more should we trust in God's divine defence system, it never fails. *If God is for us, who can be against us?* (Romans 8:31, NKJV).

Power to Kill

As a young man, I was very curious about how the armed forces operate. I later discovered that certain operatives within a government's armed forces can be officially authorized to use lethal force in pursuit of specific objectives, they are, in effect, licensed to kill. For instance, U.S. special forces are empowered to engage in deadly missions globally as part of their mandate to protect national interests. They have the power to kill.

This authority became especially prominent during the United States' intensified war on terrorism. A central aim of these elite units is to locate and neutralize terrorist leaders, even in their most remote hideouts. As one special forces source explained, *"The people in these units are available 24 hours a day, seven days a week, anywhere in the world."* While these operatives do kill, they do not necessarily commit murder.

Is there a difference between killing and murder? Yes, there is. Many Bible commentators make a distinction: murder is the premeditated, unlawful taking of a life; and killing can refer more broadly to the act of taking a life, but not always with unlawful or malicious intent.

For example, Exodus 22:2–3 makes a legal distinction: If a thief is caught breaking in at night and is struck and killed, the defender is not guilty of bloodshed. But if it happens after sunrise, the defender is guilty of bloodshed. This implies that some instances of killing may be justified, while others constitute murder. Examples of divine judgment in the Bible include:

- The Flood – God destroyed humanity (except Noah's family) due to extreme wickedness (Gen. 6:7).
- Egypt's firstborn – God struck down the firstborn of Egypt during the Exodus as a final act of judgment (Exod. 13:15).
- The conquest of Canaan – God commanded Israel to destroy idolatrous nations to prevent moral and spiritual corruption (Deut. 20:16–18).
- Sodom and Gomorrah – God destroyed these cities for their grievous sin, though He was willing to spare them if even ten righteous people were found (Gen. 18:32).

These acts were not random or impulsive, they were deliberate acts of divine justice, designed to uphold righteousness and protect God's redemptive plan through Israel.

While God has the sovereign right to take life, humans do not share that right unconditionally. The Sixth Commandment, *You shall not murder* (Exod. 20:13), reminds us that only God, or those to whom He delegates authority (e.g., civil governments), may justly take a life. Even then, God is not eager to destroy. His preference is for mercy: *The Lord is not slow in keeping his promise… He is patient with you, not wanting anyone to perish, but everyone to come to repentance* (2 Pet. 3:9, NLT).

God waits, giving people time to turn from sin. But when they persist in rebellion, His justice may require Him to take life, to maintain holiness, protect the innocent, or fulfil His purposes. The power to kill belongs to God. He does not kill without cause, and He never murders. All His actions are governed by perfect justice and love. Although He may delegate authority to humans (e.g., governments or armies), life ultimately belongs to Him alone.

Power to Hate

"Hate" is a strong and often misunderstood word, especially when attributed to a loving God. In a world where love is celebrated as the highest virtue, the idea that God possesses the power to hate may seem uncomfortable or even contradictory. Yet Scripture is clear: God is not only a God of love, He also hates. His hatred, however, is always righteous. It is targeted at evil and aimed at preserving justice, holiness, and truth. *There are six things the LORD hates, seven that are detestable to him: haughty eyes, a lying tongue, hands that shed innocent blood, a heart that devises wicked schemes, feet that are quick to rush into evil, a false witness who pours out lies, and a person who stirs up conflict in the community* (Prov. 6:16–19, NIV). In this passage, God's hatred is not directed at individuals per se, but at their wicked actions—actions that violate His nature, harm others, and corrupt justice.

But what is hatred? Hatred is a deep and intense form of dislike, often accompanied by anger, resentment, or revulsion. While frequently viewed as wholly negative, hatred is a double-edged force. Depending on its source and target, it can either fuel devastating evil or channel righteous indignation against sin and injustice.

History bears tragic witness to the destructive power of human hatred:

- In 1994, approximately 800,000 Rwandan Tutsis and moderate Hutus were slaughtered in just 100 days by Hutu militias (BBC, 2011).
- In 2017, about 700,000 Rohingya Muslims fled persecution and the destruction of their homes in Myanmar—a crisis described by the UN as "a textbook example of ethnic cleansing" (BBC, 2018).
- During the Holocaust, Nazi Germany and its collaborators systematically murdered six million Jews—nearly two-thirds of Europe's Jewish population.
- In the Balkan conflicts, 20,000–25,000 Albanians were massacred by Serbian and Montenegrin forces.
- The Southern Poverty Law Centre identified over 900 active hate groups in the U.S., with hate-related engagement on social media reportedly rising by 900% in two years.

Why do people hate? Experts in human behaviour provide several psychological explanations:

1. Fear of the Other – People often hate what they perceive as different or

threatening. According to Marsden and Patrick Wanis, group identity plays a significant role in defensive hatred.

2. Projection of Inner Fears – Clinical psychologist Dana Harron suggests people often hate in others what they fear or deny in themselves.

3. Lack of Self-Compassion – Therapist Brad Reedy notes that rejecting parts of ourselves may lead us to attack those who mirror our inner conflicts.

4. Distraction from Pain – Bernard Golden explains that hatred can be a defence mechanism to mask feelings of helplessness or shame.

5. Cultural and Societal Conditioning – Silvia Dutchevici argues that cultures of war, competition, and disconnection can normalize and perpetuate hate.

But God's hatred is holy. It is not like human hatred, which is often fuelled by ego, revenge, or bias. God's hatred is a righteous revulsion toward sin. He hates not out of malice, but because of His moral perfection. He detests anything that distorts truth, defiles His creation, destroys human dignity, or defies His will. *For you are not a God who is pleased with wickedness; with you, evil people are not welcome. The arrogant cannot stand in your presence. You hate all who do wrong* (Psa. 5:4–5, NIV). Even Jesus, the embodiment of divine love, expressed hatred, not for people, but for evil:

- He overturned the tables in the temple, driving out those who exploited others in the name of worship (Matthew 21:12–13).
- He rebuked the Pharisees for their hypocrisy and spiritual abuse (Matthew 23).
- He denounced sin consistently, while extending mercy to the repentant.

Let those who love the Lord hate evil… (Psalm 97:10, NIV). This is the power God gives His people, the power to hate what is evil, while still loving people and working for their redemption. Believers are called to share in God's holy hatred. Christians are not called to hate others, but we are commanded to hate evil: *Love must be sincere. Hate what is evil; cling to what is good* (Rom. 12:9 NIV).

We need this power today—to reject injustice, to stand against sin, and to renounce evil in all its forms, even when it is disguised as good. This kind of hate fuels moral courage and strengthens our resolve to pursue godliness, no matter the cost.

The power to hate is not about anger or vengeance, it is a righteous indignation rooted in God's holy character. As God's people, we are called to align our affections with His, to love what He loves and hate what He hates. That is the power of discernment, the power of moral clarity, and the power to stand for truth in a compromised world.

Hatred is spiritual as much as it is psychological. While psychology offers important insights, hatred is not merely a mental or emotional issue, it is also spiritual. The Apostle Paul describes hatred as a work of the flesh (Gal. 5:19–20), a symptom of a life governed by sin. It originates in a mind that is hostile to God (Rom. 8:7).

At its core, sinful hatred is rooted in spiritual rebellion. The Devil despises God and His creation. He rebelled against divine authority, corrupted humanity, stirred up violence in Noah's day, sought to destroy the infant Jesus, and continues to wage war against redemption. Every act of hate born from sin draws its power from this fallen spirit.

By contrast, God's hatred is based on His holy standard, perfect righteousness and justice. He hates sin, injustice, and wickedness. When Jesus bore the world's sin on the cross, He experienced separation from the Father, who cannot look upon iniquity. Scripture is clear about the things God hates:

- *Jacob I loved, but Esau I hated* (Rom. 9:13)
- *There are six things the Lord hates, seven that are detestable to Him...* (Prov. 6:16–19)
- *The Lord examines the righteous, but the wicked, those who love violence, His soul hates* (Psa. 11:5 NIV)
- *I hate divorce, says the Lord, because it covers one's garment with violence* (Mal. 2:16)

God does not hate indiscriminately, His hatred targets sin and unrepentant wickedness. While His love is offered to all through Christ, those who reject this gift choose judgment over mercy. *Hate what is evil* (Rom. 12:9 NIV).

Hatred must be understood in its spiritual context. Destructive hatred arises from our sinful nature and is empowered by the enemy of our souls. But righteous hatred, a Spirit-born detesting of evil, is aligned with the heart of God. The Godhead abhorred sin so deeply that Jesus endured brutal suffering to redeem creation. This redemptive act was powered by the Holy Spirit. In the same way, believers can only resist the power of sin and death through the Spirit.

As children of God, we are not powerless. We are given the authority to hate what is evil and love what is good (Rom. 12:9). This means rejecting both sinful actions and the inner attitudes that lead to them: *Put to death, therefore, whatever belongs to your earthly nature: sexual immorality, impurity, lust, evil desires, and greed, which is idolatry.* (Col. 3:5 NIV)

We live in a world where hatred devastates nations, families, and souls. But hatred itself is not the enemy, it is how we use it. Let us hate injustice, pride, deceit, and all that opposes the love and truth of God. And let us do so by the power of the Holy Spirit, never in our own strength. Resist the hate that destroys. Embrace the hate that purifies.

Power to Love

Love is not merely a feeling or a virtue, it is a divine force. The power to love transcends emotion and taps into the very nature of God. Scripture tells us plainly: *God is love* (1 John 4:8). This means that love is not just something God does; it is who He is. When we love others truly, sacrificially, and unconditionally, we reflect the image of God.

The greatest commandment Jesus gave was centred on love: *Love the Lord your God with all your heart and with all your soul and with all your mind. This is the first and greatest commandment. And the second is like it: Love your neighbour as yourself* (Matt. 22:37–39 NIV). Yet loving as God loves requires supernatural power. It is not natural to love those who hurt us, betray us, or are different from us. It takes the indwelling power of the Holy Spirit to love the way Jesus commands: *Love your enemies and pray for those who persecute you* (Matt. 5:44 NIV).

God's love is powerful, it heals, restores, transforms, and even saves. Romans 5:5 reminds us that *God's love has been poured out into our hearts through the Holy Spirit.* This divine outpouring empowers believers not only to receive love but to give it, even when it's hardest.

True love is not weak. It is bold. It corrects, forgives, bears burdens, and even lays down its life for others: *Greater love has no one than this: to lay down one's life for one's friends* (John 15:13 NIV). Jesus on the cross is the ultimate demonstration of love's power, love that conquers sin, death, and hate.

Maggot (2004) wrote: *There is no power in the universe or, indeed, in infinity itself that is greater than love. God Himself is love and created all things in, through, and by that love.* His love is the foundation that sustains all creation. Love has even been proposed as a biological function that keeps human beings connected and promotes the continuation of the species (Fisher, 2004). But what, exactly, is love?

Definitions of Love

Love is among the most complex concepts to define. Common interpretations include:
- A strong feeling of attraction and emotional attachment (Merriam-Webster, 2000)
- Compassionate and affectionate actions toward others, oneself, or animals (Fromm, 1956)
- A wide range of positive emotional and mental states, from sublime virtue to deep interpersonal affection—even simple pleasure (Oxford English Dictionary)

In all its forms, love is a major force that sustains interpersonal relationships.

Philosophical Views of Love

Philosophers have tried to define love in deeper terms:
- *To will the good of another* – St. Thomas Aquinas
- *Absolute value* – Bertrand Russell

- *Delight in the happiness of another* – Gottfried Leibniz
- *A feeling of unity* – Meher Baba
- *An active appreciation of intrinsic worth*
- *Unconditional selflessness* – Jeremy Griffith
- Simply: *Giving without expecting in return*
- Cultural and Historical Perspectives

The ancient Greeks identified several types of love:

1. Storge – Familial love
2. Philia – Deep friendship
3. Eros – Romantic love
4. Xenia – Hospitality or guest-friendship
5. Agape – Unconditional, selfless love that expects nothing in return

Psychological and Scientific Perspectives

Helen Fisher, a biological anthropologist, categorizes love into three overlapping stages:

- Lust – Driven by hormones
- Attraction – Linked to dopamine and reward systems
- Attachment – Promotes long-term bonding

Psychologist Robert Sternberg proposed the Triangular Theory of Love, consisting of:

- Intimacy (emotional closeness)
- Passion (physical and romantic attraction)
- Commitment (the decision to remain together)

From a biological perspective, love functions as a mechanism for survival, bonding, and family structure.

The divine Source of Love

The true source of love is God. It is reflected in His relationship with creation and in how He enables humans to love one another. As Scripture declares again: *"God is love"* (1 John 4:8), and this love was demonstrated most clearly when He gave His only Son for our salvation: *For God so loved the world that He gave His one and only Son, that whoever believes in Him shall not perish but have eternal life* (John 3:16, NIV).

Jesus endured shame, suffering, and death on the cross to redeem us. His love did not end at the cross, He gave us His Spirit so that we could become His dwelling place and experience divine love from within.

Because we are made in God's image, we possess the capacity to give and receive love. We were created to live in the rhythm of divine love—to reflect it to our Creator and extend it to others. This is the agape love Jesus spoke of: selfless, sacrificial, and unconditional.

Love is central to God's essence and eternal nature. The Apostle Paul emphasized that even among great Christian virtues like faith and hope, *the greatest of these is love* (1 Cor. 13:13). Unlike spiritual gifts that may fade, love endures because it is anchored in God Himself.

God's Love Has Never Changed

God's love has never changed, from creation to humanity's fall, through redemption, and into eternity. After Adam and Eve sinned, God covered their nakedness. Even after Cain murdered Abel, God placed a protective mark on him. God's love continues despite our failures, it is unwavering, patient, and redemptive.

God illustrated this love vividly when He commanded the prophet Hosea to love an adulterous woman, representing God's love for Israel despite their unfaithfulness: *Go and love your wife again, even though she commits adultery. This will illustrate that the LORD still loves Israel, even though the people have turned to other gods* (Hos. 3:1 NLT).

True love is costly. Loving those who love us is easy. But what about those who hurt us? The abuser? The murderer? The betrayer? The enemy? Human justice often demands punishment, sometimes even death. But divine love does something radically different. Jesus said: *You have heard that it was said, 'Love your neighbour and hate your enemy.' But I tell you: love your enemies and pray for those who persecute you.* (Matt. 5:43–44 NIV).

One of the greatest challenges is that the offender may not express any remorse for the pain they've caused. And yet, even on the cross, Jesus forgave His executioners, saying: *Father, forgive them, for they do not know what they are doing* (Luke 23:34 NIV). This is agape love, unconditional, countercultural, and divine. It resists bitterness, embraces mercy, and requires supernatural strength to live out.

Believers are Empowered to Love

Loving this way is not something we can do in our own strength. But thanks be to God, the Holy Spirit pours His power into our hearts, enabling us to love in every circumstance: *God's love has been poured into our hearts through the Holy Spirit who has been given to us* (Rom. 5:5 ESV).

The power to love is a divine gift. Use it in your family, your marriage, your workplace, your ministry, in every area of life. Let it be the force that fuels reconciliation, healing, and spiritual growth. Through the Holy Spirit, you have everything you need to love, radically, relentlessly, and redemptively.

Power to Speak

As a shy 13-year-old Form One student, I once faced an unforgettable challenge. Our secondary school prefect asked me to pray before the entire student body could eat. In a dining hall packed with over 1,000 students from Forms 1–5, I was terrified.

To make matters worse, I was the youngest and smallest student in the school, so short that most students couldn't even see me unless I was elevated. The prefect made me stand on the dining table to pray. That moment was humiliating and nerve-racking. I had a fear of public speaking—and yet there I was, forced to speak in front of a thousand peers. While it was stressful for me, many students found it amusing.

The disciples of our Lord Jesus Christ faced a similar fear. After Jesus' arrest, they were terrified to speak about Him. Peter, who had once boldly declared his loyalty, denied even knowing Jesus when questioned by a servant girl. Fear gripped their hearts, and they fell silent in the face of danger.

I, too, have experienced moments of hesitation. There have been times when I had the opportunity to share the gospel but felt intimidated. I've seen pastors and Christian leaders hesitate or remain silent when pressed by media or confronted in public forums, especially on controversial issues.

Silence in the Face of Truth

Unfortunately, the Church has often remained silent on crucial moral and societal issues. Even in countries where freedom of speech is protected, many churches avoid addressing topics like LGBTQ+ ideology, abortion, and biblical marriage, for fear of offending or facing backlash. As a result, many settle for preaching safe, agreeable messages that don't confront sin or call for repentance.

And yet, Jesus never avoided hard truths. His earthly ministry was filled with controversy and confrontation, but He never compromised. During His trial, He had the chance to escape suffering by denying the truth, but He chose to stand firm.

He warned that anyone who followed Him would face the same opposition. True to His word, many of His disciples died dishonourably in the eyes of the world, but honourably in the eyes of heaven, for speaking the truth.

In today's world, whether at the workplace, in ministry, in marriage, or even within families, people often struggle to speak openly. Fear of breaking organizational policies, offending loved ones, or being misinterpreted often silences even well-meaning voices. Tragically, even when situations call for truth, many remain silent.

But persecution for speaking truth is not new. From the early Church until today, believers have been victimized for professing their faith. Jesus and His disciples were harassed and ultimately killed for declaring God's Word. Speaking the truth has always come at a cost. The world says, Be bold, speak out! But for believers, the boldness to speak is not drawn from self-confidence. It is rooted in spiritual power. Jesus knew His disciples could not declare the gospel unless they received divine power. He told them: *But you will receive power when the Holy*

Spirit comes upon you; and you will be my witnesses in Jerusalem, and in all Judea and Samaria, and to the ends of the earth (Acts 1:8).

While Jesus was with His disciples, He gave them power to minister. But after His ascension, they needed a new source, the Holy Spirit. Without the Spirit, they would lack the boldness to share the gospel in His absence. So, Jesus instructed them to wait in Jerusalem until they were baptized with the Holy Spirit. This baptism would dispel their fear and empower them to speak boldly. After receiving the Spirit, the once-timid Peter stood and preached to a crowd—and 3,000 people were added to the body of Christ in a single day (Acts 2:14–41).

Every believer baptized in the Holy Spirit has this same power. No matter how intimidating the environment may be, the Holy Spirit will open your mouth and fill it with the Word of God. This is the word of the LORD to Zerubbabel: 'Not by might nor by power, but by my Spirit,' says the LORD Almighty." (Zech. 4:6). When filled with the Spirit, nothing can prevent you from declaring the oracles of God. Even Moses, called by God to lead Israel out of Egypt, doubted his ability to speak. He said, *O Lord, I have never been eloquent... I am slow of speech and tongue."* But God replied, *"Who gave man his mouth? ... Now go; I will help you speak and will teach you what to say* (Exod. 4:10–12).

If we remain in God's presence and walk in obedience, He will give us the words and the courage to speak. May we continually rely on the Holy Spirit for the boldness to declare His truth, even when it costs us everything.

Power to Keep

God owns and keeps the universe and everything in it. His power to keep is rooted in His nature—faithful, unchanging, and eternal: *Now to Him who can keep you from stumbling and to present you blameless before the presence of His glory with great joy...* (Jude 1:24 ESV). The Bible consistently portrays God as the one who keeps, guards, and preserves. His power doesn't only create, it keeps.

- He keeps the universe in order: *In Him all things hold together* (Col. 1:17)
- *He upholds all things by the word of His power* (Heb. 1:3).

- He keeps His people: *The LORD watches over you, the LORD is your shade at your right hand* (Psa. 121:5); *I give them eternal life, and they shall never perish; no one will snatch them out of my hand* (John 10:28)

Jesus Christ preserves the structural integrity and functional order of creation. *He is before all things, and in Him all things hold together* (Col. 1:17 NIV); *The Son is the radiance of God's glory and the exact representation of His being, sustaining all things by His powerful word* (Heb. 1:3 NIV). Our Lord holds together both the living and non-living things, as well as their interactions. He also keeps the physical and mathematical laws that govern the universe.

God has entrusted His people to Jesus Christ, giving Him the authority to keep them: *To those who have been called, who are loved by God the Father and kept by Jesus Christ* (Jude 1:1 NIV). *This happened so that the words He had spoken would be fulfilled: 'I have not lost one of those You gave me* (John 18:9, NIV). Jude affirms that those whom God has called and sanctified are given to Christ, who faithfully keeps them. Humanity, created in the image of God, has also been given both the ability and responsibility to keep what God has entrusted to us. This is seen in several biblical mandates:

- Creation Mandate: *The LORD God took the man and put him in the Garden of Eden to tend and keep it.* (Gen. 2:15)
- Moral Responsibility: *Fear God and keep His commandments, for this is the duty of all mankind* (Eccl. 12:13)
- Stewardship of Faith and Doctrine: *Guard what has been entrusted to your care. Turn away from godless chatter...* (1 Tim. 6:20)

We are called to care for God's creation and uphold His Word in ways that glorify Him. Throughout the Old Testament, God repeatedly instructed Israel to keep His commandments (Exod. 20:6; Deut. 8:6), statutes and laws (Deut. 4:40; 6:1–2; Exod. 15:26), testimonies (Deut. 6:17), covenant (Psalm 103:18), and His law (Prov. 28:7; 29:18). Obedience was the foundation of Israel's identity as God's people. It had both spiritual and practical consequences:

- It was the condition for possessing the Promised Land.

- It demonstrated reverence for the Lord.
- It guaranteed long life (Deut. 4:40).
- It led to blessing, multiplication, and prosperity (Deut. 30:16; Josh. 1:9).
- It established holiness and secured God's favour (Deut. 28:9, 13; Lev. 25:18).
- It granted access to the mysteries of God (Deut. 29:29).

In the New Testament, obedience remains central, but through faith in Jesus Christ, not performance. Jesus told the rich young ruler: *If you want to enter life, keep the commandments* (Matt. 19:17 NIV). Paul emphasized that keeping God's commands was more important than religious rituals: *Circumcision is nothing and uncircumcision is nothing. Keeping God's commands is what counts (1 Cor. 7:19).* He also urged Timothy: *Keep this command without spot or blame until the appearing of our Lord Jesus Christ* (1 Tim. 6:13–14). Believers today are still called to keep Gods commandments, not out of legalism, but by abiding in Christ. They are the framework for godly living.

Keeping by the Spirit

"Keeping" is not done in our own strength. We need supernatural power to remain faithful, especially in a world that pushes us to let go. Jesus gives us the power to keep His commands. He knew His disciples couldn't fulfil their calling without divine help. That's why He said: *You will receive power when the Holy Spirit comes upon you…* (Acts 1:8). By the Holy Spirit, we are empowered to:

- Keep the faith (2 Timothy 4:7)
- Keep a clear conscience (1 Peter 3:16)
- Keep unity (Ephesians 4:3)
- Keep going, even when weary (Galatians 6:9)

The Holy Spirit empowers believers to believe, obey, endure, and stand in a world that challenges all those things.

God also keeps what we entrust to Him. Paul affirmed this truth: *I know whom I have believed and am convinced that He is able to keep what I have entrusted to Him until that day* (2 Tim. 1:12). Even in times of suffering or temptation,

God's keeping power is active: *The Lord is faithful, and He will strengthen you and protect you from the evil one* (2 Thess. 3:3); and *No temptation has overtaken you… But God is faithful. He will not let you be tempted beyond what you can bear…* (1 Cor. 10:13). Ultimately, His promise is to keep us for eternity: *I give them eternal life, and they shall never perish; no one will snatch them out of my hand (John 10:28–29)*. What God places in our care is secured by His power, but we must remain in Christ. When we do, His power to keep flows into every area of our lives.

Power to Remember

Memory is one of God's remarkable gifts to humanity. It enables us to learn, grow, and reflect. Yet as powerful as memory is, forgetfulness is a common human experience, so much so that Scripture repeatedly urges us to remember. From Genesis to Revelation, God continually calls His people to remember: His works, His promises, His commandments, and most importantly, Himself.

Humans tend to forget. Despite our best efforts, most people forget things, appointments, names, keys, and sometimes even the kindness of God. For decades, scientists have studied the human brain to understand how we acquire, store, and retrieve information. Only a few individuals possess what science terms *hyperthymesia*—the rare ability to recall nearly every detail of their lives.

Rieland (2012) reported that there were at least 33 known individuals worldwide with this extraordinary ability. They remember exactly what they thought, felt, and experienced on any given day, after seeing or hearing something only once. Their memory is so strong, it's virtually immune to manipulation. Yet even that ability has its limits. No human can perfectly remember everything without the help of God. Many rely on memory aids, technology, or training, but even these systems occasionally fail.

Most people have what scientists describe as "fluid" memory, we retain information briefly before it's either forgotten or stored in long-term memory, where it gradually fades or becomes harder to retrieve. Sometimes, we forget events almost immediately after they occur.

The story of Joseph, Jacob's favourite son, illustrates this tendency to forget.

Joseph, a God-fearing young man, was wrongly imprisoned after Potiphar's wife falsely accused him. While in prison, he interpreted a dream for Pharaoh's chief cupbearer. After the cupbearer was released and restored to his position, he forgot Joseph's request to mention him to Pharaoh, despite having promised to do so.

Have you ever frantically searched for something you were using just minutes ago? Or left your seat to retrieve an item from another room, only to forget what it was once you got there? Have you ever grilled meat, only to remember it after the smoke alarm went off? These are common human experiences.

Maybe your situation has been even more severe. Have you forgotten to pick up your child or spouse? Or searched the entire house for car keys, only to find them still in the ignition? Or gone to the store for milk and come back with everything except the milk? Most of us have been there.

Let me share an unforgettable personal experience. In 2009, I travelled from the UK to Papua New Guinea on a business trip for a biodiversity conservation partnership. After a 21-hour flight with multiple layovers, I landed in Sydney, Australia. What followed was unexpected.

I had just 90 minutes to transfer to another airport for my connecting flight to Port Moresby. Drowsy and exhausted, I picked up what I *thought* was my hand luggage and boarded the shuttle. At the next security checkpoint, I reached into the bag to grab my laptop, and realized it was missing. I had left it in the overhead bin on the plane.

Panic set in. That laptop held all my work documents and trip data. I asked the staff to help me return to the previous terminal. By God's grace, they agreed. I rushed to the information desk, and thankfully, someone had turned in the laptop. I retrieved it and raced back to the connecting terminal just in time to catch my flight.

But the ordeal wasn't over. In the chaos, I had left my weather coat at the previous terminal. I had no time to return for it. That flight to Port Moresby remains one of the most stressful of my life. I had forgotten—not intentionally, but because I lacked the power to remember.

No created being can fully remember everything deposited in their memory, unless empowered by God. Even the rare individuals with what science calls *hyperthymesia*, the ability to recall nearly every detail of their lives, still depend on God's sustaining power. As Scripture reminds us, Jesus Christ upholds all things by the word of His power (Hebrews 1:3; Colossians 1:17).

For believers, the Holy Spirit living within us gives us access to the divine power to remember. This power isn't merely cognitive, it is spiritual. We are called to:
- Remember who we are in Christ,
- Remember what God has done in our lives,
- Remember His promises and His power, and
- Remember to rely on the Holy Spirit, the Helper, who brings to our remembrance what truly matters (John 14:26).

Power to be Content in Times of Lack and Abundance

Jeff Manion, in his book *Satisfied*, poses a compelling question: *Is there ever a point when we become satisfied with who we are, what we have, and even what we do not have?* It's a question many, Christians included, find difficult to answer. In our consumer-driven, debt-laden, advertisement-saturated culture, contentment is rare.

Discontentment is not new, it's deeply embedded in the human story:
- Satan was not content with his position in heaven, he craved God's throne.
- Adam and Eve were not content with their identity, they wanted to "be like God."
- Adonijah, though a prince, sought to usurp his father David's throne.

Even today, discontentment affects people across every social class and spiritual level.

Modern culture measures well-being through various indices, the Happy Planet Index, Human Development Index, Gross National Happiness, and more. These models focus on things like material wealth, education, social status, and political influence. But they often equate more resources with greater satisfaction. The pressure to meet these standards leaves many feeling inadequate or overwhelmed.

Even economists admit: the earth does not have enough resources to meet every human desire. In the pursuit of "more," many become frustrated, anxious, or even suicidal when their efforts fall short. And Christians are not immune to this pressure.

Some believers assume that lack is always a curse to be broken, often quoting: *The Lord is my shepherd, I shall not want* (Psa. 23:1). But Scripture also shows us that faithful, Spirit-filled believers often experience seasons of lack. God's provision does not always mean abundance—it means *enough*.

Worry stems from trying to use today's resources to solve tomorrow's problems. But God promises daily mercies: *The steadfast love of the Lord never ceases…they are new every morning* (Lam. 3:22–23). *Do not worry about tomorrow… each day has enough trouble of its own* (Matt. 6:34). God provides what we need for each day. He's not trying to teach us to store up for independence from Him, but to live dependent on Him, with gratitude for today's portion.

The Power to Plant and Harvest

Planting is an essential management practice in agriculture, forestry, and ecosystem management. The verb *plant* is also used metaphorically in Scripture to refer to the act of depositing the Word in the mind and heart of an individual. God, the Creator of the earth, designed biological systems that rely on planting, whether by seed, seedling, or vegetative material, to reproduce and multiply. Likewise, animals, birds, insects, and marine species reproduce by producing gametes, their own form of "seeds." In this way, seeds are God's divine method of ensuring the continuity of both physical and spiritual life.

The ability to plant and harvest is not just a physical process but also a spiritual principle deeply embedded in the Bible. The act of planting and harvesting symbolizes the cycles of life, growth, and transformation. Both the physical and spiritual realms rely on this powerful concept, which involves sowing seeds, whether in the soil or in our hearts, and patiently awaiting their harvest.

Growing up in a smallholder farming community, I became intimately familiar with the concepts of planting and harvesting. I often enjoyed my sleep, but I knew that Mum would soon be knocking to marshal us to the field. I wasn't wrong. At 5 a.m., her footsteps echoed, followed by a knock. Each child was assigned a certain number of ridges to make by midday.

By 11 a.m., the tropical sun was fierce, and we were drenched in sweat. We waited for Mum's cue to send our sister home to prepare lunch. But before that came her usual warning: "Anyone who doesn't finish by 12:00 will not eat." We all understood what that meant.

After completing our tasks, we rushed home for lunch and a brief nap, knowing we would return by 2 p.m. to plant. We carried dibber forks, fertilizer, and seed. Each planting session involved a team: one to dig, another to apply fertilizer, and a third to plant and cover the seed. While we were sometimes allowed to choose our preferred tasks, Mum would intervene if disagreements arose.

Planting maize (corn) was more labour-intensive than planting beans, which didn't require fertilizer. To maximize space, we inter-planted maize and beans. Birds, however, often ate freshly planted seeds unless rain fell immediately, masking the planting sites.

Later in life, I witnessed vast fields being planted using tractor-mounted equipment. These mechanical planters replicated our manual tasks, digging, fertilizing, seeding, and covering. Regardless of the method, planting always required energy and effort.

Whether seeds are planted physically, mechanically, or metaphorically, the hope is the same: that they will germinate, grow, and bear fruit. Farmers forget the toil once they see a good harvest. God gave us seed-bearing plants for food, except for the tree of the knowledge of good and evil (Genesis 2:16–17).

God is the original Sower. *Now the LORD God had planted a garden in the east, in Eden* (Genesis 2:8). He created the soil with properties that meet the needs of different seeds, providing the ideal balance of water, nutrients, and air. Seeds planted in unsuitable conditions, such as extreme cold or heat, may remain dormant or perish.

Human beings also plant metaphorical seeds, seeds of faith, encouragement, restoration, compassion, truth, creativity, and more. These seeds enrich lives and make them productive. However, humanity also plants harmful seeds: conflict, corruption, adultery, war, confusion, and destruction. These undermine our role as stewards of God's creation. Metaphorically, God planted the greatest seed, His Son, into the world through the virgin Mary. Through Christ's life, death, and resurrection, we continue to reap a spiritual harvest of souls.

The God who created planting and harvesting knows how laborious these processes are and supplies divine power to accomplish them. When restoring Israel, God declared:

I will bring my people Israel back. They will rebuild ruined cities and live in them. They will plant vineyards and drink their wine... I will plant Israel in their own land, never again to be uprooted... (Amos 9:14–15, NIV).

Rebuilding, planting, and harvesting required divine intervention, especially in the face of opposition, but God's power was sufficient. God also gave Israel specific conditions for fruitful harvests:

- *So, you shall observe My statutes... Then the land will yield its fruit...* (Lev. 25:18–19)
- *He will give rain for the seed you sow...* (Isa. 30:23)
- *There will be peace for the seed... the heavens will give their dew...* (Zech. 8:11–12)
- *Isaac sowed in that land and reaped a hundredfold, and the LORD blessed him* (Gen. 26:12)

These passages emphasize that God controls all the variables in planting, rain, soil, sunshine, and timing. Yet, there were times when poor harvests occurred: *You have sown much, but harvest little...* (Hag. 1:6); and *Ten acres of vineyard will yield only one bath of wine...* (Isa. 5:10). God's favour determined productivity, and His presence ensured success. As Paul noted: I planted, Apollos watered, but God gave the increase (1 Cor. 3:6). Jesus also told the disciples to wait in Jerusalem until they were empowered by the Holy Spirit, assuring them of His divine presence to the ends of the earth. His presence meant continuous access to the power of God.

Disciples plant the seed of the Word, but it is God who brings transformation and produces the fruit of the Spirit. Scripture outlines this pattern:

- *John the Baptist prepared the way* (Matt. 3:3)
- *Jesus commissioned His disciples to heal, deliver, and preach* (Matt. 10:1–8)
- *He instructed them to make disciples of all nations* (Matt. 28:16–20)
- All believers are called to preach the good news (Acts 1:8)

The power to plant and harvest is available to every believer. Whatever God has called you to sow - faith, love, truth, or service - go out and do it. God has equipped each believer with a spiritual toolkit, complete with divine power to meet every need. Whatever your current condition, He has already made provision. If we abide in Christ and He in us, we are guaranteed access to His immeasurable power.

The idea of planting and harvesting is foundational to biblical teaching. In Galatians 6:7–9, Paul reminds us that we will reap what we sow: *Do not be deceived: God cannot be mocked. A man reaps what he sows. Whoever sows to please their flesh, from the flesh will reap destruction; whoever sows to please the Spirit, from the Spirit will reap eternal life (Gal. 6:7–8, NIV)*. This principle applies not only to our actions but also to the attitudes of our hearts. What we plant, whether good or bad, spiritual or worldly, determines the harvest. Every small act, thought, or decision contributes to the seeds we plant in our lives and in the lives of others.

In the story of creation, God planted the Garden of Eden (Gen. 2:8), and from that point forward, the concept of planting and harvesting has been integral to human existence. God is the ultimate source of life and growth. Even though we do the work of planting, it is God who gives the increase. As Jesus said: *I am the vine; you are the branches. If you remain in me and I in you, you will bear much fruit; apart from me you can do nothing* (John 15:5, NIV*)*.

The power to plant and harvest is sustained by God's provision, grace, and guidance. Planting requires careful preparation. The soil must be fertile, and the seeds must be chosen wisely. Likewise, in our spiritual lives, we must tend to the "soil" of our hearts, removing weeds, rocks, and distractions to cultivate fertile ground for growth. As we plant good seeds through prayer, good deeds, and obedience, we invite God's blessings. As Paul wrote: *I planted the seed, Apollos watered it, but God has been making it grow* (1 Cor. 3:6, NIV)

This verse teaches us that while we plant and water, it is ultimately God who causes growth. Our role is to be faithful in planting and trust that God will bring the harvest in His perfect timing.

The harvest—whether of crops, relationships, or spiritual growth, is a time of celebration. It represents the fulfilment of what was once planted and nurtured. In the Bible, the harvest is often described as a time of blessing, reward, and joy. Galatians 6:9 encourages us:

Let us not become weary in doing good, for at the proper time we will reap a harvest if we do not give up. Similarly, Jesus told His disciples: *Do you not say, Four months more and then the harvest? I tell you, open your eyes and look at the fields! They are ripe for harvest* (John 4:35, NIV). God invites us to recognize the spiritual harvest around us, in the people we serve, the ministries we engage in, and the seeds of faith we plant in others.

The power to harvest is rooted in obedience. Harvest is not only the result of human effort; it is also the result of submitting to God's timing and purposes. Even in seasons of drought or delay, God is faithful to bring the harvest at the right time. The Bible speaks about waiting for the harvest: *Be patient, then, brothers and sisters, until the Lord's coming. See how the farmer waits for the land to yield its valuable crop, patiently waiting for the autumn and spring rains* (Jam. 5:7 NIV).

We are called to be patient and to trust God's timing. Whether we are waiting for a spiritual breakthrough, personal growth, or material provision, patience is key. The power to harvest is rooted in faith that God is at work, even when we cannot yet see the results.

The power to plant and harvest is not merely about material wealth or physical crops but is deeply tied to the spiritual harvest we can experience. Every good work done in God's name plants a seed that can grow into something greater. The seeds of faith we sow in others can yield a lasting, spiritual harvest. As 2 Corinthians 9:6 says: *Whoever sows sparingly will also reap sparingly, and whoever sows generously will also reap generously.*

We are called to be generous in every area of life, planting seeds of kindness, faith, love, and good works. As we sow, we trust God to bring about the harvest in His timing and in ways that glorify His name.

The power to plant and harvest reflects the rhythms of life that God has established, rooted in the spiritual and physical principles of sowing and reaping. Whether we are planting seeds of faith, good works, or love, we can trust that God will bring the increase. The key is to remain faithful in planting, patient in waiting, and obedient in the harvest. As we do so, we will see the fruit of our labours and experience the abundance of God's provision.

CHAPTER 9
Accessing the Power of God

What Does it Mean to Access the Power of God?
The phrase, 'accessing the power of God', can mean so many different things depending on the context. For example:

Spiritually, it might mean aligning with divine will or channelling divine power.

Philosophically, it could relate to the idea of accessing higher consciousness or universal truth.

Scientifically or fictionally, it might suggest unlocking immense power, like in sci-fi or myth.

Motivationally, it could be about tapping into your highest potential or divine purpose.

Spiritually, to access the power of God does not mean invoking a name, force, or attempting to control or manipulate His power. Instead, it means aligning ourselves with God so that His power can work through us. It is about surrender, alignment, connection, and becoming a vessel for something far greater than us. We access the power of God by surrendering to it. Like a river flows strongest when it is not dammed, the divine flows through you most freely when you are in alignment. Here is what it truly means in a biblical and practical sense:

Having access to the mighty power of God through the sealing, baptism, indwelling, and infilling of the Holy Spirit at work in us (Eph. 1:13-14; Matt. 3:11; Acts 1:8).

Trusting in God, not ourselves: accessing God's power begins with faith, relying on His strength instead of our own. This is the heart of verses like: *Not by might, nor by power, but by My Spirit, says the Lord of hosts* (Zech. 4:6).

1. Living in obedience, alignment, and surrender to the precept and the purpose of Gods' will: When we live in obedience to God's Word and are led by the Holy Spirit, we become vessels for His power. Jesus said: *If you

remain in Me and My words remain in you, ask whatever you wish, and it will be done for you (John 15:7). The more surrendered we are, the more clearly His power flows through us.

2. Prayer and intimacy with God: Power is accessed in the secret place. When we pray, we are not just asking for help, we're tapping into divine wisdom, strength, and guidance. As James 5:16 says: *The prayer of a righteous person is powerful and effective.* Key practices include prayer but not just speaking, listening, letting go of ego and trusting in divine timing, and seeking to act with love, truth, and compassion, the frequencies of God.

3. Becoming a conduit: You don't need to possess God's power, become a channel for it through:
   - Stillness: Meditative states allow the noise to fall away so divine insight can rise.
   - Obedience to divine nudges: When your intuition whispers something that feels deeper than your own thoughts, listen.
   - Living with integrity: God flows through clean vessels.

1. Boldness in Action: Harnessing God's power also means stepping out in faith-filled action. Like Peter walking on water, he tapped into Jesus' power the moment he *acted* on Jesus' word. When we speak truth, pray for healing, or show love where it's hard, that's God's power in action.

2. Letting faith be the fuel for harnessing the power of God: When faith is more than belief, when it is trust, action, and identity, you begin to move with divine authority. Exercise your faith and the power of God by:
   - Speaking affirmations rooted in scripture or spiritual truth.
   - Acting on faith even when logic says "no."
   - Declaring your life is in divine hands, and living like it's true.

In Short, to access the power of God is to: live by faith and not fear; stay connected to God through prayer and the Word; obey His leading; and let the Holy Spirit empower your words, choices, and actions.

The Power of God is Within Us

A Christian is a temple of the Godhead; therefore, the immeasurable power of Almighty God dwells in him or her and is always accessible. Consider the following:

- Christians have the power to witness for Christ: *But you will receive power when the Holy Spirit comes on you; and you will be my witnesses in Jerusalem and in all Judea and Samaria and to the ends of the earth* (Acts 1: NIV).
- God's power, at work within us, accomplishes great works: *Now all glory to God, who is able, through his mighty power at work within us, to accomplish infinitely more than we might ask or think* (Eph. 3:20 NIV).
- The Kingdom of God involves living by God's power: *For the Kingdom of God is not just a lot of talk; it is living by God's power* (1 Cor. 4:20 NIV).
- We were buried with Christ and raised to life with Him by trusting in God's mighty power: *For you were buried with Christ when you were baptized. And with him you were raised to new life because you trusted the mighty power of God, who raised Christ from the dead.* (Col. 2:12).

The Scriptures demonstrate several power-related characteristics of a Spirit-filled believer.

First, when a believer earnestly seeks fellowship with the Holy Spirit, they are baptized with the Holy Spirit and clothed with His power. A believer is filled with divine power when the Holy Spirit comes upon them. Oh, that we might catch a glimpse of the greatness of this power within us! In fact, the Apostle Paul prayed that the eyes of the Ephesian believers' hearts would be enlightened, so they might confidently know the immeasurable greatness of God's power available to those who believe (Ephesians 1:18–20). God has made the body of the believer a temple of the Godhead through the indwelling Holy Spirit, transforming it into a powerhouse of God.

Second, our new life in Christ is evidence that we have trusted in the same transforming power of God that raised Jesus from the dead and seated Him at the right hand of the Father in the heavenly realms. That same power raised us with

Christ into the newness of life, we are now a new creation in Him.

Third, God uses His mighty power working within us to accomplish far more than our limited understanding, wisdom, or imagination can grasp. His power enables us to do infinitely more than we could ever ask or think (Ephesians 3:20).

Fourth, every subject of the Kingdom of God lives by the power of God. This power is the sole engine of life for the Spirit-filled child of God.

Finally, the Holy Spirit is not only relational, He is activity-oriented. He is not passive. Every believer led by the Spirit manifests God's power through supernatural acts. There is always outward evidence of the inward presence of God. When a believer leads a life devoid of spiritual activity, the Holy Spirit is grieved or restrained. We can, in fact, quench the fire of the Holy Spirit and forfeit His power. God is principled and intentional in how He dispenses His power.

God is both effective and efficient with His resources, including His eternal power. His distribution of power is based on a precise assessment of our tasks. Writing to the Ephesians, Paul said: *"But unto every one of us is given grace according to the measure of the gift of Christ"* (Ephesians 4:7, KJV). God never gives an assignment without providing a precise measure of grace and faith for its execution. Every believer has received a gift of Christ - and with it comes a divine budget of grace and provision. As the Apostle Peter also wrote: *Grace and peace be multiplied to you in the knowledge of God and of Jesus our Lord, as His divine power has given to us all things that pertain to life and godliness, through the knowledge of Him who called us by glory and virtue, by which have been given to us exceedingly great and precious promises, that through these you may be partakers of the divine nature, having escaped the corruption that is in the world through lust"* (2 Peter 1:2–4). Peter emphasizes the importance of knowing God the Father and Jesus Christ, who called us by His glory and virtue. Jesus rescued us from the corruption of this world and grafted us into Himself - the true Vine - so that we might be united with Him. This union has two key implications:

- First, as we believe in Him and in His name, He gives us the power to become sons of God (John 1:12, KJV).

- Second, Jesus Christ has given us all things we need to live a life devoted to Him.

Additionally, the Lord has given us the Holy Spirit, who empowers us to do the will of God. His presence within us ensures that our potential, capabilities, and resources are deployed to accomplish the good works He prepared in advance for us to do (Ephesians 2:10).

Peter makes a distinction between the power to sustain life (the breath of God in us) and the power for godliness (the breath of God *living* through us by the Holy Spirit). Every activity within our life in Christ comes with a guaranteed budget of divine power. That's why Paul could boldly declare, *"I can do all things through Christ who strengthens me"* (Philippians 4:13, NKJV).

The only limitation is our own inability - or sometimes unwillingness - to apply that power to our daily tasks.

Any assignment God gives is potentially achievable, because He never calls without equipping. Throughout the Old Testament, whenever the Spirit of the Lord came upon an individual, there was a visible and powerful manifestation - often through supernatural acts. Similarly, in the New Testament, the apostles and disciples - empowered by the Holy Spirit - were sent to homes, villages, and cities to:

- Heal the sick
- Restore sight to the blind
- Bind the broken-hearted
- Open deaf ears and loosen mute tongues
- Set captives free
- And even raise the dead.

Today, Spirit-filled believers continue to carry out God's work with His power, successfully fulfilling the assignments given to them.

We carry the immeasurable power of God within us, with the potential to accomplish exceedingly abundantly more than we could ever ask or imagine (Eph. 3:20). However, the presence of the Holy Spirit and His power in us does not mean that this power automatically accomplishes our God-given tasks.

The extent to which we experience and utilize this divine power depends on our willingness to walk in righteousness under the leadership of the Holy Spirit. This requires our full cooperation, surrender, and obedience. So, let me ask you: To what extent are you harnessing the power of God?

The Eternal Power of God is Often Underutilized - or Not Utilized At All

There are moments when I retreat to solitary places to reflect on the events of my life. At times, I ask myself why some of the things the Lord has promised in His Word have not yet manifested in my life, despite the assurance that I have been adopted as a child of God. The Word of God assures me that the moment I gave my life to the Lord Jesus Christ, He sealed me with the Holy Spirit. I know that I am baptized and filled with the Spirit. And yet, I also know I have not fully accessed the eternal power of God within me.

There is a noticeable gap between the quality and quantity of power God has made available to me and what I have actually used. For the sake of satisfying my curiosity, allow me to ask you a few questions: Have you ever experienced the full power of God at work in your life? Do you believe that the same power that raised Jesus Christ from the dead and seated Him at the right hand of the Father is also at work in you? Do you share Paul's confidence when he says, *I can do all things through Christ who strengthens me* (Philip. 4:13, NKJV)? Would you confidently say you are doing everything worthy of your calling?

If your answer is "Yes" to all or some of these questions—congratulations! You are doing well. If your response is "No," don't worry. You are not alone, and the Lord is both willing and delighted to assist you. Perhaps you are uncertain whether what you have experienced is truly the power of God at work in your life. If so, you are a perfect candidate for His mercy and grace.

Why Is the Power of God Underutilized?

Every genuinely saved Christian is indwelt by the Holy Spirit and carries the eternal power of God. However, very few believers utilize this power to any significant degree. In fact, many rarely, if ever, tap into it. Let's explore a few reasons why this might be the case:

a. Insufficient Instruction

A believer may be aware of God's power within them but lack the proper instruction to utilize it. A clear example is found in Matthew 17:14-21, where Jesus' disciples failed to heal a demon-possessed boy, despite being empowered by Christ.

Was there something wrong with the power Jesus gave them? Not at all! When Jesus healed the boy, He later explained to the disciples that their failure was due to unbelief and a lack of prayer and fasting, which were necessary in that situation. They eventually learned what kind of faith and spiritual discipline was required. Their lack of instruction limited the manifestation of God's power.

b. Wrong Teaching

Some Christians have been taught that the power of the Holy Spirit, so vividly displayed in the early Church, ceased with that generation. As a result, many believers today have little or no expectation of experiencing that same power. False doctrines or traditions have quenched their faith, leaving them spiritually passive.

c. Fear or Reluctance to Act

Other Christians know they have God's power, but they are reluctant to step out in faith. Life challenges - illness, marital struggles, rebellious children - can seem overwhelming. In such times, instead of invoking the power of God, believers often feel helpless.

Have you ever faced a situation where you felt powerless to act? Are you shy or afraid to exercise the power of God in public? Do you believe you need divine boldness to share the Gospel or pray for the sick? Yes, you do, and the power of God is available for these very moments.

d. Restrictive Church Culture

In some churches, traditions or structures restrict the flow of the Holy Spirit.

When programmes are designed to cater solely to cultural norms or time constraints, the gifts of the Spirit - prophecy, healing, words of knowledge, etc. - are suppressed or ignored. Such environments can condition believers to live a life devoid of supernatural power, which is far from the life God intends for His children.

There is nothing more disheartening than knowing the eternal power of God resides in you, and yet, you cannot access or use it to fuel a godly life. This brings to mind a memorable event from the late 1990s, when I was teaching at the Natural Resources Development College in Zambia.

Twenty-six members of staff were treated to a rare trip to one of the world's great wonders. By 5 a.m., we were packed into a 27-seater minibus. The early morning was cool and dark, but we travelled smoothly. By sunrise, we had left the city behind. After a three-and-a-half-hour journey, we reached our destination, the breathtaking Kariba North Bank hydroelectric power station on the Zambezi River.

We were awestruck by the massive dam wall and the vast reservoir. We toured the dam, walked across the 120-meter-high wall, and entered the power generation room with its four giant turbines and the control centre. The station generated 600 megawatts of electricity, powering cities and industries across Zambia.

But just a few hundred meters away, hundreds of homes had no electricity. Massive transformers and high-voltage lines passed directly overhead. Locals could hear the loud hum of power, but they lived in darkness. At night, they lit candles, lanterns, or improvised lights. That sight stayed with me - it was a stark image of being so close to power yet living without it.

So, how do we access and use God's Power? That is the crucial question. Are we like those homes - so close to the source, yet disconnected? As believers, we have been connected to the greatest power source in existence - the very power that raised Christ from the dead. But connection alone is not enough; we must draw from that power and let it flow through us.

God has not only provided the power - we must also be willing vessels, properly instructed, full of faith, and unafraid to act. We must remove the blocks: false teaching, fear, cultural restraints, and passivity. So, ask yourself: Am I truly walking in the power God has given me? What would change in my life if I fully yielded to the Holy Spirit? How can I begin today to draw from the unlimited power of God within me?

How Can We Access the Power of God?

While God upholds all things by the word of His power (Heb. 1:3), a believer also needs this power to carry out the good works that God prepared in advance for them to do (Eph. 2:10). This unique power, which fuels all godly functions in a believer's life, only becomes available and active when certain spiritual conditions are met.

The life of any being created in the image of God operates somewhere along a spiritual continuum - ranging from a spiritually dead state, completely devoid of the presence and activity of the Holy Spirit, to that of a redeemed person, living with the fullness and active operation of the Spirit. The Holy Spirit is the source, distributor, and regulator of God's power in the life of a believer. Harnessing this power involves creating conditions in one's life that open and regulate the access valve to God's power, conditions that both welcome and govern the operation of the Holy Spirit.

This section briefly outlines how a disciple of Christ can access the power of God in practical and spiritual terms.

Salvation Initiates the Flow of the Power of God

At the moment of salvation, the Holy Spirit takes residence within the believer, initiating the flow of divine power. This power is not abstract, it is the very same power that raised Christ from the dead (Rom. 8:11). From that point on, the believer is equipped to live a godly life, fulfil divine assignments, and walk in supernatural authority. The Spirit enters the believer's life, not only as a seal of redemption but as a source of power for transformation, obedience, and mission. He indwells us, making us vessels through which His power can flow and operate.

Any human being who is not adopted as a child of God through Jesus Christ has no access to the eternal power of God. While God sustains all His creatures by the word of His power, the power to live a life devoted to Him is exclusively available to those who accept Jesus Christ as their personal Lord and Saviour and believe in His name. In his letter to the saints in Ephesus, Paul distinguishes between two categories of people: *As for you, you were dead in transgressions and sins, in which you used to live when you followed the ways of this world and of the ruler of the kingdom of the air, the spirit who is now at work in those who are disobedient. All of us also lived among them at one time, gratifying the cravings of our flesh... But because of His great love for us, God, who is rich in mercy, made us alive with Christ even when we were dead in transgressions, it is by grace you have been saved* (Eph. 2:1–5).

The first category includes those who are:

- *Spiritually dead* – their spirits are disconnected from the Holy Spirit and instead aligned with the spirit of the ruler of the kingdom of the air.
- *Dead in transgressions and sins* – unresponsive to the Spirit of God, deeply rooted in rebellion and violations of God's law, and living in personal offense against God.
- *Followers of the ways of the world and the prince of the world* – shaped by worldly desires and spiritual disobedience.

These are people without God, disconnected from the Holy Spirit and therefore without access to the power of God.

The second category includes those whom God has lovingly and mercifully saved from sin and spiritual death by raising them with Christ. They are saved by grace through faith in Jesus Christ. These believers are:

- *Sealed by the Holy Spirit*, with the potential to be baptized and filled with the Spirit as He leads.
- *Positioned for increasing manifestations of God's power*, which grows as the Holy Spirit works in them, and their faith matures.

The work of the Holy Spirit in the life of a believer is like an aperture - a small opening that allows light to shine through. The larger the opening, the more intense and brighter the light. Similarly, the Holy Spirit has the potential to release the full measure of God's power assigned to your calling. However, the rate of flow and degree of manifestation is directly related to how much you yield and cooperate with the Spirit's work. You are the gatekeeper of the manifestation of God's power in your life.

Salvation is the foundational stage in accessing and walking in the power of God. There must be a transformation - from the kingdom of darkness, where the spirit of sin and death governs the lives of worldly people, to the kingdom of light, where the saved are led by the Spirit of life.

Anyone who desires to access and operate in the power of God must first be saved through the death and resurrection of Jesus Christ. Don't forfeit the power of God because you are not saved. If you have not yet received Jesus Christ as your Lord and Saviour, invite Him into your life today, and you will begin to experience the power of God at work in you.

Develop and Nurture Your Union With Jesus Christ

Accessing and operating in the power of God requires a strong, intimate relationship with Jesus Christ. The Lord likened His ideal relationship with believers to the organic connection that exists between a vine and its branches. Emphasizing this union, Jesus said: *I am the true vine; you are the branches. If you remain in me and I in you, you will bear much fruit; apart from me you can do nothing* (John 15:5, NIV). Jesus highlights two key truths: (1) the organic union between the vine and the branches, and (2) the condition for bearing much fruit, remaining in Him, and He in us.

In nature, a vine is permanently joined to its branches until the plant dies, the branch dries and falls off, or it is trimmed. The term grafting has often been used to symbolize what happens when a believer is united with Christ. Grafting is a horticultural technique where tissues from two plants (the rootstock and the scion) are joined together so they grow as one. When a branch is grafted into a vine, their tissues merge, forming a shared vascular system, xylem and phloem, to transport water, nutrients, and food throughout the plant. This union allows:

- Nutrients and water to flow from the soil to the branch,
- Food and hormones to circulate throughout the plant, and
- Leaves and fruit to grow in optimal conditions where they can access light and space.

Paul uses this same image in Romans to describe the union between saved Gentiles and Christ: *But if some of the branches were broken off, and you, although a wild olive shoot, were grafted in among the others and now share in the nourishing root of the olive tree...* (Romans 11:17, NKJV). Here, Paul explains that when the unproductive branches (rebellious Israelites) were broken off, Gentiles who accepted the gospel were grafted into the nourishing root, Christ Himself. From Jesus' vine-and-branch analogy, we learn three key truths: salvation joins us to Christ; this union is meant to be sustained and continuous; and fruitfulness is impossible without abiding in Him.

The life of a branch entirely depends on its connection to the vine, from its formation to its fruit-bearing, and eventually to its end. There is no moment in the life of a branch when it can survive without the vine. If we desire to experience the full measure of God's power and grace:

- We must be fully committed to our union with Christ.
- We must abide (live) in Him, and He in us.
- We must remain consistently connected for His power to flow through us continuously.

God does not want brief visits or hurried moments in His presence. He longs for deep, quality fellowship with His children. As we dwell in Him daily, His life and power flow through us, producing lasting fruit and transforming us into effective vessels for His glory.

If you are a parent with children and you love them as you should, you understand the joy of having your children around you. Each time I have visited or spoken with my mother, she has often said, "I wish I could have all my children around me every day, just to look at them. Money doesn't matter. I just want to be with you." Despite her flaws, my mother has always had a deep desire to be with us.

God, the architect of parental love, has an even deeper and unfailing desire to always be with us. As a loving Father, He wants us to dwell in His presence. Jesus Christ loves you so much that He longs to be with you, even in your weakness. This union between Christ and the believer is the bedrock of our relationship with God. A fruitful vine requires the cooperation of both the vine and the branch.

The Lord has invested heavily in our union with Him. Paul writes to the saints in Ephesus that, in union with Christ:

- God has blessed us with every spiritual blessing in the heavenly realms (Eph. 1:3 ERV).
- He chose us in Him before the foundation of the world, to be holy and blameless before Him in love (Eph. 1:4 NKJV).
- He predestined us to be adopted as His children through Jesus Christ (Eph. 1:5 NKJV).
- He gave us His grace (Eph. 1:6 NKJV).
- We have redemption through His blood and the forgiveness of sins (Eph. 1:7 NKJV).
- He purposed to gather in one all things in Christ, in heaven and on earth (Eph. 1:10 NKJV).
- We have obtained an inheritance, being predestined according to His will (Eph. 1:11 NKJV).
- We trusted in Him after hearing the word of truth, the gospel of our salvation, and were sealed with the Holy Spirit of promise (Eph. 1:13 NKJV).

Paul emphasizes what God has done for us and what we have received through our union with Christ. One major outcome of these blessings is that they commit God to make His power available to us, if we remain within the boundaries of our relationship with Him. God cannot pour out acts of love upon us without also making provision for the release of His power to those who abide in Him.

To develop a sustained union with Christ means to live in continuous awareness of His presence, because everything within you depends on Him. Many believers only experience brief moments of His presence throughout the day. But Christ must not just visit your life, He must live in and through you if His breath is in you. Just as you breathe in and out continuously, your union with Christ should be sustained by ongoing communion with the Lord. If you have an organic union with Christ, how strong is it? What are you doing to sustain it?

Fellowship With the Holy Spirit Guarantees Access to the Power of God

Children of God who experience the full manifestation of God's power in their lives have discovered the secret: giving the Holy Spirit total freedom to operate in their lives as He wills. No creation of God can function according to His plan and purpose unless the Holy Spirit provides the power for its activities. Look at it this way: every national government on earth has a ministry or department responsible for power supply in the country.

Despite the diversity of energy sources (electricity, fossil fuels, biofuels, and wood fuel such as charcoal and firewood), the government is obligated to ensure that households, communities, and organizations have access to energy. This concept of providing power for daily life originates from God. In fact, assigning a specific body to oversee power distribution mirrors God's divine organizational structure for spiritual power.

God is the source of all power. But within the Trinity, the Spirit of Yahweh is Yahweh's active presence and power (Bernard, 2005). The Holy Spirit is the power of God driving all divine activity, including the creation and sustenance of the universe and all that is within it. For example:

- During the creation, *the Spirit of God was hovering over the waters* (Gen. 1:2, NIV).
- The psalmist said: *When you send your Spirit, they are created, and you renew the face of the earth* (Psa. 104:30).

- Job declared, *The Spirit of God has made me, and the breath of the Almighty gives me life* (Job 33:4).
- In Genesis, *The LORD God formed man from the dust of the ground and breathed into his nostrils the breath of life, and the man became a living being* (Gen. 2:7).

The power of the Holy Spirit was actively at work in the creation of living beings. When God conceives a creature in His mind, the Word gives it form and specification, and the Holy Spirit brings it into being.

All activities, whether in heaven or on earth, depend on the power of the Holy Spirit to come to pass. Nothing comes into existence apart from His operation. Even the birth of Jesus Christ was an act of the Holy Spirit's power. The angel told Mary: *The Holy Spirit will come upon you, and the power of the Highest will overshadow you* (Luke 1:35 NKJV). Although the process of Christ's conception remains a mystery, it was through the Holy Spirit that our Redeemer was united with creation. The more we yield to the Spirit of God, the more His power is released in and through us, for creation, renewal, transformation, and fruitfulness.

a. The Holy Spirit Anointed Jesus Christ for His Ministry on Earth

Jesus Christ did nothing without the power of the Holy Spirit. At His baptism, as Jesus prayed, *heaven was opened and the Holy Spirit descended on Him in bodily form like a dove* (Luke 3:21–22 NIV). From that moment, He was filled with the Holy Spirit, who then led Him into the wilderness to be tempted by the devil. It was the power of the Spirit that enabled Him to overcome the enemy.

Throughout His life and ministry, the Holy Spirit provided Jesus with the power to fulfil His divine mission. The author of Acts writes: *God anointed Jesus of Nazareth with the Holy Spirit and with power, and He went about doing good and healing all who were oppressed by the devil, because God was with Him* (Acts 10:38, NKJV). This clearly shows that the Spirit of God empowered Jesus for service.

Despite His divine status as the Son of God, Jesus still needed the anointing of the Holy Spirit to accomplish His earthly assignment. The success of His three-year ministry reflects His complete dependence on the Spirit's power. He honoured the office of the Holy Spirit and taught us to do the same. Jesus invites us to abide in Him so we can continue His works, and do even greater things, as we follow the leading of the Holy Spirit. By design, nothing is done in the kingdom of God without the involvement of the Holy Spirit and His power.

b. God's Children Need the Holy Spirit to Accomplish Their Tasks

Paul blessed the believers in Rome, praying that they would *abound in hope by the power of the Holy Spirit* (Rom. 15:13). The Holy Spirit is God's essence and action in His sphere, including the universe - performing miracles, guiding people, speaking through them, bestowing spiritual gifts, dwelling in believers, and empowering them for service.

Those who follow Christ - indwelt, governed, and led by the Holy Spirit - live lives that honour and please God. Even the Church must submit to the leadership of the Holy Spirit in its life and ministry. The fellowship of believers can manifest the power of God through prophecy, teaching, apostleship, pastoral work, evangelism, leadership, helps, administration, giving, speaking and interpreting tongues, and other good works, but only if the Holy Spirit is given total freedom to operate as He wills.

Many churches struggle to strike a balance between organizing their activities and giving the Holy Spirit room to express Himself freely. This raises a vital question: What does it really mean to give the Holy Spirit room to work in your life and in the Church?

The key to living according to God's plan, purpose, and will is having the Holy Spirit actively dwelling and working in you. In the Old Testament, the Holy Spirit would come upon individuals for specific assignments. But God's desire, fulfilled through Christ, is for the Holy Spirit to dwell permanently in us.

Jesus Christ Himself was full of the Holy Spirit, who led Him to fulfil His purpose. Being filled with the Spirit means laying down all our defences and allowing Him unlimited access to every area of our lives. It also means being ready to receive and obey whatever instructions He gives.

If God, the Holy Trinity, recognizes, values, respects, and works through the power of the Holy Spirit to fulfil His will, and if we can do nothing apart from abiding in Christ and being filled with the Spirit, then we must obey. The Holy Spirit is the very presence, power, and essence of God at work in the lives of believers.

If the Holy Spirit is so critical in the life of a believer, why is He often neglected? Why is He not as prominent as He should be in the lives of many believers and churches? Straus (2004) observed that we are living in an era in which *a religion that has none of the miracles or supernaturalism is easier to accept than one that demands supernaturalism. A regenerated man makes no effort to explain the miracles recorded in the Bible.*

While signs, miracles, and wonders performed by Jesus and His disciples served as powerful tools to draw people to salvation, many churches today struggle to follow Christ's example. We often pray for revival, but what has gone wrong? Although I do not claim to know all the challenges facing the Body of Christ, I can highlight a few:

1. Lack of Personal Knowledge of the Holy Spirit

Many believers don't fully understand who the Holy Spirit is or how He works. As noted by CBN.com, adult Christians often act as though the Holy Spirit is *hiding in the church cellar*. They may know about Him but not know Him personally, nor recognize Him as fully God, just like the Father and the Son. When they read the Bible, they're surprised to discover that the Holy Spirit was present from the very beginning: *The Spirit of God was moving over the surface of the waters* Genesis 1:2. In fact, there are over 100 references to the Holy Spirit throughout the Old and New Testaments. How close are you to the Holy Spirit?

2. Lifestyle Conflicts with the Spirit's Presence

Some believers struggle to maintain deep fellowship with the Holy Spirit because of choices or lifestyles that conflict with His holiness. They feel unworthy, often disqualifying themselves from intimacy with the Spirit, believing their flaws make them unacceptable to a divine being so pure.

3. Perceived Cost of Walking with the Spirit

There are those who understand what it means to walk with the Holy Spirit, but believe it's too demanding. They worry about what they would have to give up and are unsure if the transformation is worth the cost.

4. Overloaded Lives and Misplaced Priorities

Many believers are simply too busy. They struggle to integrate a meaningful relationship with the Holy Spirit into their fast-paced lives. Instead of centring life around God and allowing work, ministry, and relationships to flow from that centre, their relationship with the Spirit is reduced to a side note, an "appendage" to their "normal life." Placing the Holy Spirit in His rightful place in our lives, not as an afterthought but as the source of direction, power, and presence, will enable us to fulfil our God-given purpose.

a. The Spirit of God Dwells and Works in a Believer

The Spirit of God plays a pivotal role in the life of a person both before and after salvation. God has made provision for believers to be sealed, filled, and baptized with (or in) the Holy Spirit. The Holy Spirit is actively involved in every stage of the believer's journey, from choosing God's children before the foundation of the world, to preparing their hearts for salvation, conveying the good news, and enacting it within them.

The Spirit of God, who indwells believers, is the means by which they are incorporated into the body of Christ and empowered to live righteously. Every person who believes in Jesus and accepts His saving grace receives the Holy Spirit, along with the power to fulfil the righteous requirements of the law. The same Spirit who gives believers spiritual birth, as Jesus said, *unless one is born of water and the Spirit, he cannot enter the kingdom of God* (John 3:5, NKJV), now comes to dwell within them under the new covenant in Christ.

Every believer who has received the power (right) to become a child of God has also been sealed with the Holy Spirit. Paul confirms this truth in his letter to the Ephesians: *In Him you also trusted, after you heard the word of truth, the gospel of your salvation; in whom also, having believed, you were sealed with the Holy Spirit of promise, who is the guarantee of our inheritance until the redemption of the purchased possession, to the praise of His glory* (Eph. 1:13–14, NKJV). The seal or stamp of the Holy Spirit is God's mark of ownership, a pledge of protection and a guarantee of our inheritance until the full redemption of His purchased people. Child of God, you have been sealed with the Holy Spirit.

b. The Holy Spirit Regenerates, Justifies and Sanctifies Believers

The Holy Spirit plays a vital role in the believer's spiritual journey, from regeneration and justification to sanctification and empowerment for service through Spirit baptism. Each phase reveals a different facet of God's redemptive plan, grounded in His love, grace, and eternal purpose for His people.

Regeneration: The New Birth

Regeneration is the act of God by which He imparts new spiritual life to the believer, making them a new creation in Christ. This transformation is solely the work of the Holy Spirit, who convicts of sin and enables repentance and faith. He imparts God's nature on believers through faith enabling them to partake of His divine nature (2 Pet. 1:4). As J.I. Packer notes, regeneration is birth; sanctification is growth.

A regenerated person is a new creation in Christ, beginning a transformed life marked by new desires, appetites, ideals, and goals. With this new birth comes a fresh source of power and a new pattern of living. Regeneration is an instantaneous work of the Holy Spirit that occurs at the moment of salvation, when He enters the believer. The Holy Spirit empowers the regenerated believer to obey God and grow in His grace.

Justification by God, Applied Through the Holy Spirit

According to classic Christian doctrine, especially in Protestant theology, justification is a legal declaration by God (the Father) that a sinner is righteous, based on the atoning work of Jesus Christ. A follower of Christ is justified by God the Father, the ultimate judge (Rom. 3:30), through the blood of Jesus (Rom.

5:9), by the grace of God (Rom. 3:24), and by the work of the Holy Spirit (1 Cor. 6:11). While the Holy Spirit is not the source of justification, He acts as the agent who applies it, regenerating the heart and enabling faith, which is the means through which justification is received.

Since we are all guilty and condemned sinners, we need forgiveness and justification to enter the kingdom of God. When God justifies people, He gives a 'not guilty' verdict to any and all who accept to be washed by the blood of Jesus as their only hope for salvation.

Through justification a person becomes righteous by the work of the Holy Spirit. Bernard (2005) considers justification as an "objective standing" in God's sight and a "subjective transformation" based on the work of the Holy Spirit. A justified person is counted righteous by legal reckoning even though he/she is not righteous in his/her heart and conduct. Martin Luther refers to such people as "simultaneously righteous and sinful." This changes the position of a believing sinner before God, who has declared them righteous and accepted them, with the guilt and penalty of sin put away forever.

In addition to regeneration and justification, the Holy Spirit sanctifies the believer. Sanctification is an act of God by which He sets apart a person, place, or object for Himself to accomplish His purpose in the world. For example, God sanctified the Sabbath day (Gen. 2:3), a building and its contents (Exod. 39:44), a house (Exod. 19:23), a mountain (Exod. 19:23), and the prophet Jeremiah (Jer. 1:5). Jesus also sanctified Himself, saying: *For them I sanctify myself, that they too may be truly sanctified* (John 17:19). Likewise, every child of God is sanctified through a collaborative process between the believer and God.

Sanctification is a state predetermined for believers, into which they are called by grace, and which they experience as they live out their Christian life. Child of God, the Holy Spirit lives in you. He has set you apart for His divine purpose, to fulfil God's perfect will. And He absolutely has a plan for you.

God sanctifies at different stages throughout a person's life. First, there is preparatory sanctification, which occurs even before birth, according to God's foreknowledge. Jeremiah records that the word of the Lord came to him, saying: *Before I formed you in the womb I knew you, before you were born I set you apart; I appointed you as a prophet to the nations* (Jer. 1:5). God assures Jeremiah that He had already completed the process of choosing, consecrating, and appointing him as a prophet before forming him in the womb.

This shows that before Jeremiah was born, before he became a conscious follower of God, he was elected according to the foreknowledge of God the Father. This implies that God had your calling in mind as He intricately formed your body in your mother's womb. Although your fallen nature and life circumstances may obscure your real identity - your gifts, calling, and potential - your Creator knows the substance you are made of. Jeremiah saw only his limitations: youth and inexperience. But God, who made him, also had the power to remove those obstacles and reveal his real identity and abilities according to His divine design.

Preparatory sanctification is the initial, sovereign work of God that precedes any personal experience or choice. Whatever God calls you to do is not based on coincidence or your circumstances, it's based on His careful, divine planning. All three persons of the Godhead are involved in this process, and the Holy Spirit enacts it by His power.

Later, Jeremiah entered another phase of sanctification, positional sanctification, when God officially called him to serve as a prophet. At this stage, the Holy Spirit set him apart to activate and fulfil his divine appointment. God the Father revealed His plan to Jeremiah and affirmed that, from that moment, he would be consecrated as God's possession and servant. In the life of every believer, positional sanctification takes place at the moment of regeneration, when the Holy Spirit enters the believer and sets them apart for God's purposes.

Adam was created in the image and likeness of God, and he was God's possession by creative right. Isaiah also records God's declaration of ownership over His people, writing, "I provide water in the desert and streams in the wasteland to give drink to my people, my chosen, the people I formed for myself"

(Isaiah 43:20-21, NIV). You are God's child, and He takes pride in you as His creation.

All three persons of the Godhead are involved in the positional sanctification of a believer: the blood of Jesus (Heb. 13:12) and the offering of His body (Heb. 10:10) sanctify believers; God the Father calls, sanctifies, and preserves believers in Jesus Christ (Jude 1:1); and believers are washed, sanctified, and justified in the name of the Lord Jesus Christ and by the Spirit of our God (1 Cor. 6:11).

Sanctification before birth and at the time of regeneration or activating your calling is a sovereign act of God. However, practical sanctification, which builds piety and true holiness in your life, is your responsibility. Some believers use God's sovereign acts of sanctification as an excuse for not maintaining their personal sanctification. Every child of God must commit to a disciplined life devoted to Christ and fellowship with the Holy Spirit. The Word of God, prayer and fasting, active fellowship with believers, walking in the Spirit, and surrendering your will to God are activities that plug into the sanctifying power of the Holy Spirit. The Holy Spirit's power works in the regeneration, justification, and sanctification of a believer. And the Holy Spirit abides in the believer forever.

In the life of a believer, baptism with, in, or by the Holy Spirit takes place when he or she is immersed in the Spirit. Baptism in the Spirit confers power to do the good works that God prepared for you in advance according to His will, plan, and purpose.

b. Baptism With, in or by the Holy Spirit

While this section does not seek to explore all the divisive theories surrounding the baptism with, in, or by the Holy Spirit, it highlights key aspects of this divine work and its relevance to the life of a believer in Christ.

There are two main interpretations of this baptism. The first group of Christians believes in the Theory of Subsequent Experience: that believers receive the Holy Spirit at salvation when they accept Jesus Christ as Lord and Savior. At that moment, God places His seal of ownership on the believer, pledges His protection, and guarantees an inheritance until the final redemption.

This view also holds that baptism in the Holy Spirit is a second and distinct experience that occurs after salvation. This interpretation suggests that receiving the Holy Spirit at conversion is different from the baptism with the Spirit, which comes later. Proponents believe that every follower of Christ must experience both. This perspective is supported by the experience of the disciples, who first received the Holy Spirit when Christ breathed on them (John 20:22).

When Jesus first called the disciples to be fishers of men, the Holy Spirit was with them, but not in them. The Spirit came upon them for service, but He did not dwell within them. Jesus addressed this distinction when He said, *I will pray to the Father, and He will give you another Helper, that He may abide with you forever, the Spirit of truth. The world cannot receive Him, because it neither sees Him nor knows Him. But you know Him, for He lives with you and will be in you* (John 14:16–17).

In the days between Jesus' crucifixion and resurrection, the disciples' faith faltered, and they deserted Him. They lacked the indwelling presence of the Holy Spirit to anchor their faith. On the evening of His resurrection, Jesus breathed on them and said, *Receive the Holy Spirit* (John 20:22). Many view this as the moment the Holy Spirit began to dwell in them, empowering them for personal holiness, justification, and sanctification.

Still, this was not the baptism of the Holy Spirit. After this event, Jesus instructed them to wait in Jerusalem until they were baptized with the Holy Spirit (Acts 1:4–5). This promise was fulfilled at Pentecost, when the disciples, along with women (including Jesus' mother) and His brothers, were filled with the Spirit and spoke in tongues as the Spirit gave them utterance (Acts 2:1–4). This baptism empowered them to carry out the Great Commission. Therefore, breathing the Spirit upon the disciples and baptism in the Spirit are viewed as separate, non-overlapping events.

The second interpretation is that every believer is baptized with the Holy Spirit once, at the moment of salvation. While this group agrees that believers can have many subsequent experiences with the Holy Spirit, they do not equate these with baptism. Many who hold this view see the idea of a second baptism accompanied by speaking in tongues as a misinterpretation or misapplication of the biblical text.

Some commentators note that the two-stage model of Spirit baptism can unintentionally divide the Church into two groups: those who are saved and have received the Spirit, and those who have also received a post-salvation baptism with the Spirit. This has the potential to create a sense of spiritual hierarchy or inequality among believers.

Are you now wondering whether you have been baptised with the Holy Spirit or not? Let us consider some key verses on the baptism of the Holy Spirit.

- *For John truly baptized with water, but you shall be baptized with the Holy Spirit not many days from now* (Acts 1:5 NKJV)
- *I baptize you with water for repentance. But after me comes one who is more powerful than I, whose sandals I am not worthy to carry. He will baptize you with the Holy Spirit and fire* (Matt. 3:11 NIV)
- *I baptize you with water; but He will baptize you with the Holy Spirit* (Mark 1:8 NIV)
- *John answered and said to them all, 'As for me, I baptize you with water; but One is coming who is mightier than I, and I am not fit to untie the thong of His sandals; He will baptize you with the Holy Spirit and fire* (Luke 3:16 NKJV)
- *And I will pray the Father, and He will give you another Helper, that He may abide with you forever* (John 14:16 (NKJV)
- *And I knew him not: but he that sent me to baptize with water, the same said unto me, Upon whom you shall see the Spirit descending, and remaining on him, the same is he who baptizes with the Holy Spirit* (John 1:33 NKJV)
- *Then remembered I the word of the Lord, how he said, John indeed baptized with water; but you shall be baptized with the Holy Spirit* (Acts 11:16 NKJV)

The Scriptures above bring out several salient features of the baptism with the

Holy Spirit. John the Baptist, the apostles (John, Mark, Luke and Matthew), Jesus Christ (Acts 11:16; John 1:33; Mark 1:8; Matt. 3:11) and other servants of God affirm the baptism with, in or by the Holy Spirit. All three persons of the Trinity are involved in the baptism with the Holy Spirit: The Father sent the Spirit upon Jesus after His water baptism in the Jordan; Jesus baptizes His followers with the Holy Spirit; and the Holy Spirit Himself indwells believers. The author of the Acts of the Apostles said: *Therefore, being exalted to the right hand of God, and having received from the Father the promise of the Holy Spirit, He poured out this which you now see and hear* (Acts 2:33). Baptism with the Holy Spirit started with believers receiving the Spirit in the upper room in Jerusalem on the day of Pentecost and that gave birth to the Church.

Every child of God is baptized with the Holy Spirit: "For by one Spirit we were all baptized into one body—whether Jews or Greeks, whether slaves or free, and have all been made to drink into one Spirit" (1 Cor. 12:13, NKJV). The Holy Spirit incorporates believers into the body of Christ and unites them with one another.

When a believer receives the Holy Spirit at salvation, he or she is immersed in the Spirit and His power. This moment of Spirit baptism occurs simultaneously with conversion and marks the beginning of a life led by the Spirit (cf. Rom. 8:14–16).

The presence of the Holy Spirit within us is the assurance that we belong to Christ. Since all Christians receive the Holy Spirit at the moment of conversion, in that sense, all believers have been baptized in the Holy Spirit. This means they are truly saved and have everything they need to live godly and holy lives. This understanding suggests that Spirit baptism may not always be accompanied by a dramatic or experiential event but is rather the spiritual reality of being united with Christ. This is one of the points of contention among charismatics, who often view speaking in tongues as the initial evidence of baptism in the Holy Spirit. In contrast, others believe that the tongues spoken on the Day of Pentecost were specifically intended to proclaim the gospel to the diverse crowd gathered in

Jerusalem. Each person heard the message in their own native language, suggesting a focus on communication rather than a universal sign for Spirit baptism.

So, where do these two perspectives on Spirit baptism leave us today? There are important lessons we can learn from both perspectives.

First, the baptism of the Holy Spirit is for all believers. Child of God, if you have received the Lord Jesus as your Savior, the Holy Spirit dwells in you.

Second, even those who dispute the belief in two separate acts of receiving the Holy Spirit do not deny that a believer may have additional experiences with the Holy Spirit after conversion, experiences that, while meaningful, are distinct from the baptism of the Spirit.

Third, the timing of Spirit baptism varies throughout the biblical narrative, making it difficult to prescribe a strict sequence. Some received the Spirit before, during, or after water baptism. This diversity reflects God's sovereign work, which may not always follow a predictable pattern.

As one theologian wisely cautions: "We must not make the tragic mistake of teaching the experience of the apostles, but rather we must experience the teaching of the apostles." Since the book of Acts is a historical narrative, its events describe a unique period of spiritual transition rather than lay down a universal blueprint for all believers.

a. Be Filled and Led by the Holy Spirit

It is God's will and command that every believer be filled with the Holy Spirit: "Be filled with the Spirit" (Eph. 5:18). After His water baptism, Jesus Christ was full of the Holy Spirit. Throughout history, believers have continually asked God to fill them with the Spirit.

But what does it mean to be filled with the Holy Spirit? It means yielding every part of one's life to the Spirit, allowing Him to fully manifest His presence and power. The Holy Spirit is not a substance like water or air that can be divided or measured. For instance, you can pour out five litres of water and keep three litres aside, or fill a container with a measured volume of air. But the Holy Spirit, being a divine person, is indivisible. He is either present in you or not.

However, the extent of His influence in a believer's life depends on how much control we surrender to Him. Being filled with the Spirit means giving Him full access to guide, empower, and transform us. The more we yield to His leadership, the more evident His power and direction become in our lives. A Spirit-filled believer is one who is fully submitted to the Spirit's will and authority.

Believers, and the Church, are warned not to grieve or quench the Holy Spirit. While the Spirit works in and through us, resisting His voice or ignoring His prompting grieves Him and may ultimately stifle His activity. Paul warned the Thessalonian church: *Do not quench the Spirit. Do not despise prophecies. Test all things; hold fast to what is good. Abstain from every form of evil* (1 Thess. 5:19–22, NKJV).

As John D. Barry, CEO of Jesus' Economy, once said: *In this age of rationalism, where "what you see is what you get", it's easy for us to excuse the spiritual. We veto the power of the spiritual in favour of what we can see, feel, and touch. Likewise, in the time of the early church, where mystery cults emphasized spiritual experiences, Paul saw this as an issue.*

In our churches and individual lives, we can sometimes de-emphasize the role of the Holy Spirit, limit His power, and draw boundaries that restrict His work in our lives. Because we cannot see or control the Spirit, we may be tempted to neglect His role altogether, until we want Him involved in activities that serve our personal interests.

At times, we even despise the word of prophecy, especially when it calls out sin in our lives. Yet we readily accept or even seek out prophecies that seem to favour us, even when they may not align with the Word of God. Sin in the life of a believer or in the church grieves the Holy Spirit. As children of God, we must examine our hearts. Is there any sin in your life that could be grieving Him?

The baptism and filling of the Holy Spirit cultivate a deep and intimate relationship between the believer and God—one that must be nurtured to bear lasting fruit in Christ. Practices such as prayer (Acts 4:31), bold witness (Acts 4:31, 33), worship in the Spirit (Eph. 5:18–19), and a sanctified lifestyle (Eph.

5:18) help sustain the Spirit's work in us. When these spiritual disciplines decline, the Spirit's influence in our lives often diminishes. The Holy Spirit is a person, with emotions and a desire for fellowship. When we resist, ignore, or disobey Him, He is grieved, and His activity may be quenched.

In extreme cases, if a believer persistently hardens their heart and turns away from the Spirit, some argue that He may withdraw. While many believers agree that in the Old Testament, the Holy Spirit departed from individuals like King Saul (1 Sam. 16:14) and Samson (Judg. 16:20), they also point out that in those times, the Spirit did not indwell believers permanently as He does under the New Covenant. David's plea in Psalm 51 - *Do not take your Holy Spirit from me* - reflects this reality.

Some Christians believe that, under the New Covenant, once a person is sealed and indwelt by the Holy Spirit, He may be grieved or quenched but will never leave. This is a debated issue. Yet it does raise a sobering question: What happens if someone rebels so deeply that they blaspheme the Holy Spirit (Mark 3:29)?

The work of the Holy Spirit in our lives is conditioned by our willingness to receive Him and surrender to His leading. While we are not perfect, God honours our sincere desire to walk with the Spirit, and He empowers us to grow in faith and obedience.

Children of God, the baptism and filling of the Holy Spirit release immeasurable power, power to live a life that honours and pleases God and reflects your divine calling. Give the Holy Spirit full freedom to work in your life. Let Him lead, guide, and empower you for all that God has prepared for you.

Observe the Discipline of Discipleship

Discipleship involves consistent, disciplined commitment to Christ. A union between Jesus Christ and a believer is like that of a vine and its branches in a vineyard; it requires tending to produce high-quality, fruitful yields. Jesus has already completed the most difficult task: saving our souls, granting us the power to become sons and daughters of God, and equipping us with everything we need for life and godliness. He has also sealed, baptized, and filled us with the Holy Spirit to fulfil our mission on earth, and He has promised to be with us until our task is done—or until He calls us home.

God paid the ultimate price for our redemption and has given us the potential, capabilities, and spiritual resources to fully experience His power at work in our lives. Yet, we have a role to play if we are to see outward evidence of the Holy Spirit's inward presence. As believers, we can learn from the prophets, apostles, the early Church, and other Christians who have witnessed or experienced the transformative power of God in their lives and ministries.

a. Believers are Soaked in the Word of God

The phrase "Word of God" has several meanings – it can refer to divine messages from God (Luke 11:28) or the personal title of Jesus, both as Spirit in heaven and as a human on earth (John 1:1; Acts 11:1; 1 Thess. 2:13). The Word of God is the verbal or written communication of the mind or thoughts of God.

God is a communicator and has been speaking into the human realm since the beginning. He speaks through creation (Psalm 19:1), through ancient prophets (Heb. 1:1), by the Holy Spirit (John 16:13), through Scripture (Heb. 4:12), and through the person of His Son, Jesus Christ (John 14:9). We come to know God by listening for Him in the various ways He speaks. By nature, the Word of God creates, sustains, and fosters fruitfulness and multiplication because it carries the power of the Holy Spirit.

Each time God speaks or inspires the writing of His Word, He (1) communicates His thoughts, which carry the concept and design of a thing; (2) defines and mobilizes the functional and operational capacities of His creation; and (3) releases power to activate capabilities and resources, combining them to produce His desired outcome. Thus, every divine command involves God the Father – the source of the Word, God the Son – the living Word, and God the Holy Spirit – who enacts the Word.

God guarantees the power of His Word when He declares through the prophet Isaiah: *As the rain and the snow come down from heaven, and do not return to it without watering the earth and making it bud and flourish so that it yields seed for the sower and bread for the eater, so is my word that goes out from my mouth: it will not return to me empty but will accomplish what I desire and achieve the purpose for which I sent it* (Isa. 55:10–11). Whatever God has spoken in your life will come to pass, regardless of your circumstances. The only real obstacle to the fulfilment of His Word is you—your unbelief, disobedience, or failure to align with His will.

The supernatural power within God's Word ensures that, once spoken, it fulfils its purpose. Since the Godhead dwells in you through the Holy Spirit, when you speak the Word of God with divine authority, creation must respond. The Lord likens His Word to fire and a hammer that breaks rocks to pieces (Jer. 23:29). The Word has inherent power to transform, just as a hammer drives nails into hard material.

Every believer must obey the Word of God because it is the foundation of the Christian life. The author of Ecclesiastes reminds us to *Fear God and keep His commandments, for this is the whole duty of man* (Eccl. 12:13, NKJV). Jesus also taught His disciples that those who obey His commandments abide in His love (John 15:10), are His friends (John 15:14), and show their love for Him. Even Jesus obeyed the commandments of the Father.

For a child of God to walk and live in the Spirit, he or she must be soaked in the Word of God. The Bible instructs us to study and meditate on the Word of God, ensuring that we obey everything it commands: *Do not let this book of law depart from your mouth, meditate on it day and night, so that you may be careful to do everything written in it. Then you will be prosperous and successful* (Jos. 1:8 NIV); *But his delight is in the law of the Lord. And in His law, he meditates day and night* (Psa. 1:2 NKJV). These two scriptures underscore the importance of immersing ourselves in the Word of God. The Israelites were commanded to keep God's Word constantly on their lips. When we store His Word in our hearts and integrate it into our being, it naturally flows from our mouths—our speech becomes seasoned with the Word.

A simple test of whether this is happening in your life is to observe how you respond when something unpleasant or unexpected occurs. For instance, what would you do if someone insulted you without provocation? If you are filled with the Word, you might simply forgive and move on. But if not, anger may rise, and you could find yourself retaliating, perhaps with words you later regret. When the situation calms, you may feel embarrassed, wondering why you didn't let your Christian values guide your response.

Let me share a personal example. My wife has faced similar challenges near our home. Our house is situated close to a main road, but there is no official provision for entering or exiting it. We usually rely on a neighbour's access slot. However, the exit is near a bus stop, which often causes traffic obstructions.

One day, as my wife returned from work and was trying to exit the road, she encountered a man walking his dog, standing directly in front of our house. He assumed she wanted to enter our neighbour's yard. My wife politely informed him that she needed to exit the road and offered to wait while he passed. Shockingly, the man erupted in anger and hurled insults at her, even calling her a "stupid woman" for not having her own driveway. A nearby bystander had to intervene. A similar situation happened again months later, yet in both cases, my wife chose not to argue or respond with insults.

So, I ask you: when someone wrongs you, what comes out of your mouth? Are your words seasoned with grace, or do they resemble fire from hell? Do you respond with cursing before remembering you are a child of God? Or do you stay calm, allowing God's love and mercy to guide your response?

I once read a short story online that made me laugh. The author described his very spiritual mother who would wash his mouth out with soap whenever he said something inappropriate. She wanted to keep his speech clean. But the real issue was not his mouth, it was his heart. Loose, careless, and harmful speech comes from an unclean heart. What we take in determines what we speak, how we live, and what we pass on to others. Keeping the Word of God in your mouth means saturating your speech with His truth. Let every word that comes out of your mouth be conceived, filtered, and sanctioned by the Word of God, regardless of the circumstances you face. When your heart is filled with the rich spices of God's love, your words will naturally be seasoned with grace and compassion.

Engage your mouth with the Word of God by singing praises, worshiping, declaring Scripture, blessing others, giving counsel, offering instruction, and praying. However, for your mouth to overflow with the Word, your heart must first be drenched in it. As Jesus taught, *For the mouth speaks what the heart is full of* (Luke 6:45).

A believer is commanded to meditate, or ruminate, on the Word of God. This means not just reading but thinking deeply, carefully, and prayerfully. As you meditate, ask reflective questions: What does this passage mean? Who said it, and why? To whom was it spoken? Under what circumstances? What can I learn from this, and how can I apply it in my life?

God has given us the Holy Spirit, who not only inspired the Word but also offers its full, divine commentary. Fellowship with Him in meditation brings true transformation, restoring us into the image and likeness of God.

When we engage the Holy Spirit in our meditation on the Word of God, He will: teach us deep and wondrous truths; reveal the instructions God has for us; unveil the nature and power of God; build our faith; enrich our praise and worship; glorify God; strengthen our defence against the enemy; uncover God's mysteries, will, purpose, and plan; sanctify us; and increase our knowledge of God. This process enriches our spiritual life and releases the power of God. It is not surprising that King Solomon said: *Above all else, guard your heart, for it is the wellspring of life* (Prov. 4:23).

God specifically instructs the children of Israel to keep His word in their hearts because the heart is the seat of intellect, emotions, and the will. People know things in their hearts (Deut. 8:5), pray in their hearts (1 Sam. 1:12-13), meditate in their hearts (Psa. 19:14), devise plans in their hearts (Psa. 140:2), keep words within their hearts (Prov. 4:21), think in their hearts (Mark 2:8), doubt in their hearts (Mark 11:28), ponder in their hearts (Luke 2:19), believe in their hearts (Rom. 10:9), and sing in their hearts. The heart is not a passive storehouse of the Word, it is living and active. Guided by the Holy Spirit, the heart stores and intellectually analyses the Word, carefully applying it to various situations in the life of a believer. The heart is the nerve centre of our intellectual and spiritual power.

The Holy Spirit uses the Word to mould the life and activities of a believer. The Word of God is a key ingredient in the construction and maintenance of the armour of God. It forms the belt of truth that holds our spiritual defence together (Eph. 6:14); it is a foundational material for the breastplate of righteousness (Eph. 6:14); it braces our feet with the gospel of peace (Eph. 6:15); it forms the shield of faith (Eph. 6:16; Rom. 10:17), with which we extinguish the fiery darts of the enemy (Eph. 6:16); it is used to build and preserve the helmet of salvation (Eph. 6:17); it is the construction material for the sword of the Spirit (Eph. 6:17), the Holy Spirit uses the Word to both attack our enemy and protect us against him. Additionally, a believer's prayer stands firmly on the Word of God. Jesus Christ fought the devil using the Word. The entire defence system of a believer is built on the Word.

The Bible also expresses the emotions of the heart: a glad heart (Exod. 4:14); a loving heart (Deut. 6:5); a fearful heart (Josh. 5:1); a courageous heart (Psa. 27:14); a repentant heart (Psa. 51:17); an anxious heart (Prov. 12:25); an angry heart (Prov. 19:3); a revived heart (Isa. 57:15); an anguished heart (Jer. 4:19; Rom. 9:2); a delighted heart (Jer. 15:16); a grieving heart (Lam. 2:18); a humble heart (Matt. 11:29); an excited or burning heart (Luke 24:32); and a troubled heart (John 14:1). Whether you are a believer or unbeliever, the heart determines how we react to situations. However, a child of God who soaks his/her heart in the Word detoxifies the heart—rooting out emotions born of sin and unrighteousness. The Holy Spirit then uses the Word to conceive emotions that honour God.

The heart also represents the will of a person: the hardened heart refuses to do what God commands (Exod. 4:21); the yielded heart submits to God (Josh.

24:23); the heart that intends to do something (2 Chr. 6:7); the heart that is devoted to seeking the Lord (1 Chr. 22:19); the heart that decides (2 Chr. 6:7); the heart that desires to receive from the Lord (Psa. 21:1-2); the heart that is turned towards God's statutes (Psa. 119:36); and the heart that wants to follow God's will (Rom. 10:1). The heart decides the direction in which an individual moves and how they get there. If an individual abides in Christ and allows His Word to abide in him/her, he submits to God, and the Holy Spirit empowers him/her to follow God's will, purpose, and plan.

The breath of God in us needs the Word of God to thrive and accomplish the will of our Creator. The Word defines, builds, and sustains our whole being, our life and godliness. As part of God's creation, we are sustained by His powerful Word. The Word of God formed you in your mother's womb and nurtured you as you grew (Jer. 1:5); it sanctified and ordained you for your work on earth (Jer. 1:5; Eph. 2:10); it provides everything you need for life and godliness (2 Pet. 1:3); it serves as your constitution for living in God's kingdom on earth and in heaven; it outlines your job description and provides the resources for every good work (Eph. 2:10); it inspires, teaches, rebukes, and trains you in righteousness to make you complete and thoroughly equipped for every good work (2 Tim. 3:16); it qualifies you to teach others (2 Tim. 2:2); it provides an elite defence system (Eph. 3:13-18) capable of overcoming the devil's strategies; it cleanses and reclaims your life for Christ (John 15:3); and it provides the best and most incomparable health care system, for *He sent His word and healed them* (Psa. 107:20).

As the Word of God prospers your soul, so your health also prospers (3 John 1:2). The Word blesses your food and water and removes sickness from among you (Exod. 23:25). It makes your life fruitful (Josh. 1:8–9; John 15) and governs the elements of nature to support your life and godliness (Col. 1:17), for Christ holds all things together. The Word of God is the essence and power of the Christian life.

No human being can truly live unless the Word of God lives in their heart.

The greatest tragedy in human history is sin, but God has given us the remedy, His Word. The Psalmist said, "Your word I have hidden in my heart, that I might not sin against You" (Psa. 119:11 NKJV). This divine antidote enables us to overcome sin and the law of sin and death. When your heart is filled with the Word, sin has no foothold; it is immediately resisted and expelled.

We must remember that salvation does not instantly destroy our sinful nature, if it did, we would never struggle with temptation again. A saved person can still be tempted, and that is not sin. However, salvation means we have transferred authority over our lives from the devil to Christ. Christ now lives in us, and by Him, the Holy Spirit dwells in us. Therefore, when we are tempted, God in us rises to resist the enemy, and through His power, we overcome. We are no longer slaves to sin but are now slaves to righteousness (Rom. 6:18).

Jesus Christ, though sinless, was still susceptible to temptation because He took on human flesh. Yet He never sinned, because He was fully yielded to the Father and empowered by the Holy Spirit. In the same way, we can live a life devoted to God, no matter the strength or frequency of temptation, if His Word and His power abide in us.

When we soak ourselves in the Word, its truth and the fruit of our meditation become deeply rooted in our hearts. God instructed Israel to be careful to do everything written in His Word. Unless we immerse ourselves in the ocean of God's Word and diligently search it for truth, we cannot fully understand, apply, or walk in the works that God prepared for us (Eph. 2:10). Every believer must meditate thoroughly on Scripture to receive divine instruction, prosper spiritually, and live a life of success in God's eyes (Josh. 1:8).

God fully understood why He commanded the Israelites to keep His Word in their hearts. The apostle Paul echoes this in the New Testament: *Let the word of Christ dwell in you richly* (Col. 3:16), and again in 2 Tim. 3:15–17. Believers must continually read, study, meditate on, and pray over the Word of God until it richly dwells within us. This is God's way of writing His law on our minds and placing His Word in our hearts (Jer. 31:33; Heb. 10:16).

This process can be likened to erasing corrupted files on a computer's hard drive (our hearts) and replacing them with new, clean data, the Word of God and its divine insights. As this transformation happens, our thoughts, words, actions, desires, and motivations are increasingly influenced and governed by Christ.

Beyond personal obedience, God also instructed the Israelites to teach His Word diligently to their children. As it is written: *And these words which I command you today shall be in your heart. You shall teach them diligently to your children, and shall talk of them when you sit in your house, when you walk by the way, when you lie down, and when you rise up. You shall bind them as a sign on your hand, and they shall be as frontlets between your eyes. You shall write them on the doorposts of your house and on your gates* (Deut. 6:6–9, NKJV). God wanted every generation, young and old, to know, love, and obey His commandments. Therefore, He gave parents the responsibility to teach their children diligently, both at home and in everyday life.

This commandment includes practical ways to make Scripture a visible and constant part of life: share God's Word during meals, bedtime, walks, and car rides; display Bible verses on walls, doors, gates, fridges, or anywhere visible to your children. In homes where this kind of Christian education is practiced, family devotions, Bible studies, scripture-based games, and Christian worship music become part of everyday life, helping children grow up knowing and fearing the Lord.

While some modern cultures might view this as restrictive or even "abusive," from a biblical perspective, this is God's ordained way to raise children in His fear and wisdom. In today's media-saturated world, where children are constantly bombarded by messages from the internet, phones, and TV, often with harmful effects, a foundation built on God's Word offers lasting security and truth. Interestingly, even in societies critical of Christian parenting, many still send their children to faith-based schools, recognizing the moral structure it offers.

Let the Word of God become your life's operating manual and saturate your heart with it. This reminds us of the image of a sponge dipped in water. Every sponge has a certain capacity for holding water, determined by the size of its pores. When that capacity is exceeded, the sponge begins to drip.

Likewise, every person created in God's image has an inbuilt capacity to absorb and retain the Word of God. Before we accepted Christ, those spiritual storage spaces were filled with worldly influences, for example, curses or negative speech. As we study the Bible, we learn that we are called to bless, not curse. So, we cleanse those heart-spaces and refill them with blessings from God's Word. This process of studying and meditating on Scripture gradually replaces darkness with truth. The rate at which this transformation happens depends on how consistently we expose ourselves to the Word of God.

Take, for example, the way rain fills the soil. Good soil has its particles arranged in such a way that there are pore spaces for both air and water. When the soil is dry, it needs moisture. The soil also has a water-holding capacity, but the rate at which water fills these pores depends on how much water reaches the soil and how quickly it arrives.

If all the soil receives is a light shower, the moisture may remain on the surface, never penetrating deeply enough to reach the pores. But when there is a heavy downpour, a good amount of water infiltrates the soil and fills those spaces. Once the pores are saturated, the soil is soaked, and any excess water simply runs off the surface.

In the same way, a believer needs extensive exposure to the Word of God to effectively displace worldly thoughts from the heart and fill it with God's truth. To do this, one must receive a consistent and abundant supply of high-quality spiritual input from various sources.

When we immerse ourselves in the Word of God and its teachings, we allow the truth to enter our hearts from multiple angles. This begins to displace the worldly words and patterns once stored there. A believer must dedicate quality time to nourishing their spirit through:

- A daily devotion of at least 15 minutes, including Bible study
- At least one hour per week of deeper study and meditation
- Attending weekly Bible studies for teaching and discussion
- Reading Christian literature

- Listening to worship and praise music
- Watching edifying Christian programs
- Participating in Christian talks, conferences, and lectures (if possible)

Though not an exhaustive list, engaging in these activities ensures that you are feeding your spirit through different sensory and intellectual pathways.

Many believers find it difficult to consistently spend time in God's Word. But if you understand that the Word of God is the framework and substance of who you are, what you think, what you say, and what you do, then the Word will become your highest priority.

King David praised God with all his heart, saying, *For You have magnified Your word above all Your name* (Psa. 138:2, NKJV). God exalted His Word above the totality of His name, His authority and reputation, because His Word represents His nature, His thoughts, and His will. Similarly, Jesus declared that His food was to do the will of the Father.

Jesus exalted the Word above all things. He used it to overcome temptation (Luke 4:4, 8, 12) and to build His life and ministry. When tempted to turn stones into bread, He responded, *It is written: Man shall not live by bread alone, but by every word that proceeds from the mouth of God* (Matt. 4:4, NIV). The Word of God sustains both the physical and spiritual aspects of our being.

The breath of God within us is sustained by every word that comes from His mouth. So, how much of His Word have you hidden in your heart? What proportion do you apply in your thoughts, speech, and actions? Just as fish depend on water to live, Jesus relied fully on the Word of God.

God's ultimate goal is for each of His children to study His Word and integrate it into their very being, so that it becomes the sole material forming their thoughts, words, behaviour, values, and beliefs. The Word should be our only blueprint for building Christian character. It serves as a divine filter for distinguishing right from wrong.

The NIV Full Life Study Bible offers seven helpful questions believers can use to evaluate their choices:

1. Can I say or do this to the glory of God? (1 Cor. 10:31)
2. Can this be done in the name, and with the blessing, of the Lord Jesus? (John 14:13)
3. Can I do this with thanksgiving to God?
4. Would Christ do this? (1 John 2:6)
5. Will it undermine the convictions of other believers? (1 Cor. 8:1)
6. Will it weaken my desire for spiritual things, prayer and God's Word? (Luke 8:14; Matt. 5:6)
7. Will it hinder my witness for Christ?

The Word of God is the gatekeeper of the soul, guarding what we allow into our lives and shaping how we live for Him.

As the early Church devoted itself to the apostles' teaching (Acts 2:42), I urge you to immerse yourself in the Word of God so you can plug into His immeasurable power. You need the living and powerful Word of God to fulfil your earthly mission. The Psalmist, longing to keep and obey the law of the LORD, prayed that God would:

- Teach him to follow His decrees.
- Give him understanding of His laws.
- Direct him in the path of His commands.
- Turn his heart toward His statutes.
- Turn his eyes away from worthless things.
- Fulfil His promise (Word) to His servant.
- Spare him from the disgrace of disobedience (Psalm 119:33–39).

He delighted in the law of the LORD and longed for it, knowing that it preserved his life in righteousness. May the Lord grant you the grace to keep His commands in your heart and obey them fully.

a. Prayer and Fasting are Spiritual Disciplines that Help Cultivate a Godly Lifestyle

Prayer and fasting are integral, Bible-based disciplines of a godly life that every spirit-filled child of God must practice. Unfortunately, many Christians fail to consistently pray and fast as the Bible instructs. In his letter to the saints in Thessalonica, Paul writes: *Pray without ceasing; give thanks in all circumstances, for this is God's will for you in Christ Jesus* (1 Thess. 5:17-18 NIV). He also instructed the Ephesian Church to *pray in the Spirit on all occasions, with all kinds of prayers and requests* (Eph. 6:18 NIV). Paul encourages believers to remain in the presence of their Father, speaking to Him and listening to His voice. We must continually cry out to Him for His grace and blessings. So, what does it really mean to pray continually?

Let's begin by understanding what 'praying continually' does not mean. The Matthew Poole Commentary explains that it does not mean, as the Euchites and Messalians of old believed, that no other duties were required but always praying. In this context, 'continually' does not mean that believers should always be on their knees or constantly lifting their hands and verbally calling on God. Such an approach could neglect other important aspects of the Christian life. Praying continually means offering repeated prayers and requests of all kinds, on all occasions, throughout the day (Luke 18:1; Rom. 12:12; Eph. 6:18; Col. 4:21). It also means that:

- Believers should come to God daily, repeatedly, and often.
- The mind should maintain a continuous attitude of prayer.
- There should be constancy in prayer (Col. 4:2) and perseverance (Rom. 12:12; Eph. 6:18).
- Praying without fainting (Luke 18:1).
- Praying with strength (Rom. 12:12).
- Praying in everything, in every season, regardless of circumstances.
- Focusing on the course of prayer without allowing distractions."

John Piper explains three conditions for praying continually. First, there must be a spirit of dependence that permeates whatever we do. Even when we are not consciously speaking to God, there is a deep abiding dependence on Him that is woven into the heart of faith. Second, praying repeatedly and often, mention things over and over and often. Third, persevere in prayer, never giving up, come to Him repeatedly during the day and often.

The key to praying continually is keeping your heart in a conscious and subconscious communion with God such that prayers can erupt spontaneously. When your heart is conditioned to always pray, you can easily mix spontaneous prayers with other activities in your life. This may also require linking your mind to your heart to ensure your activities are consistently communing with God.

The Pulpit Commentary stresses that praying without ceasing means living in a devotional frame of mind, maintaining a spirit of prayer even while fulfilling earthly duties, with your heart continually full of God's presence and communion.

The Cambridge Bible for Schools and Colleges asserts that prayer should accompany the whole of life, an ever-flowing stream that, though not always visible or audible, forms the undercurrent of all our thoughts, shaping them with its character and tone.

What should occupy us in continual prayer? Our needs and wants are continually streaming in. We are called to new service each day, and trials and temptations keep coming. We are constantly engaged in spiritual warfare, and the need to petition God to fulfil His promises is ever-present. We also need to thank Him for fulfilling His promises and releasing our blessings. A spirit-filled child of God constantly needs God's power to live a godly life throughout the day. Our wants are continual, and God deserves our praise, worship, and adoration for all His supplies. We must also seek forgiveness for transgressions, iniquities, and sins. All these activities justify praying without ceasing. However, prayer alone cannot release the full power we need to live a completely fulfilled life.

There are certain situations that will not yield to prayer alone. After leaving the Mount of Transfiguration, Jesus Christ and three of His disciples returned to find a problem. A man had brought his demon-possessed son to be healed by the disciples, but they had failed to cast out the evil spirit. After rebuking His disciples for their unbelief, Jesus said, 'But this kind does not go out except by prayer and fasting' (Matt. 17:21 NKJV).

There are several lessons we can learn from what Jesus taught His disciples. First, the apostles had previously cast out evil spirits without prayer and fasting.

However, there was something about this affliction that could not submit to their usual prayers to exorcise demons.

Second, Jesus referred to the evil spirit as 'This kind' to teach the disciples that this type, species, or class of evil spirit had a different nature and attributes from those they had previously cast out through prayer alone. This spirit was resistant to prayer alone, which could not generate enough power to evict it. The spirit had become so entrenched in the victim, producing such painful, fixed, and alarming effects, that only prayer and fasting could expel it.

Though all things are possible by faith, some are more difficult to accomplish than others. Some evil spirits may succumb to the energy of human will, the power of the divine name, and the prayers of even weak faith—these may suffice for lower-ranking demons. However, there are spiritual "generals" that require a higher level of communion with God, which is achieved through prayer and fasting.

Fourth, the disciples of Jesus Christ were not adequately prepared to cast out the evil spirit because they were not accustomed to prayer and fasting. Matthew records that the disciples of John the Baptist raised this issue with Jesus: *Then John's disciples came and asked him, How is it that we and the Pharisees fast, but your disciples do not fast?* (Matt. 9:14, NIV). The apostles needed strong faith anchored in prayer and abstinence from food to strengthen the spirit man and subdue the flesh. Because of this lack, they fell short of the power needed to heal the demon-possessed boy. There are certain things in a believer's life that cannot be attained without cultivating strong faith through fervent and persistent prayer combined with fasting.

Fifth, Jesus Christ rebuked the disciples for their unbelief. According to Bengel's Gnomon, the disciples appear to have indulged themselves while Jesus and the three others were on the Mount of Transfiguration. The name of Jesus, when spoken with little faith, could not heal the demonic boy. Given the nature of the evil spirit they were dealing with, the disciples needed to have spent time in prayer and fasting beforehand to strengthen and inspire their faith for ministry.

While prayer seeks God's assistance and places us entirely in His hands, fasting subdues the flesh, stirs the soul to action, and activates the inner man's power. There is a measure of spiritual power released when prayer and fasting are practiced together that the two disciplines cannot achieve separately. They are synergistic; their combination has an additive effect, two are stronger than one. This is consistent with the Jewish notion that through fasting, the divine soul may bring forth what is sought. The Cambridge Bible for Schools and Colleges affirms this truth, stating, "Those only whose spiritual life and faith are made strong by self-denial (fasting) and communion with God in prayer are able to cast forth this kind of evil spirit."

Prayer and fasting equip believers to receive the power of God to accomplish every good work He has prepared in advance for them to do (Eph. 2:10). These disciplines are the spiritual boardroom and field operations centre of the Christian life, where all decisions affecting the believer's total being are made and implemented. While God may use other means to accomplish His purposes, prayer and fasting empower the core areas of a believer's walk. A Christian who avoids this boardroom forfeits divine power and unwittingly submits to the influence of the Devil and his evil spirits. Likewise, a life devoid of prayer and fasting is like a plane flying without GPS, directionless and vulnerable.

Children of God, prayer and fasting are not optional, they are essential.

Distinction Between Prayer and Fasting

Prayer is one of the most misunderstood and, at times, misused disciplines of Christian living. Many believers, either knowingly or unknowingly, breach the spiritual principles and conditions necessary for communing with God through prayer. Part of this challenge can be addressed by gaining a clearer understanding of what prayer is, and what it is not.

There are several definitions of prayer that help illuminate its multifaceted nature:

- According to Stamps and Adams (1992), the word 'prayer' refers to a multifaceted communication between believers and their Lord God.

- Matthew Poole comments that communion with God may be either mental, in the heart only, as was the case with Hannah, or vocal, when expressed audibly.
- Heller (1958) describes prayer as the outpouring of one's mind and soul to God, a going out of oneself, and a pilgrimage of the spirit in the presence of God.
- Yaovi et al. (2018) offer a more theological and functional definition, stating that prayer is:
  - A spiritual outreach of a temporal, religious man to the transcendent God.
  - Man exercising his legal authority on earth to invoke heaven's influence on earth.
  - Granting heaven, the license to interfere in earthly matters.
  - A spiritual response to God that addresses and petitions Him while contemplating His nature.

While these definitions are not exhaustive, they highlight several essential aspects of prayer:

- Prayer reflects the diversity of communication between a temporal believer and the eternal God.
- It is often initiated by the believer yet empowered by the Spirit.
- As an act of worship, it is primarily spiritual in nature.
- It involves active participation between the believer and the triune God the Father, God the Son, and God the Holy Spirit.
- It is the God-given right of every believer to speak with the Father at any time and in any place.
- Prayer invites God to be actively involved in the believer's life.

Together, these perspectives emphasize that prayer is a two-way, relational communication between the believer and the Lord God.

Prayer is the spiritual lung of a Spirit-filled believer. When we pray to our Father, we enter a sacred conversation, speaking to Him (breathing out) and hearing from Him (breathing in). A believer who does not pray without ceasing is like a person whose lungs are dysfunctional, damaged, or have ceased to function.

I once experienced this physically. Between September 2017 and October 2018, I was struck with a mysterious illness. I felt breathless every time I tried to do anything. Climbing stairs became a challenge. Walking was difficult. Even sitting in certain positions restricted my breathing. My medical consultants later told me that one of my lungs had collapsed due to an unknown disease. The flow of air into my lungs was severely limited. That is exactly what happens when a believer falters in their prayer life. God designed us to be in constant communion with Him, and only through that ongoing connection can we live a truly fulfilled life on earth.

The Bible is full of references to prayer. In the Old Testament, men and women of God—such as Enoch, Noah, Moses, Joshua, Abraham, Elijah, Daniel, Meshach, Shadrach, Abednego, Nehemiah, David, Job, Esther, and Hannah—prayed fervently to God. In the New Testament, prayer remains a central spiritual discipline. Believers including the apostles, women like Priscilla, Lydia, Phoebe, and other faithful followers of Christ maintained prayerful lives.

Jesus Christ Himself upheld a consistent and disciplined prayer life. While His life was marked by many virtues, none was more evident than His prayerfulness. As Hebrews 5:7 tells us: *During the days of Jesus' life on earth, He offered up prayers and petitions with loud cries and tears to the one who could save Him from death, and He was heard because of His reverent submission.* Jesus is the perfect model of how to live a godly life. He:

- Spent the night in prayer before choosing the twelve apostles (Luke 6:12)
- Rose early to pray alone on a mountain (Mark 1:35)
- Prayed at His baptism (Luke 3:21–22)
- Prayed before beginning His public ministry (Matt. 4:2)
- Prayed before announcing His death (Luke 9:18, 21–22)
- Prayed after major events (Matt. 14:23) and in difficult moments (John 6:15)

- Prayed before meals (Matt. 14:19), when weary (Mark 6:31–35), and before facing temptation (Matt. 26:36)

Every part of His life was grounded in prayer, and prayer was the engine of His ministry. Jesus knew how to tame His humanity, keeping His flesh in submission, and ruled over every part of His life through prayer. Even on His busiest ministry days, He found time to retreat and pray. Sometimes, He had to forgo food (Mark 3:20), rest, and sleep (Mark 6:32–45) to ensure He communed with the Father. The busier Jesus became, the more He prayed.

Great servants of God—such as Martin Luther and Adam Clarke, discovered this same secret. Salter, in his book *Imago Christi* (p. 131), emphasized Jesus' total dependence on prayer by writing: *When He arrived in a town, His first thought was which was the shortest way to the mountain, just as ordinary travellers inquire where the most noted sights are and which is the best hotel.* If Jesus Christ, the Son of God, literally prayed about everything in His life and ministry, how much more should we, frail and flawed, spend nights in prayer and maintain intimate communion with God?

Every believer who has walked with Christ understands the importance of prayer in walking with God. Recognizing the vital role prayer played in the life and ministry of Jesus, His disciples once asked Him to teach them how to pray: *One day Jesus was praying in a certain place. When He finished, one of His disciples said to Him, 'Lord, teach us to pray, just as John taught his disciples* (Luke 11:1, NIV).

Beyond simply observing Jesus pray, the disciples likely noticed that the followers of John the Baptist were more effective or disciplined in their prayers. It is difficult for us today to grasp the full weight of their request without understanding the demands and rigours of ministry in that time. But the message is timeless: any Christian who truly desires to live a Christ-centred life will quickly realize they cannot do it apart from a life devoted to prayer.

Prayer invokes the power of God to accomplish every task He has called us to do. Since we live in a world under the influence of the devil and his demons, the enemy constantly devises strategies to derail the work of God and to attack His children. The moment we received the Lord Jesus Christ as our Savior; a spiritual war was declared against us. If we truly understood the depth of this warfare, no one would ever need to persuade us to pray.

Spiritual warfare against Satan and his forces involves three major aspects:

- Declaring war against Satan according to God's purpose (Luke 4:14–19);
- Entering Satan's house, destroying his gates of bronze, shattering iron bars, breaking into his stronghold, binding him, stripping him of his armour, by fervent prayer and the proclamation of God's Word (Luke 11:20–22);
- Plundering his goods, delivering those held captive by his power and bringing them to salvation, regeneration, justification, and sanctification in Christ.

It's a ferocious battle, isn't it? No wonder many believers shy away from confronting the enemy. But God has equipped you with weapons, prayer and the Word, to pull down strongholds. Every believer must declare and enforce a state of spiritual emergency over their domain to defend their territory and push forward to expand the kingdom of God.

Prayer acknowledges God as Creator and Sustainer of all things in heaven and on earth. It affirms our belief in His existence, and it reflects our humility and reverence. The manifestation of God's power in response to prayer strengthens the believer's faith, encourages holiness, and fosters spiritual growth. Through prayer, we receive God's peace and cultivate contentment in our lives.

Prayer also facilitates intimate communion between the believer and God, often best experienced in solitude. Jesus modelled this for us. He often withdrew from public spaces to pray in quiet, solitary places (Mark 1:35). In teaching His disciples, He said: *But when you pray, go into your room, close the door and pray to your Father, who is unseen. Then your Father, who sees what is done in secret, will reward you* (Matt. 6:6, NKJV).

Jesus emphasized privacy and solitude in personal communion with God. Yet

He also prayed with others—select individuals like Peter, James, and John (Luke 9:28); the full apostolic team (Luke 9:18); and even in public settings (Matt. 14:19). While prayer generates power wherever it is uttered, distractions are minimized in solitude, making it an ideal setting for deep connection with the Father.

When we are united with Christ, prayer takes on a broader dimension than simply praying for ourselves. Jesus Himself prayed not only for personal matters, but also for God's glory on God's behalf (John 12:28), for all whom the Father entrusted to Him (John 14:16–17), for the disciples to receive the Holy Spirit, for those who would be saved through their message (John 17:9), for individuals like Peter (Luke 22:31–32), and even for His enemies (Luke 23:34). Although we are called to intercede for many types of people, we often struggle to consistently pray even for ourselves.

God has given us the power and responsibility to pray over various areas of our lives—our families, communities, nations, and even the world. However, releasing the power of God through prayer requires certain conditions to be met:

1. Praying with Faith

Jesus said, "And whatever you ask in prayer, believing, you will receive" (Matt. 21:22). A believer who prays in faith does so based on a perceived provision, God's ability to provide, a promise from His Word, and a deep conviction that what is being asked for will be granted. A man or woman of faith positionally receives their request before even approaching God.

2. Praying According to the Word

Effective prayer is grounded in Scripture. God has already provided everything we need through His promises, teachings, prophecies, and words of wisdom. But we cannot access these provisions unless we pray for them under the right spiritual conditions. Prayer is the spiritual tool that aligns our needs with what God has already prepared for us.

3. Engaging the Trinity in Prayer

Fruitful prayer involves the entire Godhead:

- We pray to God the Father, who holds the keys to our blessings.
- The Holy Spirit intercedes for us, helps us align our requests with God's will, stirs the Word within us, and gives us the strength to pray.
- We pray in the name of Jesus, invoking His power and authority. Jesus, our High Priest, presents our petitions before the Father, justifying us through His blood.
- The Holy Spirit also enables us to receive and enact the Father's response.

4. Maintaining a Life of Prayer and Fasting

A disciplined life of prayer and fasting helps us stay continually in God's presence. It strengthens our faith, removes distractions, energizes our prayer life, and increases our sensitivity to hear and obey God. We must pray perseveringly and continually—with faith (James 1:5), with thanksgiving (Phil. 4:6), with a forgiving heart, in Jesus' name (John 14:13–14), and with a heart that is right before God (James 5:16).

As followers of Christ, we must walk in His steps—He prayed:
- With God's glory in view (John 17:1; James 4:3)
- In full submission to the Father's will, with strong crying and tears (Heb. 5:7)
- With great time investment, even all night (Luke 6:12)
- With urgency and persistence

Whatever posture you assume in prayer - kneeling, standing, sitting, or lying down - your heart must be fully surrendered to God.

Fasting as an Act of Worship

Fasting is a spiritual discipline of children of God that enhances a steadfast relationship with God. Biblical fasting refers to voluntary abstinence from, or going without, food to focus on prayer and fellowship with God. We voluntarily go without food to allow our inner being to commune intimately with God. However, some scholars have broadened the scope of fasting to include abstinence from consumables other than food. It has thus been defined as voluntarily giving up something we normally consume so that we can increase our intimacy with God. Based on this understanding some believers can choose to go without food, TV, a type of food, sport or other consumables. In this context fasting is denying oneself the pleasures of life.

Some believers have gone without food to lose weight or for health reasons, but have tagged prayer to such activities. However, a typical biblical fast has involved going without food for the purpose of enriching our communion with God. Denying ourselves of other pleasures of life should be by-products of our abstinence from food rather than the main activity. There are spiritual and physical reasons for going without food as we commune with our God.

When we voluntarily go without food we comply with God's desire for us to regain mastery overall things associated with our flesh to subdue the flesh and elevate our inner being to fully commune with God. Fasting brings the body, soul and spirit in reverent submission to the Holy Spirit as we converse with God – we engage the totality of our being in communing with God. Every faculty of our lives must stop whatever they are doing and either actively participate in the conversation with God or allow it to proceed without disturbances. This tames the stubborn flesh, which is always struggling to enjoy pleasures of the world.

Praying without fasting is like parents having a serious discussion with a very important visitor while children do their own things in the background. The children may be playing games and doing naughty things, which end up distracting parents from having a rich discussion. Considering that the flesh is always fighting us while having our quality conversation with God, silencing the flesh allows us to enjoy an intimate fellowship with God.

When we deny our flesh food we feed and strengthen our inner man. Paul tells us that the desires of the flesh are at war with the desires of our heart yielded to God. If we want to walk in the Spirit, we must strengthen the spirit to the point that he is stronger than the flesh. This involves dealing with the distractions from the flesh to maintain uninterrupted and constant atmosphere of communion with God.

When we fast with a pure heart, we receive a higher voltage of the power of God, our intimacy deepens, we receive deeper revelations of God and guidance on how to walk with Him to fulfil our purpose, and we are equipped to walk in the power and authority of God. Fasting looses bonds of wickedness, frees the oppressed and breaks the yokes of bondage. More than any other discipline, fasting reveals and tames things that control us. Every child of God must fast to maximize his or her communion with God.

Prayer and Fasting as a Powerhouse of a Believer

Believers who abide in the Lord Jesus Christ can pray and fast to sustain their inner beings and access the full provisions that God has made available for godly living. While the Lord's power has already granted us everything we need for life and godliness, these provisions are wrapped in promises, prophecies, words of wisdom, words of knowledge, poetry, and even in nature. They are released in our lives through prayer and fasting. Every believer who desires to live a completely fulfilled, godly life must fully integrate prayer and fasting into their daily walk with God.

The combination of prayer, fasting, and reverent submission to God's glory brings about the full effectiveness of life and ministry in a believer. Jesus Christ fasted and prayed before entering His public ministry, teaching His disciples that fulfilling a full range of ministerial duties required them to integrate these disciplines in their own lives. Many heroes and heroines of faith (Abraham, Anna, Aquila, David, Daniel, Elijah, Esther, Hannah, Job, Joseph, Joshua, Lydia, Moses, Noah, Paul, and Priscilla) prayed and fasted. In modern times, figures like Martin Luther, John Knox, John Calvin, Kathryn Kuhlman, Dwight L. Moody, Tammy Faye, Bill Bright, John Wesley, Billy Graham, and John Stott also practiced prayer and fasting. These stalwarts of faith made a regular practice of fasting and praying. Here are some examples of individuals, groups, and nations that engaged in prayer and fasting:

- Moses fasted for 40 days and 40 nights while receiving the law on Mount Sinai (Exod. 24:38).

- The Israelites went to Bethel, where they wept before the LORD, fasted the whole day, and presented offerings to inquire of the Lord before going into battle against the Benjamites (Judges 20:26-29).
- King Darius spent the night fasting after realizing his advisors had tricked him into throwing Daniel into the lion's den (Dan. 6:18).
- The people of Nineveh, upon hearing Jonah's message of doom, declared a fast for everyone, from the greatest to the least, and even their livestock (Jonah 3:5-7).
- King Jehoshaphat, when faced with an impending attack, proclaimed a fast for all Judah to seek the LORD (2 Chron. 20:3).
- Anna, an 84-year-old widow, never left the temple but worshiped night and day, fasting and praying (Luke 2:37).
- John the Baptist taught his disciples to fast and pray (Mark 2:18).
- Paul and Barnabas appointed church leaders and committed them to God with prayer and fasting (Acts 14:23).
- While prophets and teachers in the Church at Antioch prayed and fasted, the Holy Spirit instructed them to set apart Barnabas and Saul for their missionary work (Acts 13:1-2).
- Jesus fasted for 40 days and nights in the wilderness before beginning His public ministry and facing temptation (Matt. 4:1-11).
- John Knox fasted and prayed so much that Queen Mary of Scotland said she feared his prayers more than all the armies of Scotland.

The duration of these fasts ranged from one day to several years, as in the case of the 84-year-old Anna. This period of intense prayer and abstinence from food is especially effective in times of crisis and crucial decision-making. Whenever this approach to communion with God is employed, supplicants often receive what they ask for. However, there are instances when prayer and fasting do not result in the desired outcome, especially if the subject of the fast is not aligned with God's will. For example, Jesus prayed in the Garden of Gethsemane that the Father would remove the cup of suffering, but the Father did not grant His request. Jesus submitted to the Father's will. Similarly, David fasted and prayed but still lost his son. Nonetheless, every believer must pray and fast to fulfil their divine mandate on earth.

The Benefits of Prayer and Fasting

Prayer and fasting are powerful because they address the root of disobedience, sanctify the believer, and purify the environment in which prayer is conceived and uttered. They give the Holy Spirit the freedom to search our inner being and intercede for us with minimal distractions. Additionally, fasting helps us converse with God with a clear, sober mind.

When we pray and fast, it removes the "noise" around our prayers, ensuring that our voice is clear before God. Prayer and fasting act like an aperture in an optical system, clearing the light beam so that it can focus more effectively. When we earnestly pray and fast according to biblical principles, our spiritual senses—our ears and eyes—are opened wider, allowing us to see and hear from God more clearly.

The Distractions of the Flesh and the Power of Prayer and Fasting

There are pleasures of the world and desires of the flesh that crowd our inner being, blur our prayers, and make our spiritual voice hoarse. This is a ploy of the devil to drown our prayers with the pleasures of life, diverting our attention away from our communion with God. The devil diverted Eve's attention in the Garden of Eden, shifting it from the good trees to the tree of the knowledge of good and evil. Before this disastrous encounter, Adam and Eve only knew what was good, and their communication with God was 100% pure. The moment the devil enticed Eve to eat from the forbidden tree, the first couple became aware of evil, and from that point on, their bodies, souls, and spirits had to deal with a mixture of both good and evil. Evil became the second nature of humanity, and whatever humanity spoke, did, or thought, contained traces of evil—a spiritual pollutant and distraction.

The knowledge of evil competes with the knowledge of good in humans. The seed of distraction from maintaining a healthy conversation with God was planted in the Garden when the serpent led Adam and Eve into disobedience. Even after salvation, the flesh remains a major distraction that hinders intimate communion with God. Thus, the devil employs a two-fold strategy to divert a believer's focus: first, by diverting their attention from the truth, and second, by offering an evil alternative.

The Benefits of Prayer and Fasting

When we pray and fast with a pure heart, and according to God's will, He (i) equips us to focus on our relationship with Him (Matt. 6:16-18), (ii) grants our requests (1 John 5:14-15), (iii) remains accessible when we seek Him, (iv) sees our dependence, sincerity, and humility in our communion with Him, (v) reveals His will when we inquire about it (Judg. 20:26-28), (vi) guides us in times of significant decisions (Acts 13:1-3), (vii) delivers His children from their adversaries (2 Chron. 20:3), (viii) helps us develop the willpower and discipline to control our flesh (1 Cor. 9:27), (ix) comforts us when mourning the loss of loved ones, (x) heals the sick (Psa. 35:13), (xi) strengthens us when weary (Matt. 4:2), (xii) breaks the yokes of bondage and frees the captives, (xiii) gives grace to share with others, (xiv) hears us clearly as we converse, (xv) engages with us deeply, and (xvi) enables us to grow in our understanding and grasp of God's revelation.

Prayer and fasting elevate our communion with God, deepening and broadening the scope of the benefits we receive through this relationship. These disciplines strengthen us with the power of God through the Holy Spirit in our inner being. Paul assures the church at Ephesus of the presence of God's power within them: *Now to him who can do immeasurably more than all we ask or imagine, according to his power that is at work within us* (Eph. 3:20 NIV). There are two key points: God can do things beyond our understanding and requests, and the power to release these things is actively at work within us. Prayer and fasting strengthen our inner being through the Spirit, and this empowered spirit enables our feelings, thoughts, and purposes to come more under the influence and direction of the Holy Spirit for the full manifestation of God's power.

Corporate and Individual Prayer and Fasting

We can pray and fast individually, as a family, as a house church, as a local assembly, or as part of the larger body of Christ. All these modes complement each other, and every believer should strive to engage in as many of them as the Spirit leads.

Prayer and fasting "switch on" the power control switches in our Father's house, enabling us to carry out all the activities of our mission on earth. We cannot successfully perform the good works that God has called us to do unless we plug into the source of God's power. Fasting with prayer grants us access to a higher voltage of power that cannot be accessed by prayer or fasting alone.

Child of God, do you pray and fast? How disciplined are you in practicing these two vital Christian disciplines? If you are not yet in the habit of praying and fasting, it is not too late for you to start. Begin today!

c. Believers Must Belong to the Fellowship of Saints

By design, every child of God is meant to fit and function within an organic community of believers. The family, house church or Bible study group, the local church, and the universal Church provide both a physical and spiritual environment that nurtures and develops Christians to live a holistic, godly life. A productive Christian life, lived within any Christian community, is anchored on three relational pillars: unity in Christ, diversity in Christ, and equality in Christ. The fellowship of believers is the ideal body, offering the relational connections needed to share material and spiritual resources with others while receiving from them in turn.

As believers, we must ensure that we are part of a spiritually active fellowship, ranging from our families to the global church. Even in places where traditional Christian communities do not exist, believers should seek out and join any Bible-based group with sound doctrine. For example, if you are in a university setting and there is no local parish or house church nearby, the university Christian fellowship may be the only accessible Christian gathering. It is essential to be connected to the body of Christ to live out and fulfil your calling.

The author of Hebrews encourages believers to always gather and support each other in their walk of faith: *not forsaking the assembling of ourselves together, as is the manner of some, but exhorting one another, and so much the more as you see the Day approaching* (Heb. 10:25). This scripture highlights the assembly of believers as the noble community to which every believer is automatically joined the moment they are saved. We live our lives and fulfil our calling in communion with other believers.

Imagine what would happen if a cell or cells dismembered themselves from a living body. What would be the likelihood that a zebra that strays from its dazzle will survive an attack by a pride of lions? How safe would a cheetah be if it deserted its coalition? Just as a cell in the body cannot survive independent of others, no Christian can live in isolation and still fulfil their purpose. When we forsake or neglect the assembly of believers, we disconnect ourselves from vital life-sustaining support and make ourselves vulnerable to vicious attacks by the devil and his army of evil spirits.

Listen to the wisdom of King Solomon: *Two are better than one, because they have a good return for their labour. If either of them falls, one can help the other up. But pity anyone who falls and has no one to help them up. Also, if two lie down together, they will keep warm. But how can one keep warm alone? Though one may be overpowered, two can defend themselves. A cord of three strands is not quickly broken* (Eccl. 4:9-12 NIV). King Solomon outlines several benefits of two people working together rather than each one going it alone. No matter how spiritually enterprising we may be individually, we still need the input of other believers to fully realize our potential and live a fulfilled life. Though we may sometimes be under the illusion that we can succeed by doing things alone, everything we do is shaped, in part, by the influence of others.

Orson Welles claimed that *we are born alone, we live alone, we die alone*. But this view disregards all the physical, biological, social, and spiritual relational links that individuals have in their lives. No single human being is self-created. Every human embryo (except that of Jesus) results from the union of a man and a woman. The embryo develops in the womb into a baby, which is born and welcomed into the world by parents, who nurture the baby until they are old enough to start their own life. If a mother chooses to abort the foetus, the baby may never grow to be born.

From the moment we are conceived to the point of death, numerous other humans influence our growth and development. Before birth, the father and mother influence the welfare of the baby. From birth to death, different people - such as healthcare providers, educators, religious leaders, security officers, utility companies, bus drivers, media workers, and many others - contribute to our lives. Whether knowingly or unknowingly, our entire lives are intricately interwoven with those of many other people, biologically, socially, spiritually, economically, and in several other ways. I would also argue that someone's death results in the loss of relationships and the end of the services that the deceased person provided to others.

Pope Francis said: *Rivers do not drink their own water; trees do not eat their own fruit; the sun does not shine on itself and flowers do not spread their fragrance for themselves. Living for others is the rule of nature. We are all born to help each other. No matter how difficult it is … life is good when you are happy; but much better when others are happy because of you.* We are blessed to be a blessing to others.

David recognized God's creative work in bringing us into being and sustaining our lives so that we can bear good fruit. He wrote: *You formed my inward parts; You covered me in my mother's womb* (Psalm 139:13 NKJV). When calling Jeremiah to be a prophet, God said, *Before I formed you in the womb I knew you; before you were born, I sanctified you; I ordained you a prophet to the nations* (Jer. 1:5). These scriptures show that God conceived humans in His mind, formed them in their mother's womb, nurtured them as they grew, sanctified them, and ordained them for His purposes before their birth. God secured their birth and later commissioned them for their divine calling.

Paul, writing to the Galatians, said, *I have been crucified with Christ; it is no longer I who live, but Christ lives in me; and the life which I now live in the flesh I live by faith in the Son of God, who loved me and gave Himself for me* (Gal. 2:20).

When you live your life in union with Christ, you are never alone, because you are the temple of the Godhead. Child of God, make no mistake, God in three persons is always with you by faith through the Holy Spirit.

God loved us even when we were sinners. David affirmed this when he said: *You open Your hand and satisfy the desire of every living thing* (Psalm 145:16 NKJV). Matthew also wrote *that you may be sons of your Father in heaven; for He makes His sun rise on the evil and on the good and sends rain on the just and on the unjust* (Matt. 5:45). At what point, then, does a human being live life truly alone? Unless you live outside the universe, complete isolation is impossible. Even when you choose to disobey God, you are not alone, you are simply shifting your allegiance to the devil and his evil spirits.

While an individual physically experiences birth, life, and death, none of these events happen in a vacuum. Hence, the notion that *we are born alone, we live alone, we die alone* is a misnomer. If that were true, we could choose whether to be born. If we broke the law, no one would arrest us. We could decide whether to die or not. And if we chose to disobey God, there would be no consequence. But that is not how life works. None of these choices occur in a vacuum or go without impact on others.

By default, no human being is alone at any point in time. The birth of a baby marks the beginning of new relationships, and for some, it confers new roles, parents, grandparents, aunts, uncles. Even in death, people mourn, bury the deceased, and often continue holding memorials. Some relational ties even extend beyond the grave.

God, our Maker, never designed us to function in isolation. Just as God the Father, God the Son, and God the Holy Spirit operate in perfect unity, humans are also called to function within community to fulfil our divine purpose. Within the body of Christ, our gifts, skills, and resources are meant to build one another up. As we bless others, we are also blessed by what they bring. We rely on the complementarity of believers' strengths within our community.

Just as no economy thrives with one pair of hands, King Solomon observed that two people working together yield a greater return than one working alone (Eccl. 4:9). While we can pray and study the Bible alone—and indeed should—

without anchoring ourselves in a community of believers, our spiritual growth and effectiveness will still fall short of what God intended. Scripture gives us many examples of believers praying together with powerful results. When Peter was imprisoned, the Church prayed fervently, and God sent an angel to release him from jail and from Herod's grip (Acts 12:5–15). Isolation limits your potential. Partnership unlocks your maximum spiritual output.

We need other believers for stability as we walk with the Lord (Eccl. 4:10). Solomon reminds us that if one falls, the other can lift him up. Life brings moments of weakness. When I was struck by a mysterious illness, there were times when I was so weak and in pain that I couldn't even pray. Thank God for over 15 pastors and other believers who committed to pray for me. Some even fasted. One servant of God, Rev. Francis Akagbo, was available to me 24/7 during that critical time. Beyond sickness, we support one another through spiritual attacks, marital issues, ministry challenges, career disappointments, and more. Every believer will face peaks and valleys. You need people to walk with you in your highs and to lift you during your lows.

A fellowship of believers has built-in survival mechanisms. Solomon gives a simple yet profound example: *If two lie down together, they will keep warm. But how can one keep warm alone"* (Eccl. 4:11). This natural survival strategy in cold environments is only possible when two or more warm-blooded beings are together. Curious about the science behind this, I investigated thermodynamic principles of heat transfer. Physicist Ted Pavlic, a postdoctoral researcher, explains using thermodynamics why two people lying together retain heat better than one alone. He outlines three key points.

The Power of Spiritual Community: Lessons from Nature and Scripture

Ted Pavlic explains that there are three conditions that keep two people lying down together warm:

- Heat travels from a hot object to a cold one, and the rate of transfer is determined by the temperature difference between them.

- Warm-blooded animals regulate their internal body temperature. When their temperature drops, the body uses energy to restore it, unless heat is lost faster than it can be produced.
- Heat exchange between individuals occurs at the point of physical contact, where the surfaces of the bodies meet.

This means that when you reduce the surface area exposed to the cold environment and instead bring it into contact with another warmer body, total heat loss is minimized.

My curiosity about this phenomenon led me to learn more. Many small birds - such as bluebirds, chickadees, and titmice - gather in tight flocks at night and huddle together in confined spaces to share body heat. Penguins huddle in tightly packed groups to conserve energy during the extreme cold and wind of the Antarctic. Sparrows also cluster to minimize their total surface area exposed to cold surroundings. This natural coping mechanism, huddling for warmth, is a powerful metaphor for how believers overcome physical and spiritual challenges by sticking together.

When we surround ourselves with Spirit-filled children of God, we reduce our exposure to spiritual coldness and sin. Our spiritual "surface interface" is shaped by prayer, Bible study, covenant meals, the Lord's Supper, and generosity, shared with us by those walking closely with the Lord.

The assembly of believers provides a kind of spiritual security that no isolated believer can achieve alone. King Solomon emphasized that *one may be overpowered, but two can defend themselves* (Eccl. 4:12). Similarly, Deuteronomy 32:30 says: *How should one chase a thousand, and two put ten thousand to flight, unless their Rock had sold them, and the Lord had shut them up?* In this context, two pagan Roman soldiers under divine command overwhelmed ten times more rebellious Jewish soldiers than one could alone, highlighting the multiplier effect of unity under God's direction.

Even in the natural world, two soldiers are more effective than one. They can divide enemy fire, one can provide covering fire while the other advances, and together they can deliver more rounds per minute. But this disproportionate outcome in Deuteronomy was not merely tactical, it was spiritual. The Lord handed Israel over to its enemies because of disobedience.

This stands in stark contrast to God's promise when His people walk in obedience: "Five of you will chase a hundred, and a hundred of you will chase ten thousand, and your enemies will fall by the sword before you" (Lev. 26:8, NIV). The difference is obedience and alignment with God. The passage underscores not just the numerical power of unity, but the spiritual force behind it.

When believers unite in faith - through prayer, fasting, worship, and study - they access a profound spiritual power capable of demolishing strongholds. The early Church understood this. Acts 2:42–46 (NIV) tells us: *They devoted themselves to the apostles' teaching and to fellowship, to the breaking of bread and to prayer. Everyone was filled with awe at the many wonders and signs performed by the apostles. All the believers were together and had everything in common... Every day they continued to meet in the temple courts.* So strong was their unity that believers sold their possessions to support others in need. Their fellowship was not just intimate, it was transformative. *And the Lord added to their number daily those who were being saved* (Acts 2:47).

A committed fellowship of believers is so strong that it cannot be easily dismantled, and what it sets out to do will succeed, if it aligns with the will and purpose of God. King Solomon said, *A cord of three strands is not quickly broken* (Eccl. 4:12 NIV). When believers are united in mind and heart, the spiritual bonds that hold them together are so strong that the enemy finds it difficult to pull them apart.

A well-established fellowship that follows the principles of Christian living attracts the power of God. While an individual believer can wield great spiritual authority, a group of believers can draw on an even greater measure - a higher "voltage" of God's power - through the Holy Spirit, who manifests among them in diverse ways.

For example, when the apostles, women, and the brothers of Jesus gathered in the upper room and prayed together, they received the baptism of the Holy Spirit and began to speak in other tongues as the Spirit enabled them (Acts 2:2–4, NIV). Later, after Peter and John were released from prison and warned not to speak in the name of Jesus, the believers gathered again to pray. They asked God to give the apostles boldness, to stretch out His hand to heal, and to perform signs and wonders in the name of Jesus. In response, *the place where they were meeting was shaken. And they were all filled with the Holy Spirit and spoke the word of God boldly* (Acts 4:23–31, NIV).

There is immense power available to every believer who is connected to a Spirit-filled fellowship. If you are not yet part of any Christian fellowship groups, seek them out in your area. Make it a priority to join a family fellowship, Bible study group or house church, adult Sunday school, and your local church fellowship. These communities are essential for your growth, strength, and spiritual covering.

d. Harnessing the Power of God Through the Commonwealth of Believers

As I grew up in my parents' home, I noticed that each time we received visitors, my mum prepared a special meal or snack for them. For those who came from distant places, she would often cook a chicken or beef curry with Nshima (a local staple food). Even our neighbours were assured of snacks each time they visited. My parents were also generous with material things. I remember my mother giving away some of my clothes to people she believed were in need. Likewise, my father gave away some of his expensive clothes to others who were less privileged.

As I became increasingly aware of different cultures, I realized that people around the world share many types of resources - money, vehicles, even houses. In fact, wherever people live or gather, sharing resources is the norm rather than the exception. But this raises a few questions: Is generosity an inborn trait, or is it shaped by circumstances? Is there biblical evidence that humanity has always practiced hospitality? And how does the sharing of resources influence both livelihood and godliness?

Sharing is part of God's nature. His acts of creation and sustaining the universe are built on the principle of shared resources. From eternity past, the Godhead shared the vision and responsibility of creating and maintaining the universe. In any divine activity, each person of the Trinity has a unique role, demonstrating shared responsibility. For example, God the Father conceived the earth with its plants and animals, God the Son expressed the Father's will through the Word, and God the Holy Spirit executed that Word into action.

The manifestation of God's power and essence depends on the united and cooperative work of the Trinity. The resources and responsibilities of the Father, Son, and Holy Spirit are so deeply interwoven that they cannot be separated. This divine collaboration reflects an open-access model, everything each Person has is held in common. Therefore, sharing is not just something God does; it is who He is.

When God created humanity, He demonstrated this generosity by forming man from the dust and breathing His own breath of life into him. God shared His life with us. Later, when humanity fell, God demonstrated His ultimate act of generosity: *For God so loved the world that He gave His only begotten Son, that whoever believes in Him should not perish but have everlasting life* (John 3:16, NKJV). The gift of Jesus was God's way of sharing His love and redemption with creation. The Holy Spirit continues to share God's power and presence with us today.

Through His death, burial, and resurrection, Jesus took on our sin and gave us His righteousness. As branches grafted into the true vine, we now share in God's divine nature. We are co-heirs with Christ. We have been given the right to become children of God (John 1:12, NKJV), and we have access to His incomparably great power (Ephesians 1:19). God gives consistently and lavishly, revealing His nature as the ultimate giver.

Every creature reflects God's design for mutual sharing. Plants produce oxygen, which animals and humans need. In return, humans and animals exhale carbon dioxide, which plants use for photosynthesis. This is one of countless examples showing how life is sustained by mutual exchange. The universe is an intricate ecosystem of living and non-living things, designed to coexist through interdependence. We are wired to give and receive.

Some claim they don't need anyone to survive, but even a brief reflection shows how interconnected we really are. Marriage, for example, is a relationship built on the sharing of physical, emotional, and spiritual resources. A woman shares her body with her husband and, during pregnancy, with her child. The child in turn shares love with parents and siblings. At work, employees share their skills and time, and employers share compensation and benefits. Nature too reflects this exchange, livestock, wild animals, and marine life provide food and materials, while humans manage and steward ecosystems.

In the body of Christ, sharing is central. Ministers serve others with the Word, prayer, fellowship, and material support. The Church functions as a spiritual economy where no one thrives alone. Every member brings something to the table, and every member needs the contributions of others. *But the manifestation of the Spirit is given to each one for the profit of all* (1 Cor. 12:7, NKJV). This principle of mutual benefit defines the church as a commonwealth of faith and resources.

When you join the body of Christ, your gifts, time, and life become part of a shared spiritual ecosystem. Your body, soul, and spirit become a resource for the edification of others, just as their gifts help build you up. By default, every believer becomes a public good, someone designed to give and receive in community.

The early Church clearly understood the concept of the commonwealth: *All the believers met together in one place and shared everything they had. They sold their property and possessions and shared the money with those in need"* (Acts 2:42–44, NIV). Some argue that this was merely the behaviour of a young, naïve Church, one no longer relevant or practical in today's context. However, there are two important realities we must consider.

First, this was a Church birthed out of a powerful outpouring of the Holy Spirit. Even if its practices appear idealistic, they were rooted in obedience to the Spirit's leading. Ironically, it is often when believers consider themselves "mature" in the faith that they begin to question, even dilute, God's commands.

According to Jeon (2013), giving in the early Church was a voluntary and joyful response to the gospel and its profound spiritual and social implications. The early believers demonstrated mutuality, unity, and intimacy through their commitment to Christ, most tangibly by their sacrificial generosity and shared resources. This Holy Spirit-driven unity fostered an internal vibrancy that led to numerical growth. **Second**, the early Church deprivatised the life of the believer, something that many people today resist. Their fellowship ensured that no child of God lacked basic needs. Today, we are faced with a stark paradox: the world produces enough food to feed everyone, yet one in seven people goes to bed hungry every night. According to Oxfam Canada, *"The world produces 17% more food per person today than 30 years ago. But close to a billion people go to sleep hungry every night. The problem is that many people in the world don't have sufficient land to grow, or income to purchase, enough food. Hunger is not a random condition."*

Globally, the capitalist model often leads to nations hoarding resources while others struggle. The principle of the commonwealth is simple: those with abundance share with those in need. However, in our current systems, resources are frequently used to gain control or assert dominance. While God has provided more than enough for every creature on earth, our spiritually insensitive models of stewardship have led to inequality and exclusion. The principles of commonwealth often stand in stark contrast to capitalist ideals.

Sharing resources: a biblical foundation

Sharing of resources within the community of believers is foundational to both spiritual and physical growth in the body of Christ. Several biblical passages affirm this principle:

1. Sharing Must be Part of Your Calling

Every child of God is commanded to work not just for personal gain, but to help others. Paul told the Ephesians: *"Let him that stole steal no more: but rather let him labour, working with his hands the thing, which is good, that he may have to give to him that needeth"* (Eph. 4:28, KJV). Christians are called to build livelihood systems that are designed to include capacity for generosity. While this may seem countercultural or even exploitative to some, sharing is a trait inherited from our heavenly Father.

2. Sharing Activates God's Cycle of Multiplication

Paul also writes: *"Now he who supplies seed to the sower and bread for food will also supply and increase your store of seed and will enlarge the harvest of your righteousness. You will be enriched in every way so that you can be generous on every occasion, and through us your generosity will result in thanksgiving to God"* (2 Corinthians 9:10–11, NIV). Notice how both seed and bread come from the same source. A wise farmer divides the harvest: some for food, some for future planting. Seed is stored in a way that preserves its viability. Paul emphasizes that God is the one who supplies both the seed and the increase. This ensures not only our sustenance, but also our ability to share with others.

God's economy is circular. As we give, He replenishes. When we hoard, we break this divine cycle. By denying one person what they need, we may indirectly deny many others who would have benefitted downstream through the multiplier effect.

When we choose to share what God has given us - whether spiritual gifts, money, food, or time - we complete the circuit of giving and receiving. And as Paul points out, generosity leads to thanksgiving to God. The person you bless will glorify God because of your obedience.

3. Sharing is God's Provision for Sustaining the Vulnerable in Our Midst

The author of Deuteronomy wrote, *"When you are harvesting in your field and you overlook a sheaf, do not go back to get it. Leave it for the foreigner, the fatherless and the widow, so that the LORD your God may bless you in all the work of your hands"* (Deut. 24:19, NIV). According to the books of Deuteronomy and Leviticus, Israelite farmers were instructed to: leave the corners of their fields unharvested; leave behind any produce that fell (gleanings); and not to return to collect overlooked or forgotten produce.

This system applied to grain fields, orchards, and vineyards, ensuring that foreigners, widows, and the fatherless had access to food. Through such acts of generosity, God promised to bless the work of their hands.

Today, many humanitarian organizations practice this same principle of *gleaning*, collecting surplus food to distribute to those in need. Likewise, Christians who understand that God's provision is meant not only for personal use but also for helping others - foreigners, orphans, widows, and even wildlife - embody this principle. God gives not only to sustain us, but so we can supply the needs of others and sow generously. Our works of charity confirm our submission to the gospel of Jesus Christ.

4. Sacrificial Sharing Motivated by Love, Reverence, and Obedience is An Act of Worship

In Mark 12:41–44, Jesus observed people giving offerings at the temple. He highlighted the poor widow who gave two small copper coins, everything she had to live on. Others gave from their surplus, but she gave from her poverty. Her offering, though small in value, demonstrated deep trust, worship, and obedience.

She gave not because she had enough, but because she recognized giving as worship. Ironically, she was the kind of person others might have expected to *receive* from the temple treasury, not contribute to it. Yet, she still gave.

Her example reminds us that no one is too poor to give something. And while Jesus was observing monetary gifts, the principle extends to any resource we have time, food, skills, and compassion. Whenever we give intentionally, sacrificially, and joyfully, we honour God.

5. When we Share with the Vulnerable, we Share Christ's Burden

Proverbs 19:17 says, *"Whoever is generous to the poor lends to the Lord, and he will repay him for his deed"* (ESV). Though God owes nothing to anyone (Rom. 11:35), He graciously repays those who care for His children. He treats acts of generosity as loans to Himself.

6. Sharing Activates the Law of Reciprocity

Paul wrote to the Corinthians: *"Whoever sows sparingly will also reap sparingly, and whoever sows generously will also reap generously"* (2 Cor. 9:6). And Dr. Luke added, *"Give, and it will be given to you. A good measure, pressed down, shaken together, and running over will be poured into your lap…"* (Luke 6:38, NIV). This principle teaches that: God favours acts of charity; God rewards those who give to the poor; and Generosity begets generosity.

The image of blessings being "poured into your lap" comes from an Eastern tradition where robes were gathered into a pouch-like fold above the belt, functioning like a large pocket. The overflowing blessings symbolize that what we give, we receive back in even greater measure. A hallmark of Christ's followers is generosity. Jesus taught His disciples to be known not just for their righteousness but for their liberality and kindness, even to strangers and sinners (3 John 1:5–6).

7. Believers are Commanded to Share Even with Their Enemies

Jesus said: *But love your enemies, do good to them, and lend to them without expecting to get anything back. Then your reward will be great, and you will be children of the Most High, because he is kind to the ungrateful and wicked* (Luke 6:35, NIV). This is a hard teaching. Yet, it reveals the heart of our Father, who sends rain and sun on the just and unjust alike. To be like Him, we must imitate His love, even toward those who wrong us. Paul echoes this in Romans 12:20, *If your enemy is hungry, feed him; if he is thirsty, give him something to drink.* This kind of sharing requires a transformed mind and heart, shaped by the mercy and forgiveness of Christ.

Even when giving is difficult, our attitude matters. Paul instructed the Corinthians, *"Each man should give what he has decided in his heart, not reluctantly or under compulsion, for God loves a cheerful giver"* (2 Cor. 9:7). King Solomon adds, *He that soweth wicked things shall reap evils… God blesses a cheerful man and a giver…* (Prov. 22:8, KJV). According to Ellicott's Commentary, even Aristotle rejected the title of "liberal" for someone who gave without pleasure because such a person would prefer to keep the money rather than do good.

Sharing with the needy should be voluntary and cheerful, an offering from the heart. Let your gift be given freely and willingly. It is not so much the quantity that matters, but the quality, the spirit in which the gift is offered.

A Christian who follows the initial prompting of the Holy Spirit when faced with a need will often give generously. The instinctive prompting of a benevolent heart is to give liberally. God has planted these compassionate instincts in us. If we respond to them sincerely, we will likely give as we ought. Generally, this is the safest and best guide for our giving: to give as our Spirit-led hearts prompt us when a need arises.

God desires the heart in every act of service. Only cheerful, voluntary giving, born of genuine love, can be acceptable in His sight. God, by His Spirit, stirs the believer's heart, enabling us to give without grudging or reluctance. He loves such giving because it reflects His own heart, a heart inclined to bless, to give, and to care generously. Therefore, we must examine the motives behind our giving. No matter how liberal our giving may appear, God may reject it if it lacks sincerity. We should never give:

- Out of obligation or fear of what others will think
- Because others are giving and we feel pressured to match them
- To uphold status, out of pride or vanity
- To impress a pastor, friend, or community
- Because we feel we must protect our reputation

True Christian giving should come from a deliberate, joyful decision, not from manipulation or compulsion. God looks at the will and affection of the giver, not the quantity of the gift. Anything given without a cheerful heart is, in God's eyes, wasted.

8. Supporting Ministers and Teachers

Believers are also called to share good things with their teachers, just as they share with their brothers and sisters in Christ: *Let the one who is taught the word share all good things with the one who teaches* (Gal. 6:6, NIV). In an age where prosperity gospel abuses have provoked suspicion, some have gone to the extreme of condemning all Christian giving. However, Scripture remains clear: believers have a responsibility to support those who minister the Word.

Those who are called, qualified, and sent by Christ to preach and teach should be honourably maintained. They dedicate their time, energy, and gifts to instructing the Church, and therefore should be supported in a manner that allows them to focus on spiritual matters without worldly anxieties. What we share with them should be liberal and sufficient, providing for their needs and the needs of their families, ensuring their service remains joyful and undistracted.

9. The Early Church and the Commonwealth of Saints

The concept of the commonwealth of saints hinges on unity of heart and soul. Acts 4:32 says: *All the believers were one in heart and mind. No one claimed that any of their possessions was their own, but they shared everything they had.* And Acts 2:45 adds: *They sold property and possessions to give to anyone who had need.* The Holy Spirit brought about a profound unity—a bond that fused believers together in heart, soul, and purpose. This supernatural unity manifested not only in doctrine and prayer but also in their handling of possessions. Their hearts were knit together, and their affection and understanding were harmonized in the Spirit.

Commentators such as Gill and Ellicott point out that this unity went beyond emotional connection. It extended into practical living. Believers did not regard their possessions as exclusively theirs, but as resources entrusted to them for the good of the community. Their mindset was one of stewardship, not ownership.

Though the early Church may seem like a "fairy tale" to some today, it happened, and it can happen again, but not by human willpower or economic systems. Only through the Spirit of the Lord (Zech. 4:6) can such unity and generosity be revived in today's Church.

10. The Modern Church and the Challenge of Unity

This early Church model holds a sobering message for the modern Church, especially concerning the responsibility of wealth and the claims of brotherhood. In a time when individualism dominates, the idea of holding things in common feels foreign, yet it reflects the very essence of Christian discipleship: *By this everyone will know that you are my disciples, if you love one another* (John 13:35). We must not dismiss the principle of shared resources just because some have abused it. The early believers did not renounce ownership legally, but they let go of the attitude of ownership. They held their possessions loosely and used them for the benefit of others as needed. Their unity of heart and soul was a miraculous work of the Holy Spirit. When believers are filled with the Spirit, they are drawn into deep love, selflessness, and shared purpose. That same Spirit is available today.

As a child of God, you are called to be part of this spiritual commonwealth, a community where there is shared doctrine, shared burdens, shared resources, and mutual care. This is the true Church, living by the teachings of Jesus, walking in sincere love, and manifesting the unity of the Spirit in every area of life. Let us live with one heart and one soul, not in theory but in practice, until the Lord returns.

11. Sharing is a Practical Expression of the Love of Christ

The Lord desires His brothers and sisters to be as charitable as He is. Obedience to His command ensures that all our brethren can live honourable lives. Reiterating this call to love, John, by the Spirit of God, provides a sobering litmus test for our love for Christ: *But whoever has this world's goods, and sees his brother in need, and shuts up his heart from him, how does the love of God abide in him?* (1 John 3:17, NKJV). This verse challenges us to reflect honestly:

- Have you seen a brother or sister in need?
- Did you have the resources to meet that need?
- Did you consider sharing what you had with them?

We must remain sensitive to promptings of the Holy Spirit. He will not bring someone's need to our attention unless He knows we have the means to help. Let us purpose in our hearts to help those in need—especially our brethren in the faith. This is how we show that the love of Christ truly dwells in us. Let us purpose in our hearts to help people in need, especially our brethren.

e. Believers Access the Power of God Through Shared Meals

Eating is a spiritual activity that draws power from God, provided it is not abused. King Solomon said, *A person can do nothing better than to eat and drink and find satisfaction in their own toil. This too, I see, is from the hand of God, for without him, who can eat or find enjoyment?* (Eccl. 2:24–25 NIV). The power and ability of humans to eat, drink, and find joy in their labour proceed wholly from God. Although the acts of eating and the utilization of food in the body appear to be merely physical and physiological processes, they are driven by the hand (power) of God.

Beyond their spiritual aspects and their role in meeting the body's energy, growth, development, and defence requirements, meals have social functions in the life of a believer and the community of saints. Sharing a meal with others is an outward expression of the unity of those involved. Friends, families, colleagues, royals, businessmen, religious individuals, statesmen, and other groups in society share meals as an expression of their shared values.

Families, the basic building blocks of the Church, communicate this value very well, especially those that are deeply rooted in Christ. Families usually share meals and hence enjoy several benefits associated with this practice.

In many cultural settings, mealtime is a special time for being together to enjoy each other and a time for sharing knowledge and wisdom on matters of common interest. Families that eat together are generally more productive than those that do not. Sharing meals ensures that:

- Everyone is fed.
- Members of the family are consistently connected, they know what is going on in each other's lives.
- Everyone is emotionally supported.
- All family members contribute to the preparation of meals.
- Everyone develops a sense of routine.
- Parents and children find out about each other's day.
- The family shares news items and finds out what each individual thinks about them.
- Children have proper meals.
- Good eating habits improve children's performance in school.
- Chances of children indulging in drugs or alcohol are reduced.

Families that eat together also encourage healthy eating patterns and higher nutrient intake, and reduce fat, sugar, and calorie intake because they eat homemade food.

Other studies have suggested that sharing meals in a family setting provides opportunities for individuals to learn language skills and table manners, interact in a relaxed atmosphere, celebrate cultural heritage, and give birth to traditions. Thus, rich family meal customs build family relationships, health and well-being, and rich societal values.

Many people living in the lands described in the Bible still practice mealtime customs depicted in biblical texts. Meals in this part of the world express social, cultural, symbolic, and spiritual ideas, values, and beliefs. They often convey the common Near Eastern value of hospitality (Gen. 18:1–8; Heb. 3:12); affirm kinship, friendship, and goodwill (Gen. 31:33–54); acknowledge one's status (1 Kings 17:8–16, 2 Kings 4:8–11); and recognize the peaceful nature and commitment to non-offensive treatment of kinsmen, neighbours, and strangers. Depending on the environment and nature of the event, sharing a meal can express different non-verbal messages regarding interpersonal relationships.

Several biblical passages describe diverse meal settings and their value in different social, physical, and spiritual contexts. In ancient Israel, meals fell into three categories: ordinary, festive, and sacred. In the East, every aspect of human life is perceived as a spiritual occasion, and hence meals and the altar are inseparable. For most Jews, meals connected directly to sacrificial worship were sacred.

There are many biblical examples of Jews sharing meals with non-Jews and accepting food from non-Jews in earlier times (Gen. 14:18, 26:30; Exod. 18:12; Deut. 2:28, 23:4–7; 2 Kings 4:8, 25:29–30), but their social and spiritual meanings of meals sometimes restricted such table fellowship. The Jews expressed different forms of table worship. Some ate only after morning prayers (Acts 2:15), while others recited prayers before meals (1 Sam. 9:13, Matt. 14:19, 15:36, 26:26; Luke 9:16), celebrated special occasions with meals, or expressed thanksgiving through prayers after meals (Deuteronomy 8:10).

Bread was often served as a reference meal because it was an indispensable staple and substantial part of most meals (Gen. 37:25; Exod. 2:20; 1 Sam. 28:22–25; Matt. 6:11). It was not cut but typically broken with hands, which is reflected by the common expression "to break bread" (Lam. 4:4; Luke 24:35; Acts 2:42, 46).

Biblical writings show that several communities in the ancient Mediterranean had different, unique, symbolic, and significant meal customs, although they were not always consistent. This historical, social, cultural, and spiritual significance of meals explains the prominence of table worship in both the Old and New Testaments.

In the Near East, a meal was a significant component of covenant-making, a covenant was sealed with a meal. The bond was sealed by both parties vowing, often by oath, that each, having equal privileges and responsibilities, would carry out their assigned roles. The covenant-making process often comprised a sacrifice, a covenant meal, a memorial to remind parties of their commitments, and a curse attached to one who broke the covenant. It was a solemn event and a serious commitment between the parties involved.

An example of a covenant meal and its attendant peace is found in Genesis 31:51–54, where Laban and Jacob come to a truce and solemnize their pact by breaking bread. Exodus 24:1–11 records an extraordinary covenant meal, Moses and the elders of Israel sat and ate in the presence of God at the foot of Mount Sinai. Several other covenant meals are recorded in the Bible:

- Melchizedek shared bread and wine with Abram (Gen. 14:18).
- Isaac and Abimelech ate together at Beersheba (Gen. 26:26–31).
- Laban and Jacob had a covenant meal over a heap of stones at Galeed (Gen. 31:43–54).
- Joshua and the representatives of Gibeon shared a covenant meal in Gilgal (Josh. 9:14).
- Noah ate a covenant meal in the presence of God after the flood (Gen. 8:20–22; 9:9).

- God prepares a table before His people in the presence of their enemies (Psa. 23).

In ancient times, eating with others was a significant act, for only those at peace could dine together. Sharing a meal also entrusted the host with responsibility for the guest's safety. Covenant meals were often understood to take place in the presence of God.

In the New Testament, Jesus instituted the Lord's Supper, enabling believers to share in His body through the breaking of bread and in His blood through the cup of blessing (1 Cor. 10:16–17). This covenant meal, first shared between Jesus and His Jewish disciples, preceded the communal meals of the early Church, and all believers are now welcome to partake in it. As the High Priest in the order of Melchizedek, Jesus instructed His followers to share this meal regularly until He returns.

Jesus valued eating with others. Mark records: *While Jesus was having dinner at Levi's house, many tax collectors and sinners were eating with him and his disciples, for there were many who followed him* (Mark 2:15, NIV). He also dined with Zacchaeus, the tax collector (Luke 19:1–11). The Lord shared meals with sinners to demonstrate His love and to bring them salvation. In Revelation 3:20 (NIV), Jesus declares: *Here I am! I stand at the door and knock. If anyone hears my voice and opens the door, I will come in and eat with that person, and they with me.* This open invitation expresses His desire to fellowship with and save the lost.

After His ascension, the early Church developed the practice of sharing meals. Dr. Luke records that the believers *continued steadfastly in the apostles' doctrine and fellowship, and in breaking of bread, and in prayers* (Acts 2:42, KJV). The early Church understood that the sharing of meals, both in secular life and in Christian community, was not a random ritual, but one rich with spiritual symbolism.

Even today, a meal can be an expression of love and a sign of fellowship. Sharing meals with other believers is a meaningful way to foster peace among the brethren and to show a hurting world the love we have for one another. Every believer should participate in fellowship meals at church. If possible, share a meal with someone in the congregation you do not know well.

God, the Creator of heaven and earth, owns all resources, including the food we eat. He also gives us the power and ability to enjoy it. The Lord, who sustains us, ensures that all bodily processes related to eating and nutrition function properly. Sharing meals with fellow believers, and even with those who don't yet believe, demonstrates reverence for God and obedience to His commandments. Therefore, when we share meals in accordance with His will, He is present, and His power is made accessible to us. Sharing meals with a God-consciousness invites His presence and power.

Other Modes of Accessing the Power of God
a. Seek First the Kingdom of God and His Righteousness (Matt. 6:33)

Access to the power of God requires aligning your life's purpose with God's purpose. In Matthew 6:33, Jesus admonishes His followers to seek the will of God in everything they do. When you seek first the Kingdom of God first and His righteousness, you prioritize God's will above all else. Whenever we live in union with Christ, God takes full responsibility for meeting all our needs, ensuring our lives are sustained by His storehouses.

Seeking God's will is an expression of our total dependence on His providential care. In our society, where people look to money, insurance, and others for security, wholehearted dependence on God is rare. Consider a simple instruction: give 10% of your income or agricultural produce to God and live on the remaining 90%. How often do we fail this test? Why do we struggle with this instruction? We live in a society built on safety nets, so much so that even after accepting Christ, these safety nets often linger in our subconscious.

When we face difficulties, we often turn first to our "nets"- friends, family, or bank accounts -before remembering to call on the name of the Lord. A devoted follower of Christ lives as if there are no human-made safety nets, depending entirely on God to deliver or guide them, even when He ultimately works through those nets.

When we seek first God's kingdom and His righteousness, we plug into His immeasurable power. Beyond the power universally available to all creation, we gain access to the power reserved for those who live in union with Christ. As a child of God, strive to seek His will in all things, and you will fulfil your life's purpose.

b. Dwell in the House of the Lord

In the business world, apprentices attach themselves to mentors to learn a trade. They work closely with them, observing, learning, and applying skills under supervision. In some cases, apprentices even live with their mentors. Believers who walk with God adopt a similar model of cultivating intimacy with Him.

David boldly declares: *One thing I ask from the Lord, this only do I seek: that I may dwell in the house of the Lord all the days of my life, to gaze on the beauty of the Lord and to seek him in his temple* (Psa. 27:4, NIV). Although we often read this verse casually, the Psalmist expresses deep longing and a rich relationship with God. Under painful circumstances - being a king on the run, bearing the consequences of his sins, and denied the opportunity to build the Lord's temple - David distilled all his longings into one desire: to be in the presence of the Lord.

Imagine being given one opportunity to ask God for anything. Would your request reflect your deepest desire? Consider your current situation, financial strain, illness, addiction, relationship issues, rebellious children. It would be understandable to bring those before God. Yet David shows us that all challenges pale in comparison to being in God's presence. There are several lessons from Psalm 27:4:

1. Unity of desire: David had one singular, focused desire. This expressed a unified heart and life.
2. Wholehearted pursuit: Once he identified his desire, he pursued it with all he had. Have we defined our heart's desire and invested fully in it?
3. Constant fellowship: David wanted to dwell in God's house all his life, not just physically, but spiritually and emotionally, even outside the temple.
4. Gazing on His beauty: What could be more pleasurable than beholding the beauty of the Creator Himself?
5. Seeking Him is noble: Seeking the Lord in His temple is the most

honourable pursuit. Dwelling in God's presence is an expression of love and trust in the One who empowers us to live God-centred lives.

c. Know your identity and nurture it

One of the greatest hindrances to fulfilling our earthly mission is a failure to recognize and live out our identity. Imagine an electrical appliance that has been wrongly wired, it will malfunction and might even cause harm. That's exactly what happens when someone lives out a false identity. God will not connect His power to a misaligned identity.

When Jacob wrestled with the angel at the brook, he was asked to identify himself. Upon confessing his name, the angel gave him a new identity, Israel, because he had wrestled with God and with men and prevailed.

Many people walk around with stolen or masked identities. These suppress their authentic selves. But God never releases His power to a distorted identity. He desires to showcase His glory through your unique potential and design. As a believer, discovering and living out your God-given identity must be a top priority. Only then can you truly harness the power of God.

d. Exercise the full package of the gifts of the Spirit through fellowship

Believers are called to express the gifts of the Holy Spirit in their ministries. These include:

- **Word of Knowledge**: Divine insight and understanding about a person or situation.
- **Word of Wisdom**: God-given ability to apply knowledge rightly.
- **Faith**: Supernatural confidence that what God has revealed will come to pass.
- **Healing**: Restoration of health through the power of God, often connected to a word of knowledge or wisdom.
- **Working of Miracles**: Supernatural acts that manifest God's power, rooted in divine revelation.
- **Discerning of Spirits**: Ability to detect the presence or absence of spiritual forces and respond accordingly.

- **Prophecy**: Speaking or communicating God's message to individuals or groups.
- **Speaking in Tongues**: Speaking a language unknown to the speaker, given by the Holy Spirit.
- **Interpretation of Tongues**: Explaining the meaning of the message spoken in tongues so others can understand.

These gifts are not just personal blessings; they are tools to edify the Church, strengthen the body of Christ, and glorify God. Fellowship among believers is the environment in which these gifts thrive.

Many Christians believe that only certain people can manifest spiritual gifts. While it is true that some individuals are vocationally called to specific gifts, God can sovereignly use any believer to manifest multiple gifts as the Spirit leads. The key to this is submission to the authority of the Holy Spirit. The degree to which God's power operates in and through you depends on your willingness and determination to be led by Him. We should never limit the Lord, let Him do what He wants with our gifts.

A believer indwelt by the Godhead carries the same power that raised Jesus Christ from the dead and seated Him at the right hand of the Father. Regardless of the stature of the person carrying this power, it is fully capable of accomplishing the purpose for which it is applied. However, when a Christian invokes the power of God, its operation requires a strong spiritual foundation.

The full expression of God's power in our lives depends on the measure of faith apportioned to us based on our spiritual gifts, calling (vocation), and ministry. But faith feeds on the Word of God and requires the presence of the Holy Spirit operating in a spiritually healthy environment.

The Word and the Holy Spirit do not operate in a vacuum, or in a person who passively hosts them. They move and manifest through Christians who actively walk in God's presence, live lives saturated with the Word, practice devoted prayer and fasting, and are fully submitted to the Spirit's leading.

Just as a crane anchored on steel plates on solid ground can lift and move heavy loads, a Christian firmly anchored in Christ can overcome any challenge in their sphere of life and time. When you are firmly grafted into Christ, the glorious power of God will carry you through life's storms. Having experienced both lack and abundance in his walk with the Lord, Paul confidently declared: *I can do all things through Christ who strengthens me* (Philip. 4:13, NKJV). What an incredible truth this is! But if the story ended here, it would only be half the truth.

While believers have access to God's glorious power, the process of living in that power is not always straightforward. As Paul recognized, it is a battle between two laws: the law of life in Christ and the law of sin and death (Romans 7–8). God's eternal power is available to every believer, but only those who seek Him and live in His presence have the access code to stay continually plugged in. Are you plugged into the eternal power of God?

Affirmation: I am a vessel of divine power, not by might, nor by strength, but by the Spirit. May my life reflect the light and love of the Source.

CHAPTER 10
How God's Power Works?

The LORD, our God, has established mechanisms for creating and sustaining things in the universe using His eternal power. By default, humans, who are created in His image, also require this same power to carry out all the activities He has assigned to them. Although the creation story in Genesis 1 and 2 does not explicitly state that God gave Adam and Eve access to His power, other parts of Scripture (such as the Acts of the Apostles) demonstrate that humans need supernatural power to function as stewards of God's creation and to fulfil their earthly duties.

The Bible clearly shows that the eternal power of God is indispensable in our daily lives. Yet, many of us underutilize this power, often because we do not fully understand how it operates or how to deploy it in our own circumstances.

Have you ever witnessed a situation where a mother gives her child a premium-grade mango or apple to eat? She gives the child time to enjoy it, but before long, she realizes he has abandoned the fruit and tossed it to the ground. Curious, the mother picks it up and finds that he's only taken a few bites, the fruit is nearly intact. "If only you knew how nutritious and expensive this fruit is, you wouldn't waste it," she mutters. But the child doesn't have the same understanding as the mother. To him, it's just another snack.

We shouldn't blame the child—after all, he's only little. But the incident illustrates how many believers approach the power of God. Without full understanding and appreciation, we may misuse, neglect, or even discard it. This chapter highlights some of the ways the power of God operates, so we can effectively and efficiently utilize it.

Understanding Our Productive Nature

God has created us in His image to be fruitful, to multiply, and to govern the earth in ways that glorify Him. Whether or not this outcome is realized depends on our understanding and application of three key things God has given us.

1. **God created you and me with latent qualities**, designed to fully express ourselves as stewards of creation, redeemed from sin, and living Christ-centred lives. Our spiritual DNA is wired to reflect the image of God, despite the fall. Sin suppresses this potential, but it is never erased, and the enemy knows it. You may question whether this is possible because of your past. But your God-given identity and purpose remain intact. If the right spiritual conditions are present, that potential will begin to shine through. You can develop, succeed, and fulfil the mission God carved out for you.
2. **God also defined your maximum output, your full potential, when He formed you.** In every area of life, God has embedded algorithms (divinely designed processes and rules) and resource combinations that, when activated, will yield your best performance. Whether you are a mother, a father, a teacher, an engineer, a nurse, a pastor, a cleaner, a business owner, or a student, you have a God-defined capacity to perform with excellence. The key is walking with the Holy Spirit to discover and align your potential with God's design for your life.

God specified your potential and capacity based on His purpose for your life. Paul helps the Ephesian saints understand who they truly are: *"For we are His workmanship, created in Christ Jesus for good works, which God prepared beforehand that we should walk in them"* (Eph. 2:10, NKJV). Contrary to what society tells us - that our identity is shaped by what we learn, do, or experience in our environment - your identity (your qualities and potential) was defined before you were even conceived in your mother's womb. Therefore, the likelihood of achieving your potential and fully exercising your capacity depends on your ability to align your identity with God's original design for you.

Paul teaches that God crafted us in Christ Jesus for good works, works which were already prepared at the point of our design. These good works reveal our potential and capacity. If we discover what they are and commit ourselves to doing them, we create the possibility of reaching our full potential—once the right conditions are in place.

However, your potential and capacity alone are not enough to bring about the right outcomes in your life. You also need an enabling environment and the necessary resources to carry out these good works. God, in His wisdom, understood this from the beginning and has made available a wide range of resources - His Word, His power, wisdom, knowledge, understanding, common sense, the fellowship of believers, and more - to ensure we are fully equipped to fulfil His purposes. When you combine a clearly defined potential, the application of your capacity, and the right resources and environment, you will be fruitful.

As a student of economics, I was taught that achieving high output from a production system depends on finding the right combination of inputs. The same principle applies to our spiritual lives. While many believers understand what is required to live a Christ-centred life, we often overlook the need to define the optimal combination of the three key factors of fruitfulness, especially the operation of the power of God. It is possible to have access to God's power, yet either underutilize it or never use it at all, simply because we do not understand how it operates.

How the Power God works
Activate the Power of God

Although the power of God is accessible to believers, it often remains untapped until we activate it through obedient action. This principle is beautifully illustrated in two events from the book of Joshua: the crossing of the Jordan River and the collapse of the walls of Jericho.

God had already empowered the Israelites to cross the Jordan at a time when it had overflowed its banks. However, the manifestation of this power remained invisible until the priests, carrying the Ark of the Covenant, stepped into the river. As Joshua records: *Now the Jordan is at flood stage all during harvest. Yet as soon as the priests who carried the ark reached the Jordan and their feet touched the water's edge, the water from upstream stopped flowing* (Josh. 3:15–16, NIV).

The presence and power of God were already with the Israelites, but nothing happened until they took a step of faith. Once the priests' feet touched the water, the river parted, and a supernatural dam formed upstream, holding back the water. The priests then stood on dry ground in the middle of the river while the entire nation crossed safely. Without that initial action, God's power would have remained dormant.

A second example is the fall of Jericho. The Lord told Joshua: *"See, I have delivered Jericho into your hands, along with its king and its fighting men. March around the city once with all the armed men. Do this for six days. Have seven priests carry trumpets of rams' horns in front of the ark. On the seventh day, march around the city seven times, with the priests blowing the trumpets. When you hear them sound a long blast, have the whole army give a loud shout; then the wall of the city will collapse"* (Joshua 6:2–5, NIV). God had already delivered the city into their hands—but the Israelites still had to act. Their part involved a series of unusual instructions: marching, blowing trumpets, and shouting. Humanly speaking, these actions could not have brought down the massive walls of Jericho, estimated to be 1.5–2.0 metres thick and 3.7–5.2 metres high. Yet, they became the instruments through which God's power was released.

These events teach us a critical spiritual principle: God often intervenes in our situations through instructions that require obedience to unlock the miracle. Many believers miss their breakthroughs not because God is unwilling, but because they are either insensitive to His voice or reluctant to take the required step of faith.

We must remember that God is Spirit, and His transactions take place in the spiritual realm. To see His power manifest in the physical realm, we must partner with Him through obedience and trust. God's power is already present, but it is activated when we respond in faith to His guidance.

Let's suppose you are praying for your brother to be saved. The Lord may soften his heart and make him receptive to the gospel, but He may also require you to share the Word of God with him. Similarly, if you are praying for a job, the Lord may open a door for you, but you still need to follow the leading of the Holy Spirit, by finding the vacancy, submitting your application, and attending the interview. God releases His power to work in our situations, but we must take action to activate its flow in our lives.

The Power of God is an Enabler

The power of God does not define the course of action; it makes things happen. In the creation story, God conceived the universe with all its components. What He had were architectural plans of creation, but it was His power that translated those plans into the actual heavens, the earth, and everything in them. This has serious implications for how we approach accessing the power of God.

First, we must recognize that despite its potency, the power of God does not determine what needs to be done. Either God or humans must define the desired outcome, what, how, when, and where. Second, the power of God transforms intentions into actions that produce results. No matter how good our plans may be, they remain only ideas unless the power of God brings them to life.

Think about this: What happens if you pray for a job but do nothing to pursue one? Or ask God for wisdom to pass an exam but never study? Suppose you want God to use you to reach the nations, but you never pray, never prepare, and never go? Or imagine a young man prays and fasts, believing God has revealed his future wife, yet never approaches her. Would the power of God deliver the outcome? While the sovereign Lord can work miraculously, He usually expects us to define our course of action with the help of the Holy Spirit, and then ask Him for the power to carry it out.

As children of God, we must recognize His power as an enabler in our walk with Him. Remember: the sovereign God has given us freedom of choice and spirit-led decision-making, and He has also granted access to His power to help us fulfil our assignments. God's power is not a substitute for our Spirit-guided obedience and action.

The Power of God is a Catalyst

According to *Britannica*, a catalyst is any substance that increases the rate of a reaction without itself being consumed. It initiates or accelerates the reaction but is not the main reagent. The reaction can still occur without the catalyst, but it would proceed much more slowly. In a broader sense, a catalyst can also refer to a person or agent that precipitates an event or change.

The conversion of the Ethiopian eunuch (Acts 8:26–40) is a good example of how the Holy Spirit used Philip as a catalyst. Philip, an evangelist, was led by the Spirit to approach the eunuch, a high-ranking official in the court of Candace, queen of the Ethiopians. Though the eunuch had just returned from worshiping in Jerusalem, he was not yet saved. As he travelled in his chariot, he read aloud from Isaiah 53:7–8: *He was led as a sheep to the slaughter; and as a lamb before its shearer is silent, so he does not open his mouth. In his humiliation he was deprived of justice. Who can speak of his descendants? For his life was taken from the earth.*

Troubled by the passage, the eunuch asked whom the scripture referred to. Philip, guided by the Holy Spirit, explained that it spoke of Jesus. Immediately, the eunuch believed and requested to be baptized. This account shows that the eunuch already had a desire to know God, he was searching. It's possible he might have eventually come to the truth on his own, but God sent a catalyst (Philip) to accelerate his understanding and decision. Importantly, the search did not begin with Philip; it began with the eunuch.

Another powerful example of a catalyst is given by the apostle Paul: *In the same way, the Spirit helps us in our weakness. We do not know what we ought to pray for, but the Spirit himself intercedes for us through wordless groans* (Rom. 8:26, NIV). As believers, we pray to the Father through Jesus Christ. But due to our human weakness, our communication can be unclear or incomplete. As a catalyst, the Holy Spirit helps bridge this gap, interpreting our prayers and helping us align with the will of God. He "edits" our messages to reflect our deepest needs and "decodes" divine responses so that we can better understand what God is saying.

In both examples, the catalyst does not replace the process, it enhances and accelerates it. The Holy Spirit, or a God-sent person, ensures we remain aligned with God's will, which is essential for accessing His power. When we recognize and cooperate with the catalysts God provides, we position ourselves to receive His power and fulfil His purpose.

The Power of God Works When We Couple Our Spirit Man With the Holy Spirit

For several years, I worked for the Government of Zambia as a Lecturer at the Natural Resources Development College. During that time, we participated in various technical cooperation programmes established through agreements between the Zambian Government and other nations. One key lesson I learned from these programmes was that their effectiveness depended heavily on the quality of the relationship between our government and the donor country. Funding could be increased, maintained, reduced, or even withheld depending on the state of that relationship. This closely mirrors what happens when we desire to harness the power of God.

A believer cannot access the power of God unless their spirit is firmly connected to the Holy Spirit. The Godhead has designed the flow of divine power in such a way that it is channelled through the Holy Spirit, who connects only with the spirit man, the innermost part of our being. The condition of our spirit determines how much of God's power we can receive and channel.

Just like a power system needs stable infrastructure to function, the power of God requires a supportive spiritual structure for its flow to be consistent and effective. The Holy Spirit is the source of power, and our spirit is the conduit. To maintain a healthy and effective relationship between the two, we must build a strong foundation of Christian disciplines: immersing ourselves in biblical teaching, cultivating a life of prayer and fasting, engaging in fellowship, sharing meals, participating in the Lord's Supper, and other practices that keep us rooted in the presence of God. To harness the power of God, we must nurture a sound and growing relationship between our spirit and the Holy Spirit.

God's Power Can Occasionally Work Against Our Will

Although believers typically harness the power of God through a sound relationship with Him, God still reserves the right to exercise His power independently of our will. A vivid example is found in the story of Jonah. God sent Jonah to preach repentance to the people of Nineveh in Assyria, but Jonah resisted, he preferred to see the city suffer God's wrath rather than receive His mercy. The moment Jonah took this stance, he effectively lost control of the situation and became subject to the power of God rather than a vessel of it.

The power of God stirred up a violent storm that battered the ship Jonah was using to flee his mission. He was thrown into the raging sea, endured a harrowing three-day journey inside the belly of a great fish, and ultimately found himself preaching repentance in Nineveh. Despite his resistance, the people of the city turned to God. Jonah, overwhelmed and frustrated by God's mercy, asked to die. This story clearly shows that God's power is sovereign, He can and will overrule human will when it stands in opposition to His divine purpose.

Have you ever done something, only to regret it later upon realizing it went against God's will? Have you ever judged or resented someone God later chose to bless? These are reminders that God's power is not ours to control or direct according to personal bias. It was never designed to be used for oppression, revenge, or persecution. Rather, God desires that His power operates in us according to the measure of grace He has apportioned to each believer.

God's Power is Expressed Through Fulfilment of Promises

Many of the things God gives to believers come in the form of promises, which He fulfils in His own time. These promises cannot be fulfilled without the operation of God's power. However, they are often conditional, requiring believers to respond in obedience and faith. The apostle Peter taught that our union with Christ has granted us *His divine power*, which has given us *exceedingly great and precious promises*, so that through them, we *may be partakers of the divine nature* (2 Pet. 1:3–4 NKJV). These promises are reserved for those whom Christ has adopted as His children, those who are not only recipients, but also active participants in the journey toward their fulfilment.

In the late 1990s, during a period of commodity scarcity in Zambia, certified government workers received monthly allocation coupons. These coupons promised access to essential goods, but access was conditional. To claim the goods, the recipient needed to present valid ID and appear at the specified time and place. This illustrates how the promises of God work: God specifies the promise, the terms, the timing, and the place—but we must respond in faith and obedience.

Before His ascension, Jesus told His disciples: *Do not leave Jerusalem, but wait for the gift my Father promised, which you have heard me speak about. For John baptized with water, but in a few days you will be baptized with the Holy Spirit* (Acts 1:4–5 NIV). This promised gift - the Holy Spirit, the very embodiment of God's power - did not come upon them immediately. The disciples returned to Jerusalem and *joined together constantly in prayer* in the upper room (Acts 1:14). They waited and prayed for 10 days, demonstrating faith, unity, and obedience, conditions that aligned them with the promise.

The disciples also received a promise of Christ's return from the two angels at His ascension (Acts 1:11), and Jesus had previously assured them in John 14:1–3 that He was preparing a place for them in His Father's house. These unfulfilled promises continue to give hope and direction to every believer today.

Are you not excited that Jesus has prepared a room for you in His Father's house, where you will dwell with Him forever? Scripture is full of promises, some fulfilled, others still awaiting their appointed time. But as Psalm 119:38 (NIV) says, *Fulfil your promise to your servant, so that you may be feared*. This verse reveals an important principle: believers are called to engage actively with God's promises. We must know them, pray them, believe in them, and prepare to receive them with reverence. This same principle applies to accessing the power of God. Promises, and power, are not passively absorbed. They are stewarded, pursued, and activated through alignment with God's will.

The power of God operates in a Christian through a dynamic relationship with the Holy Spirit, grounded in faith, obedience, and alignment with God's

Word and will. So, considering the many conditions for gaining access to the power of God, the question remains: To what extent are we, as believers, harnessing this power?

CHAPTER 11
When Is God's Power Available to Us?

The followers of Jesus Christ have access to the immeasurable power of God to carry out good works in His vineyard. The LORD, who created us in His image, has built into our very nature the potential and capacity to fulfil our earthly mission using the vast resources He provides. However, these works may never materialize if our lifestyle restricts our access to the power of God. There are spiritual "power trippers", things that disrupt our connection with the divine source of power. These interruptions weaken our spiritual walk and hinder us from fulfilling our God-given purpose on earth. This chapter explores some of the causes of spiritual power cuts in our walk with the Lord, and how we can avoid or overcome them.

Neglecting the Work of God
When believers neglect the assignment God has given them, it leads to a kind of spiritual power outage, rendering their efforts incomplete and ineffective. After 70 years in exile, when the Israelites returned to Jerusalem, they focused on building their own houses, while neglecting the reconstruction of God's temple. Through the prophet Haggai, the LORD questioned the governor of Judah (Zerubbabel) and the high priest (Joshua), asking why the Israelites were living in well-built houses while His temple lay in ruins (Hag. 1:4).

God was not against them building comfortable homes, but He took issue with their misplaced priorities. As shown in Haggai 1:2, where God says: *These people say the time has not yet come to rebuild the house of the* LORD, it's clear that the Israelites intended to build the temple, just not before completing their own homes.

Any healthy relationship with God is built on the principle of putting Him and His work first. Matthew reinforces this when he says: *But seek ye first the kingdom of God, and His righteousness; and all these things shall be added unto you* (Matt. 6:33, KJV). Every creature depends on God for provision, but our ability to fully benefit from His blessings is tied to how we prioritize our relationship with Him. If we fail to place this relationship above all else, we limit our access to His abundant supply. So, what were the consequences of the Israelites prioritizing their own affairs over God's?

Focusing on their own homes while the temple remained in ruins was equivalent to deserting God and neglecting worship. This is implied in God's condition for restoring His favour: *Rebuild the temple; then I will be pleased and will be worshiped as I should be* (Hag. 1:8, GNV). Despite their well-constructed houses, the Israelites struggled to meet their basic needs because the Lord Himself restrained the productivity of their resources. He withheld rain, sent scorching winds and hail, and ruined their crops. They planted much but harvested little; ate and drank, but were never satisfied; wore clothes, but couldn't keep warm; worked hard, but earned too little; even livestock underperformed (Hag. 1:6–11). As long as the temple remained in ruins, God's presence was absent, and with it went His peace and prosperity.

Even worse, God considered the people defiled. Through Haggai, the LORD declared: *The same thing applies to the people of this nation and to everything they produce; and so, everything they offer on the altar is defiled*" (Hag. 2:14, GNB). This situation reveals three important truths:

1. **Neglecting God's work disconnects us from His power.** This weakens our ability to build, create, and thrive, and diminishes our capacity to benefit from the environment and resources God has provided.
2. **When we ignore God's priorities, He may actively work against our efforts.** He can blow away the little we manage to gather, or allow the devourer to plunder what we have, leaving us powerless to stop it.
3. **Neglecting God's temple invites opposition from His power.** This can lock our potential, hinder productivity, and block access to the resources He gave us for our purpose on earth.

It's also important to remember that "God's temple" includes our bodies (1 Cor. 6:19). Neglecting our spiritual health and obedience can block the flow of God's power in our lives. Sustained access to His power requires reverence and obedience. When the Israelites finally obeyed God and began rebuilding the temple, everything changed. God was pleased and:

- Promised to be with them (Hag. 1:13),
- Stirred their spirits to complete the work (Hag. 1:14),
- Declared that He would shake the heavens, earth, sea, and nations to bring treasure into His temple (Hag. 2:7, 21–22),
- Promised to bless them (Hag. 2:19), and
- Appointed Zerubbabel as His chosen servant to lead (Hag. 2:23).

Their situation turned from hardship to abundance. The secret? They returned to God, and His presence reconnected them to His power and blessings.

Living in Sin Limits God's Power

When we disobey God's commandments, we limit the manifestation of His power in our lives. God hates sin (Eph. 5:3; Prov. 6:16–19; Ps. 5:5) to such an extent that He sacrificed His Son to set sinners free. We need God's presence to access His power, and anything that pulls us away from His presence disconnects us from that power.

Led by the Spirit, the prophet Isaiah declared: *Behold, the Lord's hand is not shortened, that it cannot save; nor His ear heavy, that it cannot hear. But your iniquities have separated you from your God; and your sins have hidden His face from you, so that He will not hear* (Isa. 59:1–2, NKJV). This implies that sin breaks communication with God: iniquities separate us from Him, and sins conceal His face from us and silence our voices, so that He does not hear, thereby denying us access to His power.

Sin disarms a believer because God neither hears nor responds to their prayers. Speaking through Zechariah, God said: *Because they would not listen to the message I sent through the prophets, who lived long ago, I became very angry. As they did not listen when I spoke, so I did not listen when they prayed* (Zech. 7:12–13, GNB). To sin, we must first step out of God's presence. However, there are also times when we unknowingly drift away because of unrecognized sin.

When the people of Bethel sent representatives to inquire whether they should continue fasting in memory of the temple's destruction (Zech. 7:2–3), God responded through Zechariah: "Tell the people and the priests, 'When you fasted and mourned in the fifth and seventh months... was it really for Me that you fasted? And when you were eating and drinking, were you not just feasting for yourselves?'" (Zech. 7:5–6, paraphrased). Although the Israelites believed their actions were righteous, their fasting and mourning did not honour God.

Sin is the Devil's most effective mechanism for keeping people locked out of the Kingdom of God. When we persist in unconfessed sin, we forfeit the "access code" to God's eternal power. Unconfessed sin blocks our access to God's presence, leaving us exposed to the enemy's schemes. The only antidote is genuine confession and repentance.

In response to Solomon's prayer at the temple's dedication, the LORD declared: *If My people, who are called by My name, will humble themselves, and pray, and seek My face, and turn from their wicked ways, then I will hear from heaven, and will forgive their sin, and heal their land* (2 Chron. 7:14, KJV). Sin cripples both the individual and the systems that sustain them. Confession not only brings forgiveness but also unlocks healing and restoration. When a believer steps out of God's presence due to sin, four conditions must be met for re-entry:

1. Humility – Acknowledging our need for God's mercy.
2. Prayer – Humbly coming before God in repentance.
3. Seeking His face – Desiring intimacy with Him above all else.
4. Turning from wicked ways – A complete change in direction.

Diligently examine your heart and confess your sins, so you may consistently live in God's presence and continually access His power.

Mishandling Trials and Temptations

We all face trials and temptations, but how we respond to them determines whether we continue walking in the light of God or are pushed into the dark alleys of the enemy. Trials are rarely pleasant, and we often pray they never come our way. But when they do, believers typically respond in one of three ways.

First, some vigilantly pray for the trial to end immediately. They view it as an inconvenience, an unnecessary source of pain to be avoided at all costs.

Second, after realizing that the trial is not going away, some believers choose to walk through it with God. Although we believe trials can refine our faith like fire purifies gold, we often struggle, especially when others wrongly associate trials with personal disobedience. Still, some believers accept trials as a necessary part of faith development.

Finally, there are those who endure trials with a measure of resentment. They are reluctantly dragged through the storm, constantly looking for the nearest exit. They regularly pray for God's intervention or deliverance, but without peace in their hearts.

Which of these three responses best describes how you handle trials? When a believer chooses a path contrary to God's will, they may miss His providential care. James teaches that trials are sometimes necessary for spiritual growth: *Consider it pure joy, my brothers and sisters, whenever you face trials of many kinds, because you know that the testing of your faith produces perseverance. Let perseverance finish its work so that you may be mature and complete, not lacking anything* (Jam. 1:2–4, NIV). In the secular world, trials are rarely seen as a source of joy. Instead, they are often interpreted as signs of failure, mismanagement, curses, or punishment for sin.

Remember Job's friends when he faced a wave of intense suffering. They assumed his trials were self-inflicted; evidence that he had sinned and abandoned God. Job's friends attributed his suffering to sin:

1. Eliphaz asked job, *Have you ever seen a righteous man suffer like this?* (Job 4:7, paraphrased).

2. Bildad accused Job's children of sinning when he said, *Your children must have sinned against God, and so He punished them as they deserved* (Job 8:4, GNB).

3. Zophar urged, *Put your heart right, Job. Reach out to God… Then all your trouble will fade from your memory* (Job 11:13–16, GNB).

If they had known the true cause of Job's suffering, they wouldn't have made such unjust, insensitive, and offensive claims. Sometimes our harsh judgments are completely misplaced.

James emphasizes that a variety of trials is necessary to develop perseverance, a key ingredient for a mature, Christ-centred life. Perseverance must be allowed to complete its work if we want to grow in faith and spiritual character. Trials are like the surgical blade a doctor uses to remove a harmful growth. The body must endure pain during the procedure, but once it's complete, peace and healing follow. That's why James encourages believers to rejoice when facing many kinds of trials.

It's also true that few people would reject trials if they knew in advance God's purpose for allowing them. That's why James urges us to seek wisdom: *If any of you lacks wisdom, let him ask of God, who gives to all liberally and without reproach, and it will be given to him* (James 1:5, NKJV).

Wisdom helps us discern the divine purpose behind our trials. The good news is that God gives wisdom freely when we ask. However, if we resist the trials - whether by praying for them to end prematurely or enduring them with resentment - we hinder God's refining process. When we resist this process, we risk cutting off the flow of His power in our lives.

Inadequate Knowledge

When believers spend little time studying and meditating on the Word of God, they become spiritually malnourished and cannot draw enough power to carry out the assignments God has given them. The Prophet Hosea said, *My people are destroyed for lack of knowledge; because you have rejected knowledge, I will also reject you, that you shall be no priest to Me; seeing you have forgotten the law of your God, I will also forget your children* (Hosea 4:6 NKJV). There are three things that could deprive a believer of the knowledge they need to remain in the presence of God and accomplish their mission on earth: the inability to study and meditate on the Word, rejecting the Word, and forgetting the Word. These vices cripple your relationship with God for several reasons.

First, if we lack knowledge, we cannot identify and root out sin in our lives, nor can we bear much fruit. Jesus Christ said, *You have been made clean by the teaching I have given you* (John 15:3). The Word of God is a spiritual reagent that washes the spiritual filth that defiles believers.

Second, the knowledge we gain from studying the teachings of Christ builds our faith. Paul concludes, *So then, faith comes by hearing, and hearing by the Word of God* (Rom. 10:17). Starving the spirit man through inadequate study of the Word restricts our capacity to function. For example, the failure of the disciples to cast a demon out of an epileptic boy was due to unbelief and lack of knowledge (Matt. 17:15-21). Jesus told His disciples that if they had faith as small as a mustard seed, they could command mountains to move, and they would move, nothing would be impossible for them (Matt. 17:20). Unbelief and lack of knowledge undermine our faith and deny us access to the immeasurable power of God, which could be damaging to our Christian mission.

The disciples asked Jesus why they could not cast the evil spirit out of the boy. Apart from unbelief, they didn't know that the spirit in the boy required them to pray and fast. In a separate case, the seven sons of Sceva attempted to cast out a demon from a man in Ephesus using the name of Jesus, but they were humiliated (Acts 19:11-20). After observing Paul perform extraordinary miracles in the name of Jesus, they thought they could do the same. They didn't know what Paul knew or the anointing he carried. The failure to cast out the demon in both cases clearly demonstrated the effect of a lack of knowledge.

Third, knowledge ensures that we stay on track. The Psalmist said, *Your word is a lamp to my feet and a light to my path* (Psa. 119:105 NKJV). The Word is like a car's headlights that pierce through the darkness, allowing the driver to keep the car on the road. What could happen if the car's battery power were drained? If the strength of the headlights decreases, the driver may struggle to drive or even abandon the trip. Feed the spirit man, and he will maintain the flow of the power of God.

Fourth, the Word of God is intricately connected to the Holy Spirit (the carrier of the power of God) and is mission oriented. The Word always fulfils its mission if it is released with faith. *So shall My word be that goes forth from My mouth; it shall not return to Me void, but it shall accomplish what I please, and it shall prosper in the thing for which I sent it* (Isa. 55:11 NKJV). The Word of God in a believer's life can perform extraordinary things. A believer who knows the Word can send it on errands. However, it is not enough to have the Word if you cannot commission it to do what it is meant to achieve.

Lack of Commitment to Our Christian Discipline of Discipleship

The power of God may elude us because we fail to observe the disciplines that come with life in the presence of God. A believer who lacks commitment to studying the Word, prayer and fasting, fellowship/community, sharing meals and the Lord's Supper, and helping widows, orphans, and foreigners limits their access to the power of God. The following questions can assist you in conducting an inventory of some key disciplines of Christian discipleship:

- Are you part of a Christian fellowship – such as a Bible study group, local church, or Christian groups (e.g. house fellowship, women's, men's, or youth groups)?
- How much time do you devote to personal Bible study? Have you considered sharing what the Holy Spirit teaches you with others?
- Do you regularly pray and fast? If so, how often?
- How often do you share meals with family members, fellow believers in Christ, and strangers? How often do you participate in the Lord's Supper – individually, with your family, and in the local church? Have you specifically shared meals with widows, orphans, and strangers?
- Have you given things or possessions to brothers or sisters in need? Is this something you regularly do? Do you support charities to help the poor?
- Do you tithe and give offerings in your local church?

The list of questions above is not exhaustive but highlights a few key areas of our Christian life. When we neglect these essential disciplines of discipleship, we compromise our fellowship with God and deny ourselves access to His power.

Believers Fail to Access God's Power Because They Don't Ask for it or Ask Wrongly

Many of the spiritual blessings are wrapped up in the promises in the Word of God. The Lord expects us to ask for them as and when we need them. James tells us that we do not have because we do not ask (Jam. 4:2). Of course, this only happens when we ask in the name of Jesus and according to God's will.

While the Lord knows all our needs even before we approach Him, He still expects us to ask before He can fulfil that promise. I must also mention that God can sovereignly choose to give us some things even if we don't ask for them. However, there are moments when God doesn't give us what we ask for. There are several reasons why He may choose not to grant our request: maybe He has something better than what we're asking for, our request may be contrary to His will, or the Lord may want to satisfy His own desires regarding a certain aspect of our lives. It could also be that God is keen to give us something, but in the context of eternity. In this case, death may be His answer to prayer. There may be other reasons we may never understand as mere mortals.

God can also reject your prayer request because your motives, attitude, and desires are wrong. James, admonishing the saints, said, *You ask and do not receive, because you ask with wrong motives, so that you may spend it on your pleasures* (Jam. 4:3, NASB). If you ask God for a prestigious car, an exclusive mansion, a lucrative business, or wealth to show off and make others feel inferior to you, He may not give it to you because your motive is wrong. So, could it be that your request is driven by the lust of the eyes, the lust of the flesh, or the pride of life? God wants to bless you, but everything must be for the glory and praise of the Creator. Before you present your request to God, ask yourself, will this request glorify God? Anything that does not meet this litmus test may be blocking the power of God. Worse still, it may attract the wrath of God – His power may work against you.

If You Do Not Have the Right Perspective of Eternity, God May Not Release His Power

Sometimes, disciples of the Lord Jesus Christ were self-centred and wanted good things to happen to them. Although they had an eternal perspective on their lives, some of their desires were wrong. Just after the Lord's announcement of His imminent crucifixion, death, and resurrection, the mother of Zebedee's children and her sons came to Him, worshipped Him, and presented her request: *Grant that these two sons of mine may sit, one on Your right hand and the other on Your left, in Your kingdom* (Matt. 20:21, KJV). In response, Jesus told them that their request was beyond what He could guarantee at that stage. However, the other disciples were not happy with the request. There were twelve disciples, and two of them had asked for privileged positions in the kingdom to come, putting their interests first.

At times, when we are pressured by difficult circumstances, we can easily lose our eternal perspective. Paul, writing to the church at Corinth, said: *That is why we never give up. Though our bodies are dying, our spirits are being renewed every day. For our present troubles are small and won't last very long. Yet they produce for us a glory that vastly outweighs them and will last forever! So we don't look at the troubles we can see now; rather, we fix our gaze on things that cannot be seen* (2 Cor. 4:16-18, NLT).

When I was struck by a mysterious disease, the skin on my face and scalp became very dark, forming scales that peeled off on their own. I had never seen anyone with that kind of appearance. This was happening amidst other complications: the skin on my neck, earlobes, and chest was cracking and forming painful sores, and my joints were swollen, deformed, and painful. This mysterious disease moved me from a steady state to a calamity in a matter of days. My only prayer at that moment was, "Let Your will be done." However, through it all, I drew inspiration partly from Paul's letter, which encouraged the saints never to give up.

It is true that while our bodies are gradually dying, our devotion to the Word of God, prayer, fasting, fellowship, sharing meals, the Lord's Supper, and other disciplines renew our spirits daily. How wonderful it is to know that our momentary and light troubles produce an eternal glory that far outweighs them. However, there is always a temptation to focus on and amplify our little troubles and fail to see them in the context of eternity. Yes, it is a difficult thing to do, but it is necessary. Anytime we fail to trust God and view life as one small experience within a far greater picture, we reduce the greatness of God in our lives.

Failure to Recognize and Deal with Our Inadequacies

Many believers struggle to do God's will because they are not fully equipped to do it. Recognizing this problem, the author of Hebrews, in his benediction and final greetings, said: *May the God of peace ...... equip you with everything good for doing His will* (Hebrews 13:21 NIV). This doxology implies that:

- A saint needs to have certain knowledge and skills to do the will of God.
- Believers are usually deficient in certain areas and cannot competently do the will of God.
- Our lives may contain certain things that may not be good when pursuing the will of God.
- We need God to equip us with everything good to do His will.

Assessing what you know and can do allows God to equip you for His work. You need to know what you don't know for you to know what you need to know, know your knowledge gap. As a training consultant, one of the major tasks is to determine and compare the current level of knowledge and skills of a potential trainee with the required knowledge and skill set for their position (Job description). This activity defines the gap between the actual and the required level of knowledge. The gap which can be narrowed through training is a training need. Training equips the employee with knowledge and skills s(he) needs to perform duties specified in the job description. Similarly, when we accept Christ there is a gap between what we know and what we need to know to do God's will.

If we don't spend time to assess our knowledge and understand what we need to know, we are likely to underperform and underutilise the power of God. God works according to His will and His power is apportioned according to the tasks a believer is given within the will of God. Any task performed outside the will of God does not qualify for His power.

Weak Relationship with the Holy Spirit

Failure to recognize that the Holy Spirit is actively involved in creative activities and their sustenance may partly explain why a relationship between a believer and the Holy Spirit is weak and devoid of miraculous power. Every believer needs to be filled with the Holy Spirit (Eph. 5:18; Acts 6:3; Mic. 4:8; Exod. 31:3; 35:31; Acts 11:24; Luke 1:41; Luke 4:1; Acts 13:9; Acts 9:17; Luke 1:67). God expects us to be full of the Holy Spirit, who fully leads and empowers our activities.

Jesus Christ, the Son of God, needed the full measure of the Holy Spirit: *Jesus, full of the Holy Spirit, returned from the Jordan and was led around by the Holy Spirit in the wilderness* (Luke 4:1). The Son of God completely submitted to the leading of the Holy Spirit into and throughout the wilderness and His earthly ministry. This explains why He performed numerous miracles, overcame all sin, and accomplished His assignment on earth. Therefore, compromising our relationship with the Holy Spirit restricts the power of God in our lives.

God's creation needs nothing less than the immeasurable power of God to fulfil the purpose and will of God for our lives. Our Creator has given us conditional access to this power, but He has provided us with everything we need to meet these conditions. However, when we choose to entangle ourselves with worldly things that compromise our position in the Lord, He limits our access to His power. In some cases, His power may even work against us. Every believer must strive to avoid anything that compromises their position in the presence of God.

CONCLUSION

Many believers have the potential to access the immeasurable power of God, but they either underutilize it or don't use it at all. God has given everyone the potential, inherent capacity, and enough resources to do every good work to fulfil His will and purpose. Despite this unique provision, many Christians roam the earth underachieving in most of their God-given assignments because they lack knowledge of the power of God available to them and how to access it. Inadequate understanding of the manifestations of the eternal power of God contributes to misconceptions surrounding its nature and potency. These misconceptions include dismissing the work of the Holy Spirit as activities associated with the early Church, specific individuals (like selected men and women of God), or false teachings.

For believers who understand what they have in Christ, limited access to God's power could be attributed to a lack of devotion to core Christian disciplines. Such Christians may consider devout Christian principles, beliefs, and practices too restrictive or may question the philosophy of Christianity itself. Some believers, influenced by the science-faith debate, question certain aspects of Christian doctrine. These reactionary views undermine the conditions required for accessing the power of God.

Recognizing that fulfilling God's purpose requires a measure of faith, grace, and power, understanding how to access this power is a crucial aspect of Christian living. Believers who want to walk with God and fully access His power must fear and obey His commandments. The early Church provides important lessons on how to harness the power of God. After the outpouring of the Holy Spirit and the birth of the Church, there was a phenomenal manifestation of God's power, evidenced by both numerical and spiritual growth. This Church growth was precipitated by the believers' devotion to apostolic teachings about Christ's life and teachings, fellowship (community), prayer and fasting, sharing meals and the Lord's Supper, and supporting the needy among them. The disciples of Christ were sealed, baptized, filled, and led by the Holy Spirit.

Believers who desire to be fruitful in their walk with God seek His will in everything they do, die to self so that Christ may increase in them, build and sustain a living faith, fear and obey God's commandments, and are fully grafted into the true vine. The branch and the vine must be well integrated to allow the free flow of God's power. Believers must strive to consistently dwell in God's presence to continually access His power.

God gives believers unlimited access to His power if they walk in His presence. However, we can unilaterally vacate the presence of God or be forcibly removed if our conduct displeases Him. Some things that could limit our access to God's power include rebellion against God or living in sin, inadequate devotion to Christian disciplines, resisting or quenching the Holy Spirit, mishandling trials and troubles, failure to identify and address our inadequacies, lack of knowledge, not asking God for what we need, or asking with wrong motives, and mishandling 'unanswered prayers.' If we allow any of these issues in our lives, they could limit the manifestation of God's power.

As children of God, we should regularly assess our knowledge and competencies to identify our inadequacies. This will allow our Father to equip us to do His will. Considering the significance of the power of God in your life, ask yourself these questions: Do I understand what the power of God is and how it works? If I don't, what should I do to address this inadequacy? How devoted am I to Christian disciplines? To what extent am I filled and led by the Holy Spirit? Am I enjoying the full measure of God's power to do His will? If not, what are the major limitations to accessing this power, and how can I address them? God loves you and values you so much that He has provided you with His power to fulfil your purpose on earth. Just surrender yourself to the Holy Spirit and let Him lead you in your walk with the Lord.

One needs to be a follower of Christ to access the power of God and to live a life devoted to Him. If you have never invited Jesus Christ into your life, your time of the Lord's favour is now. All you need to do is to wholeheartedly pray the prayer below and believe every word in it.

Sinner's Prayer

Lord Jesus, I know that I am a sinner and cannot save myself. I believe that You are the Son of God who came to earth and died on the cross for my sins. Thank You for bearing my sins in Your body as You hanged on the cross. I believe that You died for me on the cross, You were buried and rose from the dead on the third day as a guarantee of my own resurrection. Lord Jesus, thank You for Your gift of eternal life. I confess and repent of all my sins. I invite You to come into my life and be my Lord and Savior. I am ready to trust and follow You all the days of my life. Thank You for accepting me as I am. In Your name, I ask for this. Amen!

www.ingramcontent.com/pod-product-compliance
Lightning Source LLC
Chambersburg PA
CBHW011717220426
43662CB00019B/2409